Understanding the Internet

CHANDOS INTERNET SERIES

Chandos' new series of books are aimed at all those individuals interested in the internet. They have been specially commissioned to provide the reader with an authoritative view of current thinking. If you would like a full listing of current and forthcoming titles, please visit our web site **www.chandospublishing.com** or contact Hannah Grace-Williams on email info@chandospublishing.com or telephone number +44 (0) 1223 891358.

New authors: we are always pleased to receive ideas for new titles; if you would like to write a book for Chandos, please contact Dr Glyn Jones on email gjones@chandospublishing.com or telephone number +44 (0) 1993 848726.

Bulk orders: some organisations buy a number of copies of our books. If you are interested in doing this, we would be pleased to discuss a discount. Please contact Hannah Grace-Williams on email info@chandospublishing.com or telephone number +44 (0) 1223 891358.

Understanding the Internet

A glimpse into the building blocks, applications, security and hidden secrets of the Web

EDITED BY
KEVIN CURRAN

Chandos Publishing
Oxford • Cambridge • New Delhi

Chandos Publishing
TBAC Business Centre
Avenue 4
Station Lane
Witney
Oxford OX28 4BN
UK
Tel: +44 (0) 1993 848726
Email: info@chandospublishing.com
www.chandospublishing.com

Chandos Publishing is an imprint of Woodhead Publishing Limited

Woodhead Publishing Limited
Abington Hall
Granta Park
Great Abington
Cambridge CB21 6AH
UK
www.woodheadpublishing.com

First published in 2009

ISBN:
978 1 84334 499 5

British Library Cataloguing-in-Publication Data.
A catalogue record for this book is available from the British Library.

Typeset by Domex e-Data Pvt. Ltd.
Printed in the UK and USA.

Contents

List of figures and tables

Figures

Tables

About the authors

Dr Kevin Curran is a senior lecturer in Computer Science at the University of Ulster, Belfast, Northern Ireland, and group leader for the Ambient Intelligence Research Group. His achievements include winning and managing UK and European Framework projects and Technology Transfer Schemes. Dr Curran has made significant contributions to advancing the knowledge and understanding of computer networking and systems, as evidenced by over 400 published works in this area. He is perhaps most well known for his work on location positioning within indoor environments, pervasive computing and Internet security. His expertise has been acknowledged by invitations to present his work at international conferences, overseas universities and research laboratories. He is a regular contributor to BBC radio and TV news in the UK and is currently the recipient of an Engineering and Technology Board Visiting Lectureship for Exceptional Engineers and is an IEEE Technical Expert for Internet/Security matters. Dr Curran was awarded the Certificate of Excellence for Research in 2004 by Science Publications and was named Irish Digital Media Newcomer of the Year Award in 2006. Dr Curran has performed external panel duties for various Irish Higher Education Institutions. He is a member of a number of professional organisations including the Association for Computing Machinery (ACM), Institution of Electrical Engineers (IEE), Institute of Electrical and Electronics Engineers (IEEE), British Computer Society (BCS) and the Higher Education Academy (HEA). He is a senior member (SMIEEE) of the IEEE and a fellow of the higher education academy (FHEA). He has chaired sessions and participated in the organising committees for many highly respected international conferences and workshops. He is the Editor in Chief of the *International Journal of Ambient Computing and Intelligence* and is also a member of 15 journal editorial committees and numerous international conference organising committees. He has served as an advisor to the British Computer Society in regard to the computer industry standards and is a member of BCS and IEEE Technology Specialist Groups and various other professional bodies.

He can be contacted on *kj.curran@ulster.ac.uk*

Derek Woods is Senior Lecturer in Computer Science at the University of Ulster; Nadene McDermot is Software Solutions Manager at the Western Health and Social Care Trust; Derek Hawkes is Duty officer/Recreation Assistant at Omagh Distict Council; Elaine Smyth is Accounting Technician at Drenagh Sawmills Ltd; John Honan is a postgraduate student at the Open University; Scott Hulme is Placement Engineer at Asidua Ltd; Gary Doherty is an undergraduate student at the University of Ulster; David O'Callaghan is an undergraduate student at the University of Ulster; Leanne Doak is a freelance Web designer; Damien Armstrong is an undergraduate student at the University of Ulster; Sheila McCarthy is a PhD postgraduate student at the University of Ulster; Karen Lee is a PhD postgraduate student at the University of Ulster; Darren McClenaghan is an undergraduate student at the University of Ulster; Ashlean McNulty is Business and IT Teacher at Magh Ene College; Padraig O'Kane is a software developer at Allstate; Stephen Norrby is a technical consultant at NYSE Technologies; Martin Christian is a software engineer at Asidua Ltd; Jason Downey is an undergraduate student at the University of Ulster; Danny Otterson is a computer technician at C3 Computers; Danielle McCartney is an undergraduate student at the University of Ulster; Karen McCleanm is an undergraduate student at the University of Ulster; David Pollock is an undergraduate student at the University of Ulster; Mairead Feeney is Lecturer, Letterkenny Institute of Technology; Rory McGarrigle is Hygiene Controller, Daniel Doherty Ltd; Colleen Ferguson is a software engineer at Allstate; Francis Doherty is a programmer at Allstate Insurance; Conrad Deighan is a PhD postgraduate student at the University of Ulster; Gerard Galway is at Health Services Executive West; Joan Condell is Lecturer in Computer Science at the University of Ulster; Winston Huang is a software engineer at Fujitsu Siemens; Niall Smyth is a software engineer at Intel; Brian McGrory is a software developer at Fujitsu Services; Gary Tracey is a software developer at Invision; Edwina Sweeney is Lecturer at the Letterkenny Institute of Technology; Xuelong Xi is Senior Lecturer at the University of London; Roisin Clarke is an undergraduate student at the University of Ulster; Jude McGlinchey is a software engineer at Invista; Cliona Murphy is a Web developer at Marley Design; Stephen Annesley is programmer at Microsoft; Peter Breslin is a systems administrator at Assetco PLC; and Kevin McLaughlin is a Web developer at Go Ape TV.

Introduction

Kevin Curran

On 22 May 1973, a young man named Bob Metcalf authored a memo that described 'X-Wire', a 3-Mbps common bus office network system developed at Xerox's Palo Alto Research Center (PARC). It was also called the Alto Aloha Network protocol but it became more commonly know as *Ethernet*. There are few networking technologies from the early 1970s that have proved to be so resilient. Metcalf deservedly went on to everlasting fame in the networking community (he also founded the global company 3COM) and his story should have ended here. However, in 1995, he predicted that the Internet would self-destruct from overload.[1] His argument was that network load (messages, packets) was growing exponentially, while network bandwidth (fibre capacity, switch performance) was growing linearly, and that at some point these two curves would cross, the result being that demand would exceed capacity. To cut a long story short – he was wrong. The Internet is still around and so is Bob, but his predictions are not now taken quite as seriously by those in the industry. This anecdote is used here not to ridicule a great man such as Bob Metcalf but rather to serve as a warning to those of us who think that they know how a complex beast such as the Internet is about to behave in the days ahead. You will be pleased to hear that I keep my predictions to a minimum in the remaining pages.

On a different note, mention to a young person that the Internet was not around 'when you were young' and you can visibly see their face change as they attempt to comprehend how on earth a race of people could survive without it. I remember my epiphany concerning the power of the Web back in the early 1990s when I was reading a book outside enjoying the sunshine when I was stung by a wasp. I simply got up after the shock and without any serious thought I returned to my office and entered the query 'sting wasp cure'. It was later that day that I realised that the Web had become an extension of myself. Today, a student seeking answers from a park bench can quite easily look it up on their iPhone.

There are no shortcuts to true knowledge and insight can only come from understanding principles and facts surrounding a subject area. This book does not dwell on the history of the Internet. Suffice to say that it was a combination as usual of military demands and industry/university collaboration. I doubt, however, that many of those involved back then could have foreseen the impact that early bandwidth-limted network would have on society. Interestingly, however, the building blocks have not changed much since those initial days. Protocols are crucial to providing functionality and their standardisation enables widespread adoption.

Mobile communications is a continually growing sector in industry and a wide variety of visual services such as video-on-demand have been created which are limited by low-bandwidth network infrastructures. The distinction between mobile phones and personal device assistants (PDAs) has already become blurred with pervasive computing being the term coined to describe the tendency to integrate computing and communication into everyday life. The new g-phone with the Android operating system from Google labs and the iPhone from Apple are the start of the newer generation of smart phones. We often forget that quite a sizeable portion of the Earth's population are still not on the Internet and that many of those that are likely to be accessing the Web from a mobile device rather than the usual desktop model. It is little wonder that many of the large corporations such as Microsoft, Google and Apple are concentrating so much on this space.

This book is divided into sections that allow the reader to dip straight into. Some will be mostly interested in aspects of network security, and Section 5 will therefore be of most appeal. Others may find the aspect of mobility and the Web to be of most interest and they are therefore referred to Section 4.

Section 1, 'The network beneath', provides an overview of protocols and how they provide the necessary functionality to move packets of information from source to destination. It discusses the problems of delay and what happens when packets become corrupt. This section introduces wireless networks and the model of mesh networks. It also provides insight into cognitive radio and streaming multimedia over the Web. Internet traffic is essentially the load on the network, or the number of packets of data traversing the network. When the Internet was first developed, it was never visualised as being a public service, so the increase in network traffic was no real cause for concern. Indeed, the growth in the rate of Internet traffic has posed severe problems for the measurement of this traffic, which is essential to our understanding of Internet congestion. A common complaint regarding traffic measurement studies is that they do not have ongoing relevance in this environment where traffic, technology and topology change faster than we can measure them. So future proposals on Internet congestion can only estimate the actual load on the network at any particular time. Internet traffic in general is said to be 'Bursty', that is, that bursts of traffic rather than a steady flow are transmitted. The most serious effects of congestion are seen in the form of congestion collapse. This section discusses such issues in depth.

Section 2, 'Internet building blocks – protocols and standards', provides an overview of Web operating systems, really simple syndication (RSS), Javascript, XML, E4X and AJAX, the Semantic Web, VoiceXML and Web services. The online community steadily grows each year and with this escalation, the number of services provided increases in an attempt to meet the demands of a computer-literate audience. There is a progression from a human-orientated use of the Web to an application-driven concept referred to as Web services. We discuss the factors leading to this development and the inspiration behind Web services and we also detail the languages, platforms and systems involved in these services.

Section 3, 'Internet trends, applications and services', introduces Web 2.0, mobile social software, long tail, podcasts and blogs, and Web accessibility for users with disabilities. Web 2.0 is a social phenomenon referring to an approach to creating and distributing Web content itself, characterised by open communication, decentralisation of authority, freedom to share and re-use, and the market as a conversation. Web 2.0 is about making sure that users add value to a site as a side-effect of what they are actually using the site for. In effect, Web 2.0 is making use of the long tail such as Amazon when it collects user reviews of their products. Most of us are used to software being developed, packaged, picked up in the shop, and kept updated through downloaded and installed patches. In the Web 2.0 world, applications are run online, with no installation, updates are constant and continuous, and access is instant from any computer with a browser. This section provides a clearer definition of Web 2.0 and the technologies and Web sites which utilise the Web 2.0 principle along with related areas such as Web accessibility and electronic survellience.

Section 4, 'The mobile Internet', introduces WiMAX, hybrid web applications, browsing the Web through a phone and mobile adaptive applications. The mobile Web refers to the World Wide Web accessible to mobile devices such as cell phones, PDAs, and other mobile devices connected to a public network. Accessing the mobile Web does not require a desktop computer and as it can be accessed with a number of mobile devices, the Internet can be accessed in remote places previously unconnected to the Internet. Currently, mobile visitors browsing the Web with wireless mobile devices such as PDAs and Smartphones are the fastest growing community of Web users. We also outline here the quest to provide mobile devices with the abiltity to detect and respond appropriately to changes in network connectivity, network connection quality and power consumption in addition to other topics.

Section 5, 'Internet security', provides an introduction to cryptography, honeynets, wireless (WiFi) security, SPAM and hacking. Wired networks have always presented their own security issues, but wireless networks introduce a whole new set of rules with their own unique security vulnerabilities. Most wired security measures are simply not appropriate for application within a wireless locan area network (WLAN) environment; this is largely due to the complete change in transmission medium. However, some of the security implementations developed specifically for WLANs are also not terribly strong. Email has become very useful and practically universal. However, the usefulness of email and its potential for future growth are jeopardised by the rising tide of unwanted email, both SPAM and viruses. This threatens to wipe out its advantages and benefits. An important flaw in current email standards (most notably SMTP) is the lack of any technical requirement that ensures the reliable identification of the sender of messages. A message's domain of origin can easily be faked, or 'spoofed'. This section investigates the problem of email spam and provides an overview of methods to minimise the volumes efficiently along with other such issues of security.

Finally, section 6, 'The hidden web', introduces the invisible web, digital watermarking and steganography, vertical search engines and Web intelligence. A Web crawler or spider crawls through the Web looking for pages to index and when it locates a new page it passes the page on to an indexer. The indexer identifies links, keywords and other content and then stores these within its database. This database is searched by entering keywords through a interface and suitable Web pages are returned in a results page in the form of hyperlinks accompanied by short descriptions. The Web, however, is increasingly moving away from being a collection of documents to a multidimensional repository for sounds, images, audio and other formats. This is leading to a situation where certain parts of the Web are invisible or hidden. The term known as the 'deep Web' has emerged to refer to the mass of information that can be accessed via the Web but cannot be indexed by conventional search engines. The concept of the deep Web makes searches quite complex for search engines. This section provides an overview of the 'invisble Web' along with related topics such as Web intelligence.

Notes

1. Metcalf, B. (1995) 'Predicting the internet's catastrophic collapse and ghost sites galore in 1996', *InfoWorld*, 4 December 1995.

2

Internet protocols

Kevin Curran

This chapter introduces the problems of streaming media to mobile resource-constrained multimedia devices as a result of a variety of factors including monolithic protocol stacks, bloated middleware and fluctuating conditions in the underlying network infrastructure. The problem to be addressed is introduced along with existing approaches to the problem and the proposed solution put forward by this body of work.

Introduction

In the early days of computing every time a new communications application was developed, a set of communications routines for handing the communications hardware had to be developed. The result was that even when these routines did work, they did not work very well. There were simply too many types of communications hardware for every application to be able to work on every machine. There were also too many opportunities for errors to creep into the code handling the communications hardware. The solution was to develop a set of routines built into the system for each piece of communications hardware attached to the computer. The applications could then access these routines via a set of standardised calls. Doing this meant that applications could be moved from one computer to the next without substantial change. Furthermore, as the routines only needed to be written once for each piece of communications hardware, any software errors could be detected and fixed more quickly.[1] Once the concept of assigning different levels of controls to different sets of standardised routines caught on, network designers developed *reference models*.

Reference models are standard ways of breaking the task of communications into different *layers*. Each layer performs tasks for the layer above it and calls upon the layer below it to perform certain tasks for it in turn. The International Standards Organisation has developed a network model that contains seven layers. Internet protocol (IP) is a connectionless protocol that gateways use to identify networks and paths to networks and hosts. In other words, IP handles the routing of data between networks and nodes on those networks. The transmission control protocol (TCP) is an end-to-end protocol that is used for push-and-pull communication via a point-to-point link. TCP is the primary transport protocol in the Internet (as well as intranets and extranets) suite of protocols providing reliable, connection-orientated, full-duplex streams and uses IP for delivery. RTP is a real-time transport protocol providing supporting applications transmitting real-time data over unicast and multicast networks.[2] This chapter discusses these major building blocks of the Internet.

Background

When a user launches a browser and requests an action to be performed the browser interprets the request. It sends information to the appropriate site server where the requested information is stored and this site server sends the information back. The Internet is actually a packet-switching network which sends requests via packets of data (datagrams). Each packet contains the IP address of the sender and receiver, and the information being requested. On any one request there can be more than one packet. This is because each packet is of a fixed size and some requests for information, such as a large page of online text and graphics, may result in multiple packets being sent in order to retrieve all the elements and information on that page. This means the request must be broken up into the appropriate number of packets. The route taken to obtain the requested information depends on the sender's geographical location and that of the receiver. If there are many packets along a certain route they will all be queued or find a different route until they reach their destination. The destination cannot send any information until all the associated packets have been received. When all the packets have been received the destination sends the requested information back in packets via routers to the sender. The same problem arises in relation to routes and bandwidth.[3] The TCP is a communication protocol which enables two hosts to establish a connection and exchange streams of data. It sends information to a client/server and must receive a response or it will send the information again. The client TCP breaks down the information into smaller packets and numbers it. The server TCP then reconstructs it so the original data can be viewed. When a user types in a URL into the address box and presses 'go' a domain name service (DNS) lookup is performed. When the DNS lookup is complete the client connects to the server via a TCP connection. The request is broken down into equal-sized packets. Each packet, containing the IP address of the destination server, is then passed through the Internet via routers. Each router resolves the next router in line using a routing algorithm. This process is repeated by every router until the destination server is reached with the request. The server then responds to the requesting client in the same way until the request has been fulfilled.[4] Between the server and the client is the most likely place for a congestion to occur. This is why it is so important that the size of the information the user has requested should be as small as possible.

The ISO (International Standards Organisation) has developed a network model which represents a different level of abstraction with each layer performing a well-defined function with minimum information flowing across layer boundaries (as described above). Another principle was that there should be a manageable number of layers.[5] Figure 2.1 shows the structure of the seven-layer OSI (open systems interconnection) reference model. The network access layer has been broken up into three separate layers comprising the network layer,

Figure 2.1 The seven-layer OSI reference model

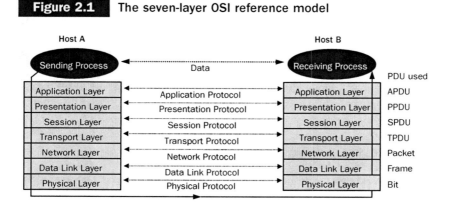

the data link layer and the physical layer. Two additional layers have been placed between the application layer and the transport layer: the presentation layer and the session layer. The application layer provides interfaces for using high-level network protocols such as the file transfer protocol (FTP) and the hypertext transfer protocol (HTTP).

Each layer is regarded as talking to its layer in the destination host (indicated by the dotted lines). The protocol data units (PDUs) used by the network layer are more specifically referred to as *packets* in the OSI reference model where a packet contains a fragment of the data being transmitted rather than all the data. Sending packets rather than all the data at once allows the network to be shared more evenly between hosts. The seven-layer OSI reference model passes the data from one layer down to the next where each layer typically adds its own header information to the data before passing it down.[6] The layers below regard the combined header and data as a single block of data adding their own header to the beginning.

In Figure 2.2 the header added by the application layer is indicated by AH (application header), the header added by the presentation layer is indicated by PH (presentation header) and so on. The data link layer adds both a header (DH) and a *tail* (DT), which contains a checksum. The physical layer then transmits this as a sequence of bits. When the data arrive at the receiving host, the equivalent layer in the receiver strips out the header information. The remaining data are then passed up to the layer above and this is repeated until the receiving process is given the data originally sent by the sending process.[7]

Figure 2.2 Each layer parcels the data received from the layer above into a PDU

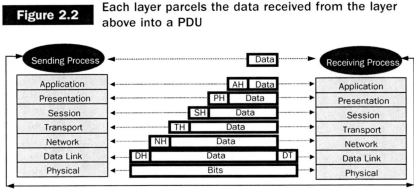

Actual data transmission path

Internet protocols

IP is a connectionless protocol that gateways use to identify networks and paths to networks and hosts. In other words, IP handles the routing of data between networks and nodes on those networks. In addition to defining an address scheme, IP also handles the transmission of data from an originating computer to the computer specified by the IP address. It does so by breaking up larger chunks of data into easily manageable IP packets that it can deliver across the network in a connectionless fashion. In an effort to manage network traffic better, IP specifies the protocol for breaking single messages into a slew of portions. Each portion is responsible for finding its way across the network based on changing traffic congestion and the IP protocol. Each time a message arrives at an IP router, the router decides where to send it next. There is no concept of a session with a pre-selected path for all traffic. Routers can send data along the path of least resistance regardless of local network traffic congestion. Packets are sent across the Internet from subnet to subnet via gateways or routers as illustrated in Figure 2.3.

The Internet gateway is designed to be transparent to the end-user application in the host computers and the subnet it is attached to. The gateway routes the IP packets to the appropriate subnet. Routing takes place in the Internet layer of the gateway that enables TCP/IP to work on different types of LAN using different media and different protocols. The TCP usually resides in the transport layer and provides a reliable end-to-end communication service that uses acknowledgements to ensure that packets have been delivered. A different protocol called UDP (user datagram protocol) can be used instead of TCP. The UDP sends IP packets but does not use acknowledgements (and is therefore unreliable).

Figure 2.3 Gateways and subnets combine to form the Internet

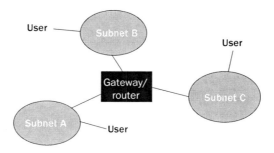

This type of service is more suitable for status information, video conferencing and voice communication applications where the loss of the occasional packet can be safely ignored.[8] Each application process must identify itself by a *port number*. The port number is equivalent to the service access point (SAP) found in the OSI model. Typically, ports 1–1023 are reserved for system use. Applications may use any of the other ports as long as no other application is currently using them. Multiple programs may communicate with a single application via a port but a port can be used only once on any host. In addition to ports, TCP/IP-based protocols use an identifier called a *socket*. A socket allows an application to communicate with a particular machine via a port using low-level read/write commands (in the same way as it would communicate with files).[9] TCP/IP is a two-layered protocol. The *higher layer*, TCP, manages the assembling of a message or file into smaller packets that are transmitted over the Internet and received by a TCP layer that reassembles the packets into the original message. The *lower layer* (network layer), IP, handles the address part of each packet so that it gets to the right destination.[10] TCP's reference model differs from the OSI seven-layer model as can be seen in Figure 2.4.

The TCP/IP model traditionally has four layers (the data link layer and the physical layer are combined into a single layer called the host-to-network layer but it is also common to show these layers separately). There is no session layer or presentation layer in the TCP/IP model (if necessary, their tasks are made the responsibility of the application layer). The TCP/IP layers that exist are essentially the same as those in

Figure 2.4 The differences between the OSI and TCP/IP reference models

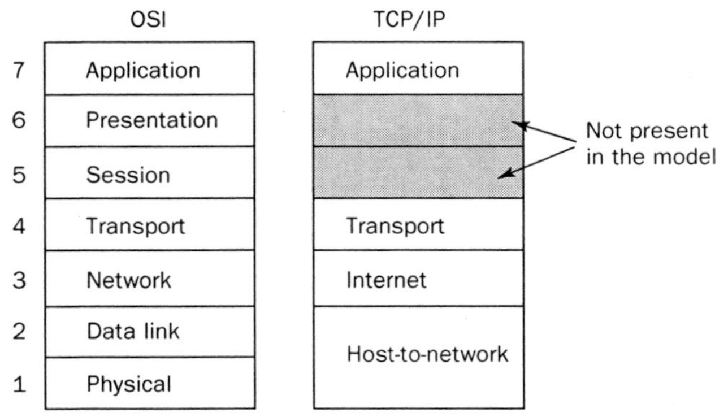

	OSI	TCP/IP	
7	Application	Application	
6	Presentation		Not present in the model
5	Session		
4	Transport	Transport	
3	Network	Internet	
2	Data link	Host-to-network	
1	Physical		

the OSI reference model. The *host-to-network* layer is responsible for sending bits across the network and for link error control and link flow control (i.e. data link layer and physical layer combined). The *Internet* layer switches packets around the network and places packets on (or removes them from) the network using IP. The *transport* layer accepts data (and instructions) from the application layer and breaks the data up into packets. It reassembles received packets into data streams and passes these data to the appropriate port number (e.g. port number 1066) and is also responsible for end-to-end flow control. Finally, the *application* layer contains all the higher-level protocols such as TELNET, FTP and SMTP that are used by applications.

RTP is a real-time transport protocol providing supporting applications transmitting real-time data over unicast and multicast networks.[11] RTP is used in MBone audio/video tools in addition to numerous commercial implementations.[12] RTP services include payload type identification, sequence numbering and time stamping. Delivery is monitored by the closely integrated control protocol RTCP (RTP control protocol). Although RTP provides end-to-end delivery services, it does not provide all of the functionality typically provided by transport protocols and it therefore generally resides on top of UDP to utilise UDP's multiplexing services. End-to-end support includes multi-party functions, such as synchronisation of multiple streams, and reconstruction of streams based on timestamps. Sequence numbers allow the identification of packet positions in a stream that may arrive out of order (e.g. to aid in video decoding). RTP bridges can act as synchronisation points along a path to transcode data into a more suitable format for the destinations that they serve.[13]

Each RTP data packet consists of an RTP packet header and payload. The packet header includes a sequence number, a media-specific timestamp, and a synchronisation source (SSRC) identifier while the RTCP provides mechanisms for data distribution monitoring, cross-media synchronisation and sender identification. The control information transmission interval (sent to all participants) is randomised and adjusted according to the session size to maintain the RTCP bandwidth below some configurable limit. RTCP's primary function is to provide session feedback on data distribution quality, which is useful for diagnosing failures and monitoring performance, and can be adopted by applications for dynamic adaptation to congestion. Monitoring statistics such as sender reports (SR) include the sender's cumulative packet count and cumulative byte count while the receiver reports (RR) statistics include cumulative count of lost packets, jitter, short-term loss indicator and round-trip time estimation time-stamps. RTP's design is based on the IP multicast group delivery protocol, in which data sources broadcast to a group's multicast address without knowledge of the actual group membership. Real-time applications such as adaptive audio or video conferencing tools are often based on RTP so that they can work in loaded networks so long as a minimal amount of bandwidth is available. Real-time applications make use of RTP's support of intra- and inter-stream synchronisation and encoding detection with RTP being frequently integrated into the application software rather than being implemented as a separate layer. In accordance with the application level framing (ALF) principle, the semantics of several RTP header fields are application dependent and several profile documents specify the use of RTP header fields for different applications (e.g. the marker part of the RTP header defines the start of a talk spurt in an audio packet and the end of a video frame in a video packet).[14] RTP in effect is integrated into the application processing rather than being implemented as a separate layer. This also means that it is not concerned with whether IPv4, IPv6, Ethernet, ATM or another communication mechanism is being used. It normally runs on top of UDP, using the latter's framing services such as multiplexing and checksum.

ALF is a protocol that explicitly includes an application's semantics in the design of that applications protocol.[15] ALF helps to break down the data into aggregates, which are meaningful to the application and independent of specific network technology. These data aggregates are known as application data units (ADUs). The lower network layer should preserve the frame boundaries of ADUs so that applications are able to process each ADU separately and potentially out of order with respect to other ADUs. This ensures that ADU losses do not prevent the processing of other ADUs. In order to express data loss in terms meaningful to the application RTP data units carry sequence numbers and timestamps, so receivers can determine the time and sequence relationships between ADUs. As each ADU is a meaningful data entity to the receiving application, the application itself can decide about how to cope with a lost data unit (e.g. real-time digital video might choose to ignore lost frames, whereas FTP applications may request the resending of lost packets).[15]

Conclusion

The ISO network model contains seven layers. IP is a connectionless protocol that gateways use to identify networks and paths to networks and hosts. The IP layer is the centrepiece of the Internet. Other important layers such as TCP that reside beneath the World Wide Web are implemented in many applications but, unlike IP, they are not compulsory. The IP layer takes control of the routing of the data and ensures that there is an end-to-end path. Newer protocols such as RTP provide important support for applications transmitting real-time data over unicast and multicast networks. The success of the Internet to date is a result of additions such as RTP in the Internet's core protocol collection.

Notes

1. Tanenbaum, A. (2004) *Computer Networks*, 5th Edition. New York: Prentice Hall.
2. Camarillo, G. and Garcia-Martin, M. (2005) *The 3G IP Multimedia Subsystem (IMS): Merging the Internet and the Cellular Worlds*, 2nd Edition. Dorchester: John Wiley and Sons Ltd.
3. Zari, M., Saiedian, H. and Naeem, M. (2001) 'Understanding and reducing web delays', *IEEE Computer* 34:12, 30–7.
4. Xilinx (2005) Transmission Control Protocol/Internet Protocol (TCP/IP), *http://www.xilinx.com/esp/optical/net_tech/tcp.htm*
5. Ji, P., Ge, Z., Kurose, J. and Towsley, D. (2003) Applications, technologies, architectures and protocols for computer communication archive. *Proceedings of the 2003 conference on Applications, technologies, architectures, and protocols for computer communications*. Karlsruhe, Germany, pp. 251–62. ACM.
6. Kyas, O. and Crawford, G. (2002) *ATM networks*. New York: Prentice Hall Publishers.
7. Stallings, W. (2005) *Data and Network Communications*, 7th Edition. New York: Prentice-Hall.
8. Beck, A. and Hofmann, M. (2005) 'Extending service mediation to intelligent VoIP endpoints', *Bell Labs Technical Journal* 10:1, 11–15.
9. Matthur, A. and Mundur, P. (2003) Congestion adaptive streaming: an integrated approach. DMS' 2003 – *The 9th International Conference on Distributed Multimedia Systems*, Florida International University Miami, Florida, USA.
10. Halsall, F. (2005) *Computer Networking and the Internet*, 5th edition. New York: Addison Wesley.
11. Perkins, C. (2003) *RTP – Audio and Video for the Internet*. London: Pearson Education.
12. Roussopoulos, M. and Baker, M. (2003) CUP: controlled update propagation in peer-to-peer networks. *Proceedings of the 2003 USENIX Annual Technical Conference*, San Antonio, Texas. ACM.
13. Balasubramanian, V. and Venkatasubramanian, N. (2003) Server transcoding of multimedia information for cross disability access. *ACM/SPIE Conference on Multimedia Computing and Networking*, ACM/SPIE.

14. Tsarouchis, C., Denazis, S., Kitahara, C. and Vivero, J. (2003) 'A policy-based management architecture for active and programmable networks', *IEEE Network*, 17:3, 22–8.
15. Wu, W., Ren, Y. and Shan, X. (2002) Providing Proportional Loss Rate for Adaptive Traffic: A New Relative DiffServ Model. citeseer.nj.nec.com/wu02 providing.html
15. Yan, B. and Mabo, R. (2004) QoS control for video and audio communication in conventional and active networks: approaches and comparison. *IEEE Communications Surveys & Tutorials* 6:1, 42–9.

3

What causes delay in the Internet?

Kevin Curran, Derek Woods and Nadene McDermot

Internet traffic is essentially the load on the network, or the number of packets of data traversing the network. When the Internet was first developed, it was never visualised as being a public service, so the increase in network traffic was no real cause for concern. Congestion in a packet-switching network is a state in which performance degrades due to the saturation of network resources such as communication links, processor cycles and memory buffers. Congestion is increasingly becoming a major problem for the Internet, making many types of file transfer both unstable and unreliable. This chapter outlines the main issues surrounding congestion on the Internet.

Introduction

Congestion on the Internet is becoming an ever-increasing problem. Even though the technology surrounding the Internet has improved significantly, it seems that file transfer times continue to increase, with no real solution in sight.[1] It is therefore important to understand first how congestion occurs and how it is measured, and subsequently, what mechanisms are in place to control this congestion. It is argued that three main factors – incompatibility of the newer applications with the Internet's architecture, the growth of the Internet, and privatisation and concomitant commercialisation of the Internet – are responsible for an inherent change in the Internet's dynamics.[2]

Internet traffic has grown at an alarming rate: 'When seen over the decade of the 1990s, traffic appears to be doubling about once each year.'[3] Indeed, the growth rate of Internet traffic has posed severe problems for its measurement, an essential to our understanding of Internet congestion. A common complaint about traffic measurement studies is that they do remain of relevance given that traffic, technology and topology change faster than we can measure them. Thus, future proposals on Internet congestion can only estimate the actual load on the network at any particular time. In fact, no single organization is truly measuring global Internet behaviour, because the global Internet is simply not instrumented to allow such measurement.[4] Internet traffic in general is said to be 'bursty', that is, that bursts of traffic rather than a steady flow are transmitted. The most serious effects of congestion are seen in the form of congestion collapse. This occurs when 'a sudden load on the net can cause the round-trip time to rise faster than the sending hosts measurements of round-trip time can be updated'.[5] Under these conditions the network can come to a complete standstill. 'Informally, congestion collapse occurs when an increase in the network load results in a decrease in the useful work done by the network.'[6] Due to this increase in network traffic and the pressure it puts on the available bandwidth, the fairness of the Internet is also at risk. Fairness means that no user is penalised compared with others who share the same physical connection. Congestion control mechanisms can enforce fairness. Unfairness in the Internet occurs when congestion control techniques are not implemented, such as the additive increase/multiplicative-decrease (AIMD) method of control, which will be discussed later in this chapter. Flows that do not 'back-off' when faced with congestion can utilise all of the available bandwidth, leaving other flows fighting for their share.

Maximum packet size

A modern server uses path maximum transmission unit discovery (PMTUD) heuristics to determine the maximum segment size (MSS), which is the safe packet size that can be transmitted.[7] PMTUD was adopted to address the poor performance and communication failures associated with oversized packets which are fragmented at routers with small message transfer unit (MTU).[8] Today, the PMTUD concept is imperfect as it uses the internet control message protocol (ICMP), which some network administrators view as a threat and block all such packets, disabling PMTUD, usually without realising it.[9] This led to increased packet overheads due to retransmissions and eventually connection time-outs. Lahey suggested a workaround where after several time-outs, the server network should be reconfigured to accept an altered ICMP packet with the

'Do Not Fragment' part disabled.[10] Consequently, the PMTUD feature is bypassed, but detection can take several seconds each time, and these delays result in a significant, hidden degradation of network performance.

DNS, caching and Web page delays

Domain name servers (DNSs) are the nub of the Internet infrastructure. They are responsible for translating domain names into an equivalent IP address needed by the Internet's TCP. The latency between DNS request and response is a random variable as the DNS lookup system uses the client's cache file, the hierarchical nature of the domain name and a set of DNSs operating at multiple sites to solve the mapping problem cooperatively. A survey from Men and Mice[11] showed that 68% of the DNS for commercial sites (e.g. .com zones) has some configuration errors, thus making them vulnerable to security breach and denial of service. They are normally handled by novices who do not fully understand the operation of DNSs very well. An intelligent DNS management system was recently developed by Liu *et al.* that offers administrator support in DNS system configuration, problem diagnosis and tutoring.[12]

The network delay for Web page loading is dominated by the hyper text transfer protocol (HTTP) standard. It is an application-level protocol for transfer of Web contents between clients and servers. Due to increasing Internet traffic, HTTP makes inefficient use of the network and suffers from high latencies for three reasons: (1) it takes time to transmit the unnecessarily large number of bytes, (2) TCP's three-way 'handshakes' for opening a connection add extra round-trip time delay and (3) multiple parallel TCP streams do not share the same congestion avoidance state. Spreitzer *et al.* have developed a prototype for 'next-generation' HTTP which should address these latency issues.[13]

The caching mechanism is available ubiquitously. It exists on the client's local disk and is also provided by DNSs, network servers and Internet service providers (ISPs). ISPs use cache server technology to help companies get their web pages faster to potential customers. Its rationale is to assuage congestion, reduce bandwidth consumption, improve retrieval times by temporarily storing Web objects closer to the clients and reduce the burden on the site server as it handles fewer requests. Caching is often deliberately defeated as not all Web contents are cacheable. A modern-day Web page contains both dynamic and static contents. Dynamic items are non-cacheable and typically contain interactive and changeable items that provide a far richer experience for users, but users are not happy to wait for them.[14] Cached components characteristically contain items that do not change, i.e. they are static. An intelligent cache engine has emerged that serves dynamic elements of a Web page and reduces latency time by 90%.[15] It works by estimating future client behaviour at a site based on past and present access patterns. The downside with caching is that if the user does not use the cached items, then congestion may have been caused needlessly.

Recommendations that were made to improve Web page designs have had a positive impact on page retrieval times as well as on usability. The adoption of cascaded style sheets (CSS)[16] and more compact image representations, namely portable network graphics (PNG),[17] have added reduced file sizes and speeded up page downloads without sacrificing graphics design.[14] PNG was designed as a successor to the popular GIF (graphics interchange format) files, but it was not until late 1997 when browser wars came to an end that many old browsers caught up and were able to read PNG formats. Another Web image format is JPEG, which uses lossy compression and exploits known limitations of the human eye. Weinberger *et al.* have created a new lossless/near-lossless image compression format called JPEG-LS.[18] This standard is for continuous tone images and is currently awaiting approval from the World Wide Web Consortium.

Network connection quality can be described in terms of availability, latency, jitter and capacity. Availability is the assurance that traffic will reach its destination successfully, and forms the basis of most service-level agreements. Latency is the delay that traffic experiences as it travels across the network while jitter is the change in this latency over time. Establishing a particular quality of service (QoS) level for a connection is a complex process, in part because of the stateless, best-effort paradigm upon which the Internet is based and the fact that one must balance all of the QoS parameters above.[19] There are two main approaches to QoS: the integrated services model[20] and the differentiated services model.[21] The integrated services model negotiates a particular QoS at the time it is requested. Before exchanging traffic, the sender and receiver request a particular QoS level from the network. Upon acceptance, the intermediate network devices associate the resulting traffic flow with a specific level of jitter, latency and capacity. The resource reservation protocol (RSVP), a protocol for signalling QoS requirements for a particular traffic flow, is a key component. The differentiated services model takes a different approach using traffic handling classes with various levels of service quality. These are established by the network administrator such that when the sender needs a particular kind of handling, it marks each individual packet. Through the migration from resource-based to service-driven networks, it has become evident that the Internet model should be enhanced to provide support for a variety of differentiated services that match applications and customer requirements, and not stay limited under the flat best-effort service that is currently provided.[22]

Flow control

Flow control is the method of preventing network congestion and increasing fairness by ensuring that a suitable number of flows are transmitted so that the receiving devices are not flooded with data. It is convenient to divide flows into three classes:

- TCP-compatible flows,
- unresponsive flows, i.e. flows that do not slow down when congestion occurs, and
- flows that are responsive but are not TCP-compatible.[6]

The flow control mechanism of TCP uses slow start and congestion avoidance algorithms as a mechanism to control the data transmission rate.[23] This helps to reduce loss of packets caused by congested routers. However, lost packets can be recovered using TCP's retransmission feature, but this incurs added delivery time. The aggressive behaviour of multimedia applications involving audio and video, in which developers employ user datagram packets (UDPs), compounds the problem of congestion. UDPs are not TCP friendly and they do not respond to packet drops, which typically suggest congestions. This aggressive behaviour degrades and even shuts out TCP packets such as HTTP and prevents them from obtaining their fair share of their bandwidth when they battle for bandwidth over a congested link. Lee *et al.* examined the use of TCP tunnels at core routers to isolate different types of traffic from one another.[24] Benefits include reduced TCP retransmission per connection by over 500% and more packets can be processed using the same amount of memory resources. This concept is not used extensively on the current Internet infrastructure. Whilst TCP and TCP-compatible flows are said to be responsive in the face of congestion, it is the unresponsive flows that cause network problems. These types of flows simply add to the congestion problem, as they are of very high bandwidth. Unresponsive flows also promote unfairness in that whereas other flows decrease the data being transmitted, unresponsive flows aggressively hunt available bandwidth. There are three main techniques adopted to control the flows within a network:

- Buffering – temporarily storing data until it can be dealt with.

- Source-quench messages – if a network device is showing signs of congestion (i.e. the buffer is full and packets are being dropped), then it will send source-quench messages to the sending devices so that they will reduce the transmission rate at which they are sending data.

- Windowing – the sending device sends a certain number of packets to the receiver, but requires an acknowledgement (ACK) before any more data can be sent. When an ACK has been received by the sender then another set of packets can be sent. If no ACK is received then this is an indicator of congestion. The receiver has not received enough packets to send an ACK, so some packets may have been dropped, due to an overflowing buffer etc. The sender, on not receiving an ACK, will then re-transmit the packets. This is, in essence, the additive increase/multiplicative-decrease (AIMD) congestion methodology.

Router congestion control

Routers have already been discussed here as being one of the key pieces of Internet architecture, so it is important to consider the controls that are in place to effectively manage congestion at this point in the transfer of packets across the Internet. Lefelhocz proposed a paradigm in order to maintain a fair routing system for Internet usage.[25] The proposed design incorporated four controls for congestion management, namely scheduling algorithms, buffer management, feedback and end adjustment, and these are widely implemented in the Internet today.

The two most popular scheduling algorithms are FIFO (first in first out), which forwards packets according to their place in the queue, and WFQ (weighted fair queuing), which attempts to allocate the available bandwidth fairly, thus protecting flows from unfairness on the part of others. Some form of scheduling algorithm must be implemented in order to prevent bandwidth being 'swallowed up' by greedy users. However, this alone will not prevent packets from being dropped, so other measures must be implemented simultaneously. Buffering is required at a switch whenever packets are arriving faster than they can be sent out. This buffering should take one of two forms. The shared buffer pool method does not protect flows from one another, but forwards packets using the first come first use method. By contrast, the per-flow allocation method uses a fairer method of packet forwarding in which each flow is forwarded on merit and 'well-behaved' flows are serviced first.

Feedback is another important function at the router to control congestion. There are two types of feedback. Implicit feedback 'requires the end user to monitor the performance of their data transmission for clues to the current network status.'[25] An example of this type of feedback can be seen in the TCP slow start algorithm, where packet loss is the congestion indicator. Explicit feedback takes the form of an indicator. This can be implemented in forward (FECN – forward explicit congestion notification) and reverse modes (BECN – backward explicit congestion notification). This type of congestion notification provides better control as it can be measured by the router in order to quantify the amount of congestion that is occurring.

The router relies on this end adjustment figure to give an accurate depiction of the amount of congestion that is occurring. This then controls the push of packets into the network, and thus the possible increase in congestion and pressure on the network. Routers manage traffic flow by using one of two methods: static routing or dynamic routing. Static routing is best implemented by small networks, where the topology and state of the network are known to be relatively stable. The routes taken by packets of data are hard coded by the network engineer manually and do not change unless the engineer becomes aware of changes within the network, such as a change to the network topology. Dynamic routing, by contrast, is used where the topology of the network is unknown and the route taken by packets of data is uncertain at the time of sending. Dynamic protocols are used to calculate the best path for the packets to take, considering many parameters. These dynamic routing protocols are used to discover the best paths for Internet traffic on a daily basis.

Gateway protocols

Once dynamic routing has been chosen as the preferred method of path selection the actual protocol that will be used to implement the metrics and perform the calculations must then be considered. There are two main classes of gateway protocols, interior and exterior. Interior gateway protocols are used within autonomous systems, that is a set of routers under a single technical administration.[26] Exterior gateway protocols are used to communicate *between* autonomous systems, therefore providing the links between different networks, in order for them to work together as a single unit.

Border gateway protocol (BGP) v4 is a routing protocol used in the Internet. It was designed for networks that implement TCP/IP. BGP is an exterior gateway protocol, which means that it performs routing between multiple autonomous systems or domains and exchanges routing and reachability information with other BGP systems. The protocol exchanges this information by using BGP speakers to communicate to the routers that directly neighbour it. These update messages can contain information such as withdrawn routes and network reachability information. The protocol uses a number of variables to determine the best path for a packet. Table 3.1 outlines these variables and their metrics.

As illustrated, the BGP v4 protocol does not usually take the load on the network into account when choosing the best path. The load would constantly be changing as users went online and offline and there would be a lot of routing table updates to the extent that there would be just as much traffic being generated just to maintain the routing table. The growth of the Internet has adversely affected the stability of routing in times of congestion. It has been shown that when a network is congested

Table 3.1 BGP v4 metrics

Next Hop	If it sees the next hop as being unreachable (down) that route is not considered
BGP Weighting	This is organised such that the larger the BGP weighting (cost) the greater the trustworthiness
Same Weight	Highest local preference is used
Same Local Preference	Prefer route where originating traffic came from
No Originating route	Prefer route with least AS hop count
Same autonomous systems (AS) hop count	Prefer external route
All routes are external	Prefer lowest origin count
Same codes and AS IGP Sync. Disabled	Prefer lowest MULTI_EXIT_DISC metric route. No metric=0
Internal Paths Only	Prefer route through closest neighbour
All else fails	Prefer BGP route with router ID of lowest router IP address

and packets are dropped, some of these packets could be the updated routing information of the network. Congestion in the network can hinder the propagation of routing information or peering refresh requests if the routing protocol messages are not isolated from data traffic.[27] It would seem that the very messages that are providing routers with information to stem the build up of congestion are at risk themselves [with both open shortest path first (OPSF) and BGP protocols displaying signs of unreliability under congested conditions]. This can have great implications for routing and therefore for Internet stability.

Notes

1. Yang, C. and Reddy, V.S. (1995) 'A taxonomy for congestion control algorithms in packet switching networks', *IEEE Network Magazine*, 9:5, 45–52.
2. Sarkar, M. (1996) 'An assessment of pricing mechanisms for the internet–a regulatory imperative', *The Journal of Electronic Publishing*, 2:1, 16–28.
3. Odlyzko, A. (2000) 'Internet growth: myth and reality, use and abuse', *Information Impacts Magazine*, November.
4. Murray, M. (2001) Measuring the immeasurable: global Internet measurement infrastructure, caida.org, April.
5. Nagle, J. (1984) 'Congestion Control in IP/TCP Internetworks', *Request for Comments: 896, http://rfc.sunsite.dk/rfc/rfc896.html*
6. Floyd, S. (2000) 'Congestion Control Principles', *Request for Comments: 2914*, Network Working Group.
7. Mogul, J. and Deering, S. (1990) Path MTU discovery. *RFC1191*. Available at: *http://www.faqs.org/rfcs/rfc1191.html*
8. Kent, C.A. and Mogul, J.C. (1987) Fragmentation considered harmful. *Digital Western Research Laboratory. Research report 87/3, December.* Taken from: *http://research.compaq.com/wrl/techreports/abstracts/87.3.html*
9. Knowles, S. (1993) IESG advice from experience with path MTU discovery. *RFC1435*. Available at: *http://www.faqs.org/ftp/rfc/pdf/rfc1435.txt.pdf*
10. Lahey, K. (2000) TCP problems with path MTU discovery. *RFC2923*. Available at: *http://www.faqs.org/ftp/rfc/pdf/rfc2923.txt.pdf*
11. Menandmice (2003) *http://www.menandmice.com/6000/61_recent_survey.html*
12. Liu, C.L., Tseng, S.S. and Chen, C.S. (2004) 'Design and implementation of an intelligent DNS management system', *Expert Systems with Applications* 27:2, 223–36.
13. Spreitzer, M. and Janssen, B. (2001) HTTP 'Next Generation', PARC research report, *http://www2.parc.com/isl/members/janssen/pubs/www9-http-next-generation.html*
14. Nielsen, H.F., Gettys, J., Baird-Smith, A., Prud'hommeaux, H., Lie, H. and Lilley, C. (1997) 'Network performance effects of HTTP/1.1, CSS1, and PNG', *Computer Communication Review* 27:4, 155–66.

15. Govatos, G. (2001). Accelerating dynamic Web site performance and scalability. Chutney Technologies, Inc. Available at: *www.caching.com/pdf/Preloader_final.pdf*

16. Lie, H. and Bos, B. (1996). Cascading Style Sheets, level 1. *W3C Recommendation, World Wide Web Consortium,* 17th December 1996, revised 11th January 1999. Available at: *http://www.w3.org/TR/REC-CSS1*

17. Libpng (2004) *http://www.libpng.org/pub/png/*

18. Weinberger, M., Seroussi, M. and Sapiro, G. (2000) 'The LOCO-I lossless image compression algorithm: principles and standardization into JPEG-LS', *IEEE Transactions in Image Processing* 9, 1309–24.

19. CISCO (20001) *DiffServ-The Scalable End-to-End QoS Model.* Cisco Systems White Paper.

20. Crawley, E., Berger, L., Berson, S., Baker, F., Borden, S. and Krawczyk, J. (1998) A framework for integrated services and RSVP over ATM. *RFC 2382.*

21. Fulp, E. and Reeves, D. (2001) 'Optimal provisioning and pricing of differentiated services using QoS class promotion', In *Proceedings of the First International Workshop on Internet Charging and QoS Technology (ICQT'01),* pp. 144–50.

22. Bernet, Y., Ford, P., Yavatkar, R., Baker, F., Zhang, L., Speer, M., Braden, R., Davie, B., Wroklawski, J. and Felstaine, E. (2000) *A Framework for Integrated Services Operation over DiffServ Networks.* Internet Engineering Task Force (IETF) Integrated Services over Specific Link Layers (ISSLL) Working Group, RFC2998.

23. Floyd, S. and Fall, K. (1999) 'Promoting the use of end-to-end congestion control in the internet', *IEEE/ACM Transactions on Networking* 7:4, 458–72.

24. Lee, B., Balan, R., Jacob, L., Seah, W. and Ananda, A. (2002) 'Avoiding congestion collapse on the Internet using TCP tunnels', *Computer Networks* 39:2, 207–19.

25. Lefelhocz, C. (1996) 'Congestion control for best-effort service: why we need a new paradigm', *IEEE Network* 10:1, 10–19.

26. Rekhter, Y. (1995) 'A Border Gateway Protocol 4 (BGP-4)', *Request for Comments: 1771.* Network Working Group.

27. Shaikh, A. (2000) 'Routing stability in congested networks: experimentation and analysis', *Special Interest Group on Data Communication (SIGCOMM) Proceedings* 2000: 163–17.

4

Mesh networking

Kevin Curran, Derek Hawkes,
Scott Hulme and Christopher Laughlin

Wireless mesh networks have evolved from a simple single-channel radio to a three-radio configuration, and now the technology itself seems to have reached a point of maturity where its uses have been brought outside of the military environment and have been implemented into everyday life. The main uses outside of the armed forces is offering broadband to the general public who live in areas with little or no broadband access or by people who are on the move in town areas. The topology seems to have been greatly affected by the increasing popularity of mobile wireless devices such as laptops, personal digital assistants (PDAs), phones and MP3 players. There are still several main issues that have to be addressed for mesh networking to reach its full potential. Obviously, the privacy and security of those using the network needs to be taken into consideration as they are allowing others to view and connect to their computer.

Introduction

Mesh networks can be either wired or wireless, and provide a way to design a network of nodes so that information such as data information, voice, video, instructions for nodes or any other type of information can be routed around a network without any interference, even when a node fails. Ad-hoc networks that are wireless have data forwarded by the nodes, depending on the connections within the ad-hoc network, and there is no central point within their topology; however, if the network is wired then the function of forwarding data is carried out by the routers. Mesh networking has a topology that contains nodes that communicate with each other, via other nodes within the network or directly depending on the position of the source node with respect to the destination node. Within the communication industry this type of communication between nodes is termed hopping, and for this type of network to operate effectively each node must have at least two radio pathways to communicate with the other nodes.

The area covered by the mesh network of nodes is called a mesh cloud; this mesh cloud is only effective if the nodes are listening to and communicating with each other. Mesh networks can be put into the category of ad-hoc networks, which means that mesh networks and mobile ad-hoc networking are closely related. The main purpose of the wireless mesh network is to provide a connection between the mesh client and the wired backbone of a network, or back haul; this could be anything from providing the public within a residential area with access to the Internet, to providing communication between units in the armed forces. The mesh network can be randomly structured with no central point, and is not as geometrically shaped as other topologies, which are shown in Figure 4.1.

The mesh network can also be fully connected, as shown in Figure 4.1. Within the wireless mesh network there are two types of nodes:

- Mesh routers: these devices forward data packets to each other within the mesh network, and have the ability to provide gateway/bridge functions, so that subnets (clients) can access the mesh network. Other than the routing capability for gateway/bridge functions as in a conventional router, a mesh router contains additional routing functions to support mesh networking.[1] Mesh routers can also have

Figure 4.1   Different network topologies

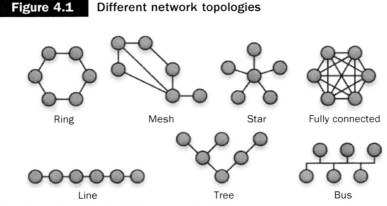

Ring   Mesh   Star   Fully connected

Line   Tree   Bus

(http://en.wikipedia.org/wiki/Network_Topology)

numerous and different types of wireless interfaces, so that a variety of wireless technologies can access the mesh network for connection into the wired backbone.

- Mesh clients: these devices do not have the capability of mesh routers, such as gateway/bridge functions. They are connected to the router either through a single wireless interface or by wire through the Ethernet; if there are multiple mesh clients at one location, a base station or access point will be connected to the clients, and from the base station a connection will made to the router/bridge within the mesh network.

The nodes in the mesh network execute the following sequence to achieve a route to the destination node:

1. The source node sends out a route request packet to the whole mesh network.
2. Nodes within the network that receive the packet revise the information already stored by them, for use by the transmitting node or source node.
3. After updating the information, the nodes set up markers or pointers back to the source node through the route tables.
4. The wireless nodes also send back other active information such as IP address, the present sequence number for the request and the identification number of the broadcast source.
5. The other nodes within the mesh network will only answer the broadcast if they are either the destination or one of the nodes on the route to the destination.

Wireless mesh was originally developed for military applications, but has undergone significant evolution in the past decade. These developments within mesh networking, which are also used by the civilian population, occurred in three stages, and were related to the configuration of the radio within the mesh network, which has improved the reliability and adaptability of the network. This improvement has been possible due to the reduced costs of radios, which in turn has led to more radios being used in mesh networks, allowing the mesh network to improve functions such as client access, transmission between client and the mesh network, and radios specifically searching continuously for other nodes, to provide faster handover between nodes whenever the network is mobile. This early stage of technological development or innovation in wireless mesh was prior to the development of IEEE standards and is known as first-generation wireless mesh.

The first mesh network generation used one radio channel to provide service to clients, and also the backhaul or transmission back to the mesh network. This type of radio configuration meant that when one node was transmitting, the other nodes in the mesh network were listening, and therefore the nodes were transmitting, then receiving, and then transmitting on the same channel. This intermittent stop-and-go behaviour adversely affects network performance, especially if the destination is far away and the traffic has to be retransmitted ('hop') across many intermediate nodes first. A diagram of the first-generation mesh network is shown in Figure 4.2.

The second generation of nodes in the mesh network improved on the performance of the mesh network by having two radios within the nodes, one to provide service for the client and the other for transmission to the mesh network or backhaul. However, as a single radio mesh is still servicing the backhaul, packets travelling towards the Internet share bandwidth at each hop along the backhaul path with other interfering mesh backhaul nodes – all operating on the same channel. This causes degradation in the performance of the mesh network, but not as severe as that with the first-generation mesh networks. A diagram of the second-generation mesh network is shown in Figure 4.2. The third generation of nodes used in the mesh network again improved on performance by having two radios in each node to service the backhaul, (uplink and downlink) and one to service the clients. This network controls the

Figure 4.2   Three generations of mesh

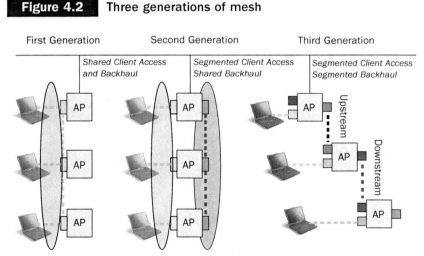

(*http://en.wikipedia.org/wiki/History_of_wireless_mesh_networking*)

channels of the radios so that the radios are on separate channels, but have the same bands, and therefore interference does not occur between nodes.

Wireless mesh network architecture

The architecture of wireless mesh networks can be of different types:

- Infrastructure/backbone uses mesh routers to form the mesh network, and these routers have gateway/bridge functions that allow connection to other networks, such as the Internet, or other subnets. The connection to the external networks can be either wired through the ethernet if the client does not have a wireless network interface card, or wireless otherwise.

- Client meshing is where the client nodes provide the actual network functions, such as routing and configuration, as well as providing the applications required by the end user customer. Therefore, this type of mesh network does not require mesh routers, and the functions and requirements of the customer's devices are thus much more extensive, as compared with the infrastructure/backbone wireless mesh networks. Client wireless mesh networks are usually formed using one type of radio on devices.

- A hybrid wireless mesh network combines both infrastructure/ backbone architecture and client mesh architecture. The infrastructure/ backbone section of the hybrid mesh network provides connections to other networks, such as sensor networks, WiFi, WiMAX and the Internet. With the client mesh section having functionalities such as routing and configuration, the connectivity and mesh cloud coverage within the wireless mesh network is improved.[2]

Design of wireless mesh networks

To improve radio communication, use of directional and smart antennas have being suggested. These antennas are very powerful both at transmitting and at receiving signals in more than one direction, and have reduced interference from external sources, in comparison with dipole antennas. Other systems such as multiple-input multiple-output and multi-radio/multi-channel were considered. All these systems and techniques were suggested to improve capacity, and increase the adaptability of wireless mesh systems.

Wireless mesh networks can be further improved by increasing control of the higher protocol layers, using more advanced radio technologies; these could include reconfigurable radios, software radios and frequency-adaptable spectrum radios. Although these radio technologies are still in their infancy, they are expected to be the future platform for wireless networks due to their dynamic control capability.[1] Standardising the radio technology used by mesh networks reduces the cost of the equipment required and the installation of the equipment, and allows compatibility between different types of equipment such as PCs and mobile phones. The organisation given the responsibility of ensuring compatibility between devices is the IEEE Standard Organisation. The IEEE has been establishing different standards for new radio technologies for various levels of the mesh network, and upgrading these standards to accommodate new technologies. These include the following standards:

- *IEEE 802.15.5* is the standard that deals with defining the media access control layer and the physical layer, so that short-range connections can be made between groups of devices that are moving, such as laptops, mobile phones and PDAs. The main problem with these devices is power source capability, which does not allow for long-range transmission, at high bandwidths. By using mesh technology, where the communication is achieved by hopping from one node to another, the area covered by these devices is increased, and still maintains a high bandwidth because of the short distances involved.

- *IEEE 802.11s* deals with the quality of service (QoS), handovers between nodes where the mesh client is mobile, and ensuring high-speed bandwidth. This standard also improved on the infrastructure and protocols used in the nodes to make connections between each other, revise the topology of the network and route configuration.

- *IEEE 802.16A* addresses the problem of interference at frequencies above 10 GHz that occurred with the standard 806.16. The new standard 806.16A incorporates the non-line of sight (NLOS) operation, which is supported by the time-division multiple access (TDMA) in the media access control layer.

- *IEEE 802.20* upgrades the previous standards to provide mobile wireless broadband, within the wireless mesh network, for both the indoor and the outdoor environment.

Scalability relates to the number of nodes that can be added to the mesh network, without compromising routing and transport protocols. If the number of nodes is increased, there are more possible hops between nodes for the data packet to reach its destination. However, with each hop there is a certain percentage loss in bandwidth, which can reduce the signal. To prevent this and ensure scalability in the wireless mesh network, every protocol from the media access control (MAC) sub-layer of the open systems interconnection basic reference model (OSI) to the application layer must be capable of adapting to the increased number of nodes or to be scalable. Initial mesh networks used a single radio, and for the source node to send the data packet to the destination node it may have had several hops; as the data packet goes through each node or hop there is a certain percentage loss in throughput. This percentage loss can reduce the distance of the transmission considerably. To overcome this problem multiple radios are added to each node, one being standard 802.11, and the other radio interface has a longer range; although the throughput is reduced, it remains at an acceptable level, for the increased distance gained.

Security in wireless mesh networks from hackers and software viruses, and the authentication of various users within a network, has to be designed into the network, so that these elements do not interfere with the normal communication of the network. The problem with wireless mesh networks is that there is no centralised trusted authority, as access points to the wireless mesh network can be numerous, and therefore unauthorised access could occur at various points. Ad-hoc networks have a certain number of security solutions, and these are being considered for wireless mesh networks, but they have not been developed sufficiently to be implemented adequately for security purposes. Transit access points (TAP) can be compromised by an attacker. This could involve the actual removal or replacement of the device, so that it can be reprogrammed to change the topology of the network for the attacker's benefit. The second form of attack is to access the device internally but make no changes to the device, but simply to monitor the passing traffic information. This form of attack is very difficult to detect. The third form of attack involves modifying the internal structure of the device; this type of attack is more easily detected, because of the use of a verifier by the wireless hot spot (WHS). The fourth type is to build clones of the TAPs, which are then placed in various locations by the attacker, and used to download information by the attacker to corrupt the routing protocols. This again can be detected by the message authentication codes (MACs). If the routing mechanism is attacked, the adversary can change the topology of the network by increasing the route lengths. This in turn reduces the speed of the bandwidth to the mesh client. The attacker could modify the topology to improve the service for them, or to monitor traffic data, which could be for malicious future use. To prevent attack by this method the operator should use secure protocols. Some TAPs only serve one mobile client, whereas others serve two or more, so that TAPs with more than one mobile client, should perhaps get half as much again of the available bandwidth. This is because the client connected to a TAP with more than one mobile client will have reduced bandwidth due to the other client on the same TAP, even though they may be paying the same price as the only mobile client connected to a TAP. This situation can be adjusted by the attacker simply increasing the number of TAPs that the mobile client's information has to travel through; this subsequently increases the number of hops, and decreases the bandwidth. To prevent this, the operator can reconfigure the wireless mesh network routinely, so that routes to TAPs from mobile clients can be optimised for traffic data.

Two of the technical challenges facing mesh networks are load balancing and routing. Load balancing is sending data packets through the mesh network so that the various paths have equal or almost equal amounts of data travelling along each, to reduce congestion, and prevent the slow down of data transmission. Routing involves having a protocol that can decide which path or route to take through the mesh network, to prevent large amounts of data queuing in any one particular route or path. Existing solutions in mobile ad-hoc and sensor networks cannot be directly applied to wireless mesh networks due to the difference in traffic patterns, mobility scenarios, gateway functionalities and bandwidth requirements.[2] Therefore, if most mesh clients wanted to access the Internet, the data traffic will be travelling either towards Internet gateways from the mesh client, or from Internet gateways to the mesh client. The consequences of this is a build up of data congestion on the routes leading towards the Internet gateways, due to the mesh routers choosing the best path to the Internet gateway. Therefore, routing algorithms need to determine routes that will balance the data traffic across the mesh network, towards access points, and not simply the best path towards access points. Load balancing within the wireless mesh network can be accomplished by the following methods:

- *Path-based load balancing*: using this method the data traffic is spread across several routes of the mesh network.
- *Gateway-based load balancing*: the data traffic load is balanced at particular internet gateways, or all of the gateways.
- *Mesh routers*: load balancing can also be carried out at the mesh routers over the wireless backbone.[2]

The protocols governing how the node should determine a path for data traffic in a mesh network are called a routing metric. There are several types of routing metrics:

- Hop count: this metric determines the most suitable path by the number of hops required to achieve the destination node.

- Expected transmission count (ETX): this metric takes into account the number of data packet losses and successful attempts ratio, along with the length of the path, which is determined by the number of successful transmissions from the media access control (MAC) layer through the mesh network.

- Expected transmission time (ETT): this determines a route by considering the different transmission times for each possible route through the mesh network. It enhances ETX by integrating the data transmission rate of each particular link into the routing metric.[2]

- Weight cumulative expected transmission time: this metric considers the different bandwidths available in each route and the variety of paths available for the transmission.

- Metric of interference and channel switching (MIC): MIC improves weighted cumulative expected transmission time (WCETT) by catching both intra-flow interference within a path and inter-flow interference between adjacent paths.[2] This method takes into account the routes used in the current link, and the previous link, to achieve the destination path. The MIC will set a larger parameter value when the current link to the destination is using the same route as the previous link; this is to take into account the intra-flow interference within each route. In order to capture inter-flow interference, MIC also captures the set of neighbours that the transmission on each current link interferes with.[2] This allows the data traffic to be routed through mesh routers that have less traffic flow.

Wireless mesh network applications

Ad-hoc networks that are mobile were mainly design for either military or for special requirements in civilian applications. This, however, is changing with users wanting to access the Internet or other more general applications, where high bandwidth is required for downloading to or from the Internet or application. This has led to the development of the ad-hoc network into a network with hierarchy, with some layers having wired or wireless connections, which is an extension of the wired infrastructure. This extension is called a mesh network, and has resulted in the ad-hoc network being part of a larger mesh network. The mesh network has many uses within the communication industry, which come under areas such as:

- *Intelligent transportation systems.* A mesh network could be set up within a city to implement the control systems for public transportation. An example of this application scenario is the Portsmouth Real-Time Travel Information System (PORTAL), a system that, as part of a city-wide public transportation communications network, aims to provide real-time travel information to passengers.[3] This mesh network allows anyone at some 40 locations throughout the city to access real-time information regarding bus arrivals, destination and present location, and the system is installed in over 300 buses.

- *Public safety.* Due to the current social, political, economic and climatic trends within countries, the need for improved communication between emergency services within disaster areas has increased. The network for emergency services must be reliable, adaptive and have a bandwidth which is high; in the past the solution has involved technologies such as mobile phones or radios, the disadvantage with these technologies being that the bandwidth is low, and therefore the rate of data transmission is slow. However, they do allow high mobility and ubiquitous coverage of the network. An agency that uses mesh networks is the police. For instance, the San Matteo Police Department in the San Francisco Bay Area has equipped all its patrol cars with laptops, and motorcycles and bicycle patrols with PDAs, employing standard 802.11b/g wireless cards for communication.

- *Internet access.* Access to the Internet has become increasingly important to the individual today, and whether for private use or for work, demand for access is increasing. This increasing demand brings problems for Internet service providers, to provide access for subscribers regardless of their physical location. The wireless mesh network provides a solution by having mesh routers located throughout either an urban or a rural environment, and because the network is wireless the cost of installation is low and affordable to the subscriber. An example of this is the metro-scale broadband city network activated on April 2004 in the city of Cerritos, California, operated by Airmesh Communications Inc., a wireless ISP (WISP) company.[3] This network has been built with Tropos-based mesh technology and covers a city area as large as eight miles using more than 130 outdoor access points, less than 20 per cent of them connected to a wired backhaul network.

- *Mesh networks in military warfare.* The first military networks were ad-hoc and used nodes that had a single radio frequency; these nodes provided connections between adjacent nodes by changing their function between mesh client and mesh router. This type of mesh network was slow and prone to interference, and in battlefield situations could leave an army with vulnerable areas for attack. This third generation of wireless mesh node has three radios, one for the mesh client, and two for the backhaul; the backhaul has a radio each for uplink and downlink, and channel management of the radios, to prevent interference from other radios. In today's modern warfare, a central radio controller for all the communications can leave a troop vulnerable, if their communication moves out of range. To prevent this occurring, if multiple wireless mesh nodes are deployed with troop squads, communication can be routed from one squad through the other squad nodes, to the intended command headquarters or squad commanders, but the network must be scalable for this to operate successfully. For this communication between squads to be maintained, the network must be capable of changing topology continuously without the user being aware of it occurring. The nodes within the network should be able to connect with additional nodes, by searching for them automatically; the nodes within the network should be able to change frequencies in a coordinated simultaneous operation without having to get permission from a central node, to prevent interference from jamming. The network should be capable of being deployed on troops, and vehicles, to allow for continuous communication between sections of the army on the move, and allow nodes to connect directly with the upper hierarchy of the network when required, or to hop between nodes to the upper hierarchy.

Wireless mesh networks have also been seen as a solution to areas which have poor Internet access as a result of either being too far away from an exchange or having no ISP in the area. However, uses for wireless mesh networks have also been found in cities and business districts in order to provide access to the Internet. This section details some mesh networks that have been implemented for the use of public and corporate communities.

In 2007, the City of London took on a project to deliver a Wi-Fi mesh network called 'The Cloud' in order to deliver Internet access to a square mile of their financial district.[4] This network has been made available through the use of nearly 130 nodes attached to the city's street lights. This network has, however, not been aimed at the general public but rather at bankers, traders and brokers. This network is not free to use; the user will actually have to subscribe through a provider who will charge fees in order to gain access. The main criticism of 'The Cloud' is that it is a Wi-Fi-based network and therefore it will work perfectly outside but will be limited to what buildings a user can gain access to while inside. Many buildings in the City of London have very thick walls which limit access indoor. Are the people working in the financial district going to use Internet access while outside? Surprisingly, there are over 350,000 users registered to use the service, which would indicate that the network seems to be of some use.[4]

Motorola has recently undertaken a project called 'MotoMesh', which uses mesh network technology to provide broadband access to the public. The aim of the project is to enable users to be able to use broadband applications seamlessly anywhere and at anytime even when on the move by foot or by vehicle. This has been done by using a form of wireless networking which is based heavily on the wired Internet infrastructure. Using this technology a person is able to use broadband applications while they are on the move, even at speeds of up to 200 mph. The technology is self-forming and self-healing, which allows users to connect to either a pre-deployed network infrastructure or connect through other users' wireless devices within range. This means that there is no need for wireless broadband towers.

One of the main developments that may see the mesh network become even more popular in the near future is the development of the IEEE standard 802.11s. There are, however, other developments being made in the technology. For instance, in order to increase the throughput using multiple radios, researchers at the Microsoft Corporation have developed what is called the 'Mesh Connectivity Layer' (MCL). MCL uses a 2.5-GHz routing protocol, which selects the best radio on each node and also selects the best path between two nodes. This protocol has also been designed to assist in sending information over varied distances by changing the frequency the packets are sent. For example, if the next node being hopped to is a long distance away then the frequency will be lowered, as lower frequencies travel further than high frequencies. In most current systems deployed on multi-hop networks a node can only send or receive a piece of data at any one time. However, a dual-radio, multiple-channel set-up is now being developed, which means that a node will be able to send and receive a packet at the same time. This will increase the capacity of a multi-hop network greatly.

Finally, Microsoft is currently researching the advantage of using mesh networks and researchers are in the process of developing a self-organising wireless mesh network. The aim of this project is to connect neighbouring houses together using wireless technology. Microsoft claim that the advantages of such a network are that everyone using the technology will not need their own individual gateway, and instead will connect through gateways distributed throughout the community. This means that packets would dynamically find a route through the nodes in the community until they reach the Internet gateway. Therefore, in less developed areas of the world, where not everyone will have their own gateway, they would still be able to connect. It also means that there would be no need to lay cables to every house in order to receive an internet connection.[5] Figure 4.3 illustrates a sole Internet gateway located in a gas station. However, all of the houses in the diagram are able to receive Internet connectivity. Microsoft has, however, run into some problems with this project such as current wireless network range, customer privacy, data security and auto configurations. These problems may be solved with completion of the new IEEE 802.11s standard, as some of these issues are being addressed within the standard.

Figure 4.3   **Microsoft mesh network**

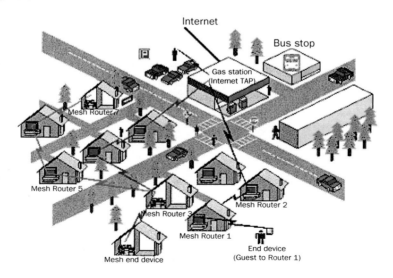

Conclusion

Wireless mesh technologies are emerging as the most effective mode of communication structure for wireless networks. The mesh network itself has many different types of technology that can be implemented into the network to improve performance, such as with broadband access to the Internet, satellite communication for military intelligence, communication networks to control transportation systems or production lines in factories using various sensors connected by a mesh network. The mesh network is also highly adaptable for today's modern dynamic environments, and can be upgraded easily by increasing the number of nodes, which increases the communication mesh with minimal loss of throughput. With new advances in radio technology, the mesh network nodes will have increased performances with regard to traffic data throughput, which should improve media output, such as video, data and sound. However, improvements remain to be made with regard to technical problems, such as load balancing, routing, protocols at the MAC, PHY layers and scalability, so that the network is more efficient at providing a service for the user in communication of various media.

Notes

1. Akylidiz I.F. and Wang Xudong, K. (2005) 'A survey on Wireless mesh networks', *Georgia Institute of Technology, IEEE Radio Communications* 43:9, 23–30.
2. Liang, M. and Mieso, D. (2007) 'A routing metric for load balancing in wireless mesh networks', *21st International Conference on Advanced Information Networking and Applications Workshops (AINAW07) IEE Computer Society*, May 2007, pp. 409–14.
3. Raffaele, B., Marco, C. and Enrico, G. (2005) 'Mesh networks: commodity multihop ad hoc networks', *IEEE Communications Magazine 2005*.
4. Cellan-Jones, R. (2007) Switch on for Square Mile Wi-Fi, *BBC News*, *http://news.bbc.co.uk/2/hi/technology/6577307.stm*
5. *http://research.microsoft.com/mesh/*

Wireless sensor networks

Kevin Curran, Gary Doherty and David O'Callaghan

Wireless sensor networks (WSNs) are used in many applications, including traffic control, military operations and health care. Sensor nodes can be of any size, and any cost. Most sensor nodes are small and energy efficient. WSNs comprise a number of small sensor nodes and a main routing node. When a signal is received by a sensor node, it sends it to the main gateway node and performs the necessary operation. WSNs provide the potential to gather, process and share data via low-cost, low-power wireless devices. As society changes more opportunities for sensing equipment and applications materialise. This chapter provides an overview of WSN technology.

Introduction

In 1901 Guglielmo Marconi transmitted signals across the Atlantic from Cornwall to St John's, Newfoundland. Throughout the twentieth century wireless transmission has advanced in a number of different technologies including radio, television, radar, satellite and mobile. As sensing, computing and communication are all following an exponential curve to zero power, size and cost, it should make sense that wireless sensor nodes, which are a combination of sensor, computers and communicators together in a small device, are also decreasing in size and cost. A sensor node is a node in a WSN that is capable of performing some processing, gathering sensory information and communicating with other connected nodes in the network. WSNs are made up of many nodes, which are important in their functionality. The sensor nodes used for wireless networks, in particular, are far more adaptable and are capable of coping in harsher environments than others.[1]

WSNs also have the ability of wireless communication over a restricted area. Because they have memory and power constraints, they need to be well organised in order to be able to build a fully functional network. It is important that the nodes build up the network using their keys after distribution. To ensure that they are correctly placed to get maximum coverage, it is sensible to plan ahead on and determine the best route for them to follow, and it is also more secure if the node picks up on more than one other node as this allows the connections to be more spread and the distribution of information to be spread further afield in case one fails. Sensor nodes in wireless networks for traffic control are required to deal with all types of weather. They are designed to cope with anything from snow to heavy winds. It is important that they are designed so they can accurately sense information and can send data (see Figure 5.1). WSNs are often used for chemical measurements in industry. For instance, offshore oil platforms transmit continuous streams of data at high speeds to land-based stations. The oil industry has successfully applied wireless communication technology for many years. WSNs represent a significant cost saving, particularly for parameter monitoring, and provide a quickly implemented, secure link from the areas such as the process plant to the control room. As they require no external field-supplied power, wireless sensors can run continuously for over five years on an internal replaceable battery while giving multiple updates per minute for the entire period. The sensor nodes that are used need to be adaptable to these environments to ensure that they function properly.[2] WSNs are also used to measure radiation levels, mainly in hospitals and power plants. Smart Dust nodes

Figure 5.1 Evolution of sensor nodes

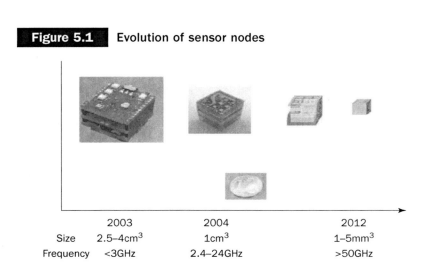

	2003	2004	2012
Size	2.5–4cm^3	1cm^3	1–5mm^3
Frequency	<3GHz	2.4–24GHz	>50GHz

are minuscule micro-electromechanical sensors (MEMSs) capable of detecting anything from light to vibrations. With breakthroughs in silicon-chip technology resulting in increasingly minuscule devices, the size of these motes could eventually be as small as a grain of sand and be able to send data to other MEMSs up to a thousand feet away.[3] Figure 5.1 shows how sensors have decreased in size and increased in performance over the last 5 years and the proposed size and frequency of sensors in 2012.[4]

The military initially used WSNs by dropping sensors in an area from a plane and the sensors themselves formed the network, providing battlefield surveillance. From here they developed into a cheaper and more powerful tool. Sensors are now being placed in very hostile areas where it would not be practical to install cables. High-technology sensors the size of a grain of sand are now being used by the military. These Smart Dust sensors are given a unique ID. The sensors are then aimed at the target from a plane and are highly inconspicuous as they resemble a grain of sand. It is thought that these sensors contributed to locating and ultimately the death of Al Qaeda leader Abu Musab al Zarqawi.[5] Figure 5.2 shows the development of sensor network applications.[6]

When referring to wireless devices people normally mention mobile phones, personal assistants or wireless laptops. WSNs, unlike these devices, are inexpensive and do not depend on pre-existing infrastructures. A WSN is a network of multiple independent sensor nodes, which are usually referred to as motes, equipped with radio transceivers and a base station which monitors the surrounding environment for various conditions such as temperature, wind speed, motion or gases. Formula 1 cars have sensors

Figure 5.2 **Sensor network applications development**

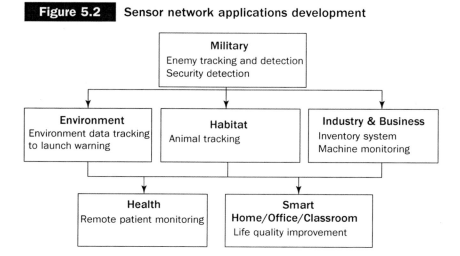

on different parts to monitor key conditions such as the engine performance, brake temperature, oil pressure and tyre pressure. These data are fed back to the control centre where the engineers can view the status of the car on a PC. A wireless ad-hoc network is normally made up of sensors. Therefore, each sensor operates a multi-hop routing algorithm, meaning that the base station can receive data packets from a number of different nodes. Most people would have seen natural-history documentaries in which an animal is captured and a collar is placed around its neck, which contains a sensor. The scientists use the data to monitor the movements of the animal, which enables them to trace its movements with a very high degree of accuracy. One of the advantages of a WSN is that, again, unlike the 'traditional' wireless devices mentioned above, the more nodes available the better the network operation. If a large number of nodes are in a small location then the network is even stronger.[2]

There are different network topologies that apply to WSNs. The star network is a simple communications topology in which a single base can send and receive data and messages to a number of remote nodes. These remote nodes can only send signals through the single base and are unable to send them between each other. The advantage of this is in its simplicity and the ability to keep power consumption of the remote nodes to a minimum. The disadvantage is that the base must be within the range of the other single remote nodes. They are unable to operate through each other, and therefore the base is vital. The mesh network allows any node within the network to communicate with and through each other. If a node is out of range of another, then it can send a message through an intermediate node to forward the message to the desired node. The advantage of this network is that if a node fails then another is available to forward any signal. This network can also operate over a longer range, where communication between nodes is generally unlimited. The disadvantage is that it uses a lot of power and the greater the distance between communication of the nodes, the longer it will take. Finally, the hybrid star–mesh network is a more versatile network and maintains the ability to keep the power of wireless sensor nodes to a minimum. Nodes with the lowest power are unable to forward messages, and therefore minimal power is maintained. However, nodes with more power in this network are able to forward these messages from those of low power.[1]

Wireless sensor hardware

Sensor nodes can vary from the size of a glove compartment to a grain of sand although the latter are yet to be released for non-military use.

Figure 5.3 Sensor node and gateway node

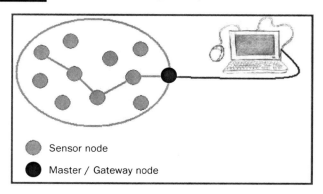

The cost of a node also varies, from as little as a few euros to hundreds of euros, dependent on the network size and the applications required. There are generally two types of sensor nodes used in a WSN, sensor nodes and gateway nodes. Sensor nodes gather required data from their surroundings by means of sensors that are attached to them. The node links with other nodes in the vicinity to transmit data to a data gateway. Sensor nodes need to be aware of the topology of the network to enable data to reach the gateway node. Gateway nodes are the interface to the system or control centre in the WSN. They are also used by the host when data are being requested from the WSN, as shown in Figure 5.3.

A sensor node consists of a power source, a micro-controller, a transceiver, external memory and sensors (Figure 5.4). The sensor acts as the eyes and ears of the node and its main purpose is to take physical data from the target area. The sensor generates a signal, which represents a drop in temperature or the presence of a car, for example. The wave

Figure 5.4 Sensor node architecture

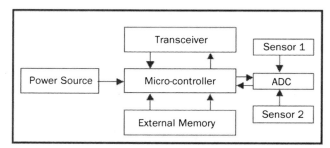

that is generated goes through the analog-to-digital converter (ADC), which creates a digital signal. The binary signal is then sent to the micro-controller. More intelligent sensors such as MEMSs have been made to provide a wider range of activities.

Transceiver

All sensor nodes have a transmitter and a receiver. These components are both contained in a transceiver, which enables a node to receive data from another node and forward the data to another node as necessary. The operational states are transmit, receive, idle and sleep. When a radio is operating in idle mode it is absorbing almost as much power as it would in receive mode. Transceivers do not have a unique global identifier. Given the large number of sensor nodes manufactured worldwide it would be unrealistic to assign one to each node. The radio band used by sensor nodes is the industrial, scientific and medical (ISM) band, which uses unlicensed frequencies. Components that use the ISM band need to be able to handle interference from other sources that may overlap. The frequency used by WSNs are between 433 MHz and 2.4 GHz. However, communication between medical devices may occupy multiple bands and use different protocols. To prevent interference in the excessively used unlicensed ISM band, biomedical devices may use the licensed wireless medical telemetry services (WMTS) band at 608 MHz.[7] There are three modes of communication that could be used with sensor nodes, laser, infrared and radiofrequency (RF). As energy consumption is one of the major problems with sensor nodes one would expect laser to be the preferred option as it uses less power than RF, does not need an antenna and is also robust as regards security. However, laser is very susceptible to atmospheric conditions. It also requires line of sight, which cannot always be guaranteed given the sometimes covert nature of sensor node deployment. Although infrared does not need an antenna it has a restricted broadcasting capability. RF, which does need an antenna, is the easiest to use.

Microcontroller

The microcontroller processes the data that it receives from other components of the sensor node. Other options include microprocessors and field-programmable gate arrays (FPGAs). FPGAs are not very power-efficient and do not work well with traditional programming techniques. They can be reprogrammed and reconfigured as necessary to eliminate deployment costs but this takes time and energy. Microcontrollers are a suitable choice for sensor nodes. They are the best choice for embedded systems. Because of their ability to connect to other devices, power consumption is less. This is because these devices can go into a sleep state while part of controller is still active. The platform on the microcontroller needs to contain an instruction-effective central processor, different HW interfaces, memory and a wake-up time. A power-effective processor guarantees fast processing time and low power consumption. In order to keep expenses low and to prevent any further components being added to the already limited space the maximum number of feasible interfaces needs to be on a microcontroller. Microcontrollers and FLASH memory are the most applicable memory types given their memory storage and price. The amount of memory required depends on whether the memory is to be used for storing application data or for programming the device. Memory should be kept to a minimum given the application software and protocol. This will ensure that costs and energy used are low.[8]

Power unit

Power consumption is one of the primary issues for WSNs. More power is required for communication than for sensing or computing. The energy cost of transmitting 1 kb of data a distance of 100 m is approximately the same as that for executing 3 million instructions by 100 million instructions per second. Depending on surroundings, two types of batteries are used, chargeable and non-chargeable, the latter being employed in hostile environments. Sensors are now being developed to recharge using solar power, thermogeneration or vibration energy. Another technology being used in sensor power units is dynamic power management (DPM). This enables devices that are not being used to be switched off and on as necessary. This is performed with help from the operating system.[9] Another power-saving method is dynamic voltage scheduling (DVS). Using this method it is possible to reduce the power by a factor of four by varying the voltage with the frequency.[10]

WSN operating system

The operating system of a node is not as complicated as that of a standard PC. WSN applications have certain tasks that would not be used on a standard PC. User interfaces are one example that would be used generally on a normal operating system but not on sensor nodes. The main characteristics of the operating system should be as follows:

- Small in size and energy efficient as sensor nodes are constrained in memory and power.
- Ability to deal with packets in real-time and on-the-fly.
- Provide a high degree of software modularity for application-specific sensors.
- Should be robust and reliable and able to work around individual device failures.

As hardware requirements for wireless network systems are the same as for traditional systems, operating systems such as eCOS and uC/OS can be used for WSNs. TinyOS is the operating system that was initially designed for sensor networks and was designed to be used in conjunction with the smart dust project. What is now known as the TinyOS Alliance began as a project between the University of Berkeley, California, and Intel Research. It has been implemented by developers worldwide, on many platforms, for a wide variety of WSNs. It is written using the nesC programming language, which is based on the C programming language but aimed primarily at sensor networks where demands on concurrency and low power consumption are high but hardware resources are limited.[11] TinyOS is free and is used on the MICA2 platform. The fact that it is open source also means that many of the software components needed to use the platform are already written. This also makes it easier for the software to interface with different hardware. It is an event-driven operating system in that it is driven by external factors detected by the sensor. The core of the operating system takes up about 400 bytes, which makes it suitable for every type of modern micro-controller. TinyOS has a two-level scheduling structure, i.e. its ability to perform extensive tasks which can be interrupted by an event. There are two interfaces, command and event. To smooth the progress of modularity, each component declares the commands it uses and the events it signals. The main tasks carried out are executing the main computation, calling lower level commands, signalling higher level commands and scheduling tasks within a component.[12]

Conclusion

A sensor node, also known as a mote, is a node in a WSN that is capable of performing some processing, gathering sensory information and communicating with other connected nodes in the network. WSNs are ideal for monitoring and analysing data. Many shops use WSNs as a means to stop thieves. These sensors are equipped with alarms to ensure security levels are kept to a maximum. WSNs are also suitable for monitoring movements in deserts and forests, allowing such areas to be monitored without the expense of labour. WSNs are used to assess the risk resulting from natural disasters as soon after the event as possible; data are sent quickly, giving people a chance to act. Security via WSNs is one of the most important areas and requires that the network is working correctly. In more urban areas less time dedicated to maintenance. Power must also be available to all security sensors at all times. A power failure can have serious consequences if timing goes wrong. Areas where WSNs have been used include monitoring disease, monitoring floods, vehicle tracking, monitoring volcanic eruptions, alarm signalling and monitoring forest fires.

Notes

1. Wilson, J. (2004) *Sensor Technology Handbook*. London: Newnes Publishers.
2. Flury, R. and Wattenhofer, R. (2007) 'Routing, anycast, and multicast for mesh and sensor networks', *Infocom*', May, pp. 946–54, Anchorage, AK.
3. Manges, W. (1999) 'It's time for sensors to go wireless. Part 1: technological underpinnings', *Sensors Magazine*, 16:4, 18–22.
4. Mainwaring, A., Polastre, J., Szewczyk, R., Culler, D. and Anderson, J. (2002) Wireless Sensor Networks for Habitat Monitoring, *WSNA '02.*, pp. 88–97, Atlanta, GA, USA.
5. Anon (2006) Smart Dust Stalked Zarqawi, StrategyPage.com, *http://www. strategypage.com/htmw/htecm/articles/20060610.aspx*
6. Khemapech, I., Duncan, I. and Miller, A. (2005) A survey of WSNs technology. *Proceedings of The 6th Annual PostGraduate Symposium on The Convergence of Telecommunications, Networking and Broadcasting.* Liverpool John Moores University.
7. Stankovic, J. (2005) Wireless sensor networks for in-home healthcare: Potential and Challenges, *Proceedings High Confidence Medical Device Software and Systems (HCMDSS) Workshop*, Philadelphia, PA, June, pp. 58–64.
8. Zhao, J. and Govindan, R. (2003) Understanding packet delivery performance in dense wireless sensor networks. *The First ACM Conference on Embedded Networked Sensor Systems (Sensys'03).* ACM.
9. Ruiz, L., Braga, T., Silva, F., Assuncao, H., Nogueira, J. and Loureiro, A. (2005) 'On the design of a self-managed WSN', *IEEE Communications Magazine*, 43:8, 95–102.
10. Yu, Y. and Prasanna, V. (2003) Energy-balanced task allocation for collaborative processing in networked embedded systems. *Proceedings of*

the 2003 ACM SIGPLAN conference on Language, compiler, and tool for embedded systems, San Diego. ACM.

11. Levis, P., Lee, N., Welsh, M. and Culler, D. (2003) TOSSIM: accurate and scalable simulation of entire TinyOS applications. *The First ACM Conference on Embedded Networked Sensor Systems (Sensys03)*.

12. Archer, W., Levis, P. and Regehr, J. (2007) 'Interface contracts for TinyOS', *IPSN*, April, 158–65.

6

WebOS – moving the operating system to the Web

Kevin Curran, Leanne Doak and Damien Armstrong

Operating systems were developed to provide system services, such as I/O, communication and storage. The role expanded over time with the addition of multiprogramming and local area networks. The role of an operating system had been fairly standard until the arrival of the WebOS. WebOS is a term used to describe Web operation systems. A WebOS in practice is a virtual desktop on the Internet. It is a simple, less featured and remotely accessible operating environment that runs in a browser delivering a rich desktop-like experience, with various built-in applications. The term 'WebOS' is not truly accurate, because it is not actually a real operating system like Windows and therefore some prefer to describe it as a 'Web desktop'. This chapter outlines WebOS in greater detail.

Introduction

There has been an increase in the number of services that are available over the Internet. In keeping with this trend, a new development has been a move towards Web-based operating systems known as WebOS. A WebOS is a framework for supporting applications that are geographically distributed, highly available and scalable.[1] WebOS includes mechanisms for resource discovery, a global namespace, remote process execution, resource management, authentication and security. A WebOS framework provides a new concept for Internet services. Instead of being fixed to a single location, services can push parts of their responsibilities out to Internet computing resources, and to the client.

These dynamically reconfiguring and geographically mobile services provide a number of advantages, including:

1. better end-to-end availability (service-specific extensions running in the client mask Internet or server failures), and

2. cost-performance (information can be moved closer to clients, and network latency and congestion can be reduced while maintaining server control).

The growth of the Internet can be attributed to its lack of central control, making the concept of a WebOS a contradiction in some ways. This concept began with office applications and the first to launch a usable suite was a company called WebOS Inc. The application was called HyperOffice[2] and contained common desktop applications including Web email, document management and file storage, online calendars, online contact management, and project management tools. It was aimed at users who wanted constant availability and remote connectivity at all times. There are various advantages to using this kind of software, especially in a business setting as the software is completely Web-based so there is no need to download or install programs from the net or from numerous CDs. It is user-friendly and easy to use with personal login details allowing for multiple users within the same company to gain access from any Internet-connected workstation regardless of browser or platform.

Traditionally, Internet applications and protocols are developed and set up without the intervention of any centralised authority. WebOS broadens this to wide-area applications running in a secure HTTP name space with the same interface, caching and performance of existing distributed file systems. There are numerous advantages of integrating the file system with application-controlled efficient wide-area communication. Figure 6.1 illustrates the architecture of WebOS: '1' indicates where the user transfers portions of their access to the server, 2 where the WebOS serves communication using secure sockets layer (SSl) and 3 where the remote server checks if proper credentials are stored in access control lists (ACLs). WebOS defines a model of trust to support applications operating across organisational boundaries providing both security guarantees and an interface for authenticating the identity of principals. One core WebOS application is *remote computer engine*, which allows remote programs to be invoked in the same way as local programs. WebOS is used to address issues such as the identity of requesting agents. This is done through authentication and programs run in a restricted virtual machine isolated from other programs to protect the local system from unauthorised access.

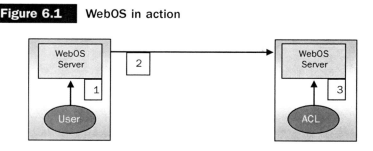

Figure 6.1 WebOS in action

The main argument at present against the WebOS approach is security. Many argue that privacy, control and reliability issues prevent WebOS from being an alternative to the standard OS. In addition, WebOS requires a fast and reliable connection to work correctly and has problems operating peripheral devices. Web applications rely on open source infrastructure and an array of technologies and formats – and these are constantly changing. Fred Oliveira of WeBreakStuff states 'after service outsourcing and personal outsourcing, we're seeing a new age of web-service outsourcing. One with no regulations only expectations and hopes. Everything is based on trust, and trust sometimes fails ... and the problem here is that even with web-services as a liability, there's no fallback mechanism, no alternative route, and no "competitor service" that can be plugged into an app in the timely manner like web 2.0 applications require. This proves that purely mash-up based applications have small foundations, and like a house with no foundations, they may fail to resist, should the unexpected happen.'[3]

WebOS implementations

Google (see Figure 6.2) has produced a number of web-based products. Gmail was their first major online application. There is now also Google calendar, spreadsheets and more. There are a number of Web operating systems such as YouOS (see Figure 6.3) and EyeOS.

Google had introduced the first iteration on their desktop search. It was a small Web server that can insert data from a local machine into browsing pages. There are three main parts to the WebOS system:

- Browser–application interface; the user views content and manages data locally and on the Internet.

Figure 6.2 Google desktop

Figure 6.3 YouOS screenshot

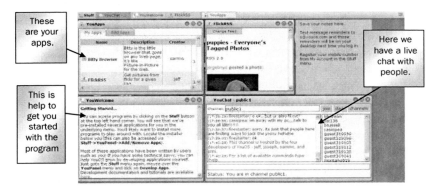

- Web applications; making the Web a richer environment for productivity, e.g. Gmail.
- Local web server; handles data delivery and display on the browser.

YouOS is another attempt to bring the web and operating systems together to form a shared virtual computer. WebOS, according to YouOS, is liberation of software from hardware.

WebOS provides operating system services to wide-area applications. On a single machine developers can rely on the local operating system to provide these abstractions. WebOS provides basic operating system services needed to build applications that are geographically distributed and highly available. One such application that demonstrates the utility of WebOS is Rent-A-Server.

Figure 6.4 illustrates the importance of keeping an eye on trends in Internet technology. Google, Yahoo, YouOS, Netvibes and WebTopOS have been among the main players on the scene actually to have developed their vision of WebOS along with a host of other start-ups. Some are already available whereas others are still their prototypes (Table 6.1). A working environment which can be accessed from anywhere is always going to appeal to certain consumers, hence the rising popularity of the current software on offer. However, Web-based applications also offer a whole new range of security issues and the possibility of uninvited access by hackers to corrupt or extract information. As with all these applications, security and data integrity are always top of the developer's agenda. Information stored on a network device can be vulnerable to attack and so must be made secure.

It is worth keeping in mind that in this case, the Web browser has access to your machine and can potentially easily interact with locally stored information and programs. A Web-based desktop needs a very high-speed connection due to the fact that all code used for the visualisation of, for example, .jss and flash files must first be stored on the workstation before it can be displayed. Coding also presents a problem. XHTML, Flash, JavaScript, CSS, etc., are not as good at providing the

Figure 6.4　Semantics of information vs. social connections

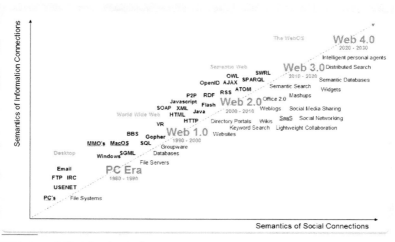

(*Source: www.radarnetworks.com*)

Table 6.1 Comparison of various Web desktops (Wikipedia, 2007)

Name	Developer	Engine	Free	Support external applications	Graphical user interface
DesktopTwo	Sapotek	Flash	Yes (proprietary)	No	Windows-like
Edeskonline	eDesk Online Pvt. Ltd	AJAX	For 3 months, then $24/ year	Yes	Windows-like
EyeOS	eyeOS Team	AJAX	Yes [open source General Public Licence (GPL)]	Yes	Mac-like
Fenestela (French)	Websilog SARL	AJAX	No	Yes	Windows-like
G.ho.st	Ghost Inc.	Flash	Yes	No	Windows-like
Goowy	Goowy Media, Inc.	Flash	Yes (proprietary)	No	Windows+ Mac-like
yourminis	Goowy Media, Inc.	Flash	Yes (proprietary)	No	Tab-based
Ironbox	Oaesys Corp.	AJAX	Yes/ subscription	Yes	Windows-like
Protopage	Protopage	AJAX	Yes	Yes	Tab-based
Purefect	Klorofil Project/ Saltanera	PHP + AJAX	Yes [open source Common Puplic Licence (CPL)]	Yes	Windows+ Mac-like
WebtopOS	WebtopOS Inc.	AJAX/ J2EE	Yes (paid plan in development)	Yes	Windows-like
XinDesk	XIN	AJAX	Invitation only (alpha)	Yes	Windows-like
YouOS	WebShaka, Inc.	AJAX	Yes (proprietary)	Yes	OS/2-like
Netvibes	Netvibes Team	AJAX	Yes (proprietary)	Yes	Tab-based

functionality and user interaction of applications built using common desktop development tools such as C or Visual Basic. They were originally designed to create web pages, so to develop actual programs which run through the browser may be much more difficult or limited.

Conclusion

The idea behind a Web operating system (sometimes referred to as Web 3.0) is a virtual desktop or 'webtop', which can be accessed from anywhere, read through a browser with various applications similar to the basic ones available on an ordinary operating system, such as filing systems and interacting windows. WebOS includes mechanisms for resource discovery, a global namespace, remote process execution, resource management, authentication and security. A WebOS framework provides a new concept for Internet services. Instead of being fixed to a single location, services can push parts of their responsibilities onto Internet computing resources, and to the client. It may indeed be possible that the future will see a world which revolves on the Web, a free-standing machine with a Wi-Fi connection and a browser installed on its hard drive. But for the present a traditional desktop and operating system handle most of our domestic and business needs.

Notes

1. Vahdat, A., Eastham, P. and Yoshikawa, C. (1997) WebOS: Operating system services for wide area applications. *Technical Report UCB CSD-97-938*, University of California, Berkeley. *http://citeseer.ist.psu.edu/vahdat97webos*.
2. *http://www.hyperoffice.com*
3. Ezzy, E. (2006) Webified Desktop Apps vs Browser Apps. *Read/Write Web Magazine*, September. *http://www.readwriteweb.com/archives/webified_desktop_apps_vs_browser_apps.php*

7

Really Simple Syndication (RSS)

Kevin Curran and Sheila McCarthy

Email has been one of the major reasons for the broad acceptance of the Internet, and although email is still a vitally important communication tool, it suffers from an increasing number of problems as a medium for delivering information to the correct audience in a timely manner. The increasing volume of spam and viruses means that email users are forced into adopting new tools such as spam-blocking and email-filtering software which attempt to block the tide of unwanted emails. This chapter provides an overview of Really Simple Syndication (RSS), a standard which allows Web content to be delivered to news readers in an active manner.

Introduction

RSS solves a myriad of problems that webmasters commonly face, such as increasing traffic, and gathering and distributing news.[1] RSS can also provide the basis for additional content distribution services.[2] The real benefit of RSS, apart from the added benefit of receiving news feeds from multiple sites simultaneously in the viewer, is that all the news feeds (i.e. news items) are chosen by the user. With thousands of sites now RSS-enabled and more on the way, RSS has become perhaps one of the most visible eXtensible Mark-up Language (XML) success stories to date. RSS formats are specified using XML, a generic specification for the creation of data formats. Although RSS formats have evolved since March 1999, the RSS icon (▨) first gained widespread use in 2005/2006. RSS democratises news distribution by making everyone a potential news provider. It leverages the Web's most valuable asset, content, and makes displaying high-quality relevant news on a site relatively easy.[3] It must be recognised, however, that RSS cannot entirely replace the primary function of email, which is to provide person-to-person asynchronous communications although it does complement it in some interesting ways.

RSS can be found as an acronym for *rich site summary, resource description framework (RDF) site summary* or indeed *really simple syndication* (which we use here).[4] The RSS format was created to facilitate 'channels' on Netscape Netcenter[5] and was made available to the general public in March 1999. Channels were a 'pull'-type mechanism where users requested certain information from various channels. The original RSS, version 9.0, was created by Netscape as a method of building portals to major news sites for news headlines. Portals are websites dedicated to specific topics. It was soon replaced by the 0.91 version, which stripped out many of the less important features, as Netscape believed that version 0.90 was simply too intricate for this undemanding task. The newly established 0.91 itself was promptly dropped by Netscape as their interest in the creation of portals declined. The now obsolete 0.91 was swiftly adopted by UserLand Software and employed as the foundation for all its Web-based concepts. Shortly thereafter, RSS version 1.0, based on a resource description framework (RDF), was developed by a third-party spin off, a group of designers who built their version modelled closely on the concepts and framework of the initial, original 9.0 (prior to its simplification into version 0.91). The RDF integrates a variety of applications from library catalogues and world-wide directories to syndication and aggregation of news, software and content to personal collections of music, photos and events using XML as an interchange syntax. The RDF specifications provide a lightweight ontology system to support the exchange of knowledge on the Web.[6,7] As a result, UserLand, indignant at being omitted from the latest increment, ignored version 1.0 and continued to advance their own brand of RSS, developing versions 0.92, 0.93, 0.94 through to their current 2.0. In reality, this means there are seven different formats to contend with. A feed aggregator, also known as a feed reader, news reader or simply as an aggregator, is client software or a Web application that aggregates syndicated Web content such as news headlines, blogs, podcasts and vlogs in a single location for easy viewing.[8] Aggregators must be flexible and comprehensive, and must be able to recognise and deal with all versions. RSS version 2.0 is currently offered by the Berkman Centre for Internet and Society, at Harvard Law School.

RSS standard

RSS has rapidly developed into a prevalent means of sharing content between websites. Many sites already use RSS, and as word spreads, new sites incorporate this feature into their sites daily. RSS looks set to become a dominant force. Numerous news sites including the BBC, Yahoo! and Wired currently use RSS to provide their subscribers with the latest headlines. Indeed, the websites of many mainstream 'giants' also incorporate RSS in a bid to keep their subscribers notified of announcements, events and advertisements. As yet, only sites which currently offer news in RSS format may be read using a news aggregator. To ascertain if a site utilises RSS is generally simple. Sites make no secret of the fact and proudly display RSS feed pictograms (such as) throughout their pages indicating which sections are available in RSS format. Right-clicking on such an icon, copying the shortcut (URL) and adding it to an aggregator creates a feed. This establishes a subscription to that particular website for the desired information. Channels to numerous sites can be created, maintained and removed if desired using most aggregators with minimal effort.

A RSS text file contains both static and dynamic information. At a high level, an RSS document is an rss element, with an obligatory attribute called version, this attribute specifying the version of RSS that the document conforms to. Here an element is a piece of data within a document that may contain either text or other subelements describing the RSS data. Succeeding the rss element is a single-channel element, which contains information about the channel (metadata) and its contents. Metadata are commonly defined as 'data about data' or data describing context, content and structure of records and their management through time. A channel may in turn contain any number of items. Items are subelements which are enclosed in matching XML start and end tags and appear as subelements of channel, listed before the closing /channel tag. Each item is identified with an opening item tag, and concluded with a closing /item tag. All child elements of an item are optional, but at least one element must be present, either title or description. An item may be a snippet of information which represents a larger article, much in the same way as a headline represents a newspaper article. If this is the case, the item's description is a synopsis of the story, and the link points to the full story. An item may also be complete in itself, and if so, the description contains the full text, and the link and title may be omitted. In this way, an RSS channel can contain many items which in turn may incorporate many differing subelements. When design and coding are complete, the validated RSS file can be registered with various aggregators, allowing the feed to be 'sucked up' by discerning subscribers. Any amendments or updates made to the RSS file will automatically be relayed to all subscribing clients.

RSS enclosures

RSS version 2.0 encompasses a powerful feature; it allows an item to have an enclosure. This can, in simple terms, be likened to an email having an attachment. In reality, enclosures hold huge potential and represent another step in the evolution of content syndication.[2] By incorporating an enclosure subelement into an item any RSS element can then describe a video or audio file. The enclosure feature has three attributes: the first, 'url', defines where the multi-media file is located; the second, 'length', determines the size of the file in bytes; and the last, 'type', describes the multi-purpose internet mail extension (MIME) type of the multi-media file. In this way an aggregator can determine the payload attributes prior to any communication, and can then apply the appropriate scheduling and filtering rules. Primarily, the most attractive feature of RSS is that it enables information from numerous websites to be viewed simultaneously, all on one page; consequently, numerous sites can be scrutinized in seconds rather than having to be tediously downloaded independently. One free newsreader is RssReader. Like other aggregators, the RssReader aggregator can sustain numerous channels, scouring each of the user's designated websites for updated feeds at regular intervals. When RssReader gathers updated headlines from the various sites, it displays an amalgamation of such in a list box positioned in the bottom right of the user's desktop (see Figure 7.1, which displays headlines from Yahoo's entertainment news feed).

If a user wishes to select a headline from the list, aggregators will provides features to open and provide a synopsis of each news article, and

Figure 7.1   RssReader's 'headline alert' screen

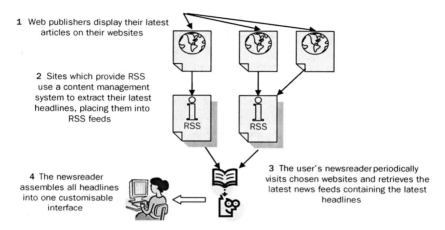

Figure 7.2   How RSS feeds work

1 Web publishers display their latest articles on their websites

2 Sites which provide RSS use a content management system to extract their latest headlines, placing them into RSS feeds

RSS

RSS

4 The newsreader assembles all headlines into one customisable interface

3 The user's newsreader periodically visits chosen websites and retrieves the latest news feeds containing the latest headlines

if the user wishes to read further on any given topic a link is provided to the specific article on each of the initiating websites. In this way, web publishers are able to channel tremendous traffic towards their sites. No longer having to wait for passing traffic, RSS provides a means of advertising ware on a much wider stage. By employing a news aggregator, a client can subscribe to any site of their choosing that provides RSS feeds. The websites that do not offer this facility may be disadvantaged, and must wait for the client to visit their page directly if at all (see Figure 7.2).

Perhaps the most compelling feature of RSS feeds is the ability to keep track of changes on the Web. It is not difficult to ascertain what websites are available today, but what is difficult is to ascertain when such sites make crucial changes. RSS feeds provide us with the necessary aptitude to overcome such problems.

RSS systems

There are an increasing number of websites that offer RSS format-producing software. Two examples are Nooked and Radio UserLand. Nooked[9] is an online service which enables users to create, publish and maintain their own RSS channels, with the minimal amount of effort and at low cost. Nooked makes RSS potentially available to users of all abilities by shielding the technical intricacies of how RSS is configured. They have a FeedWizard on their site which is web-based. It allows a feed to be created quite quickly and support podcasting and flashcasting similar to the system described here.

Radio UserLand[10] is one of the most popular weblogging tools. Radio supports the publication of weblogs, which can optionally include enclosures and also allow customers use of its own built-in news aggregator. Users can subscribe via this aggregator to feeds, allowing Radio users to achieve more than is possible with similar services which offer only weblog hosting. Radio comprises features such as the 'category' feature, which supports blogging on varied topics, and a 'multi-author weblog tool', which permits multiple authors to contribute to a community weblog.

The future for RSS

It should not be forgotten that one of the main objectives of all RSS modules is to extend the basic XML schema, which was established for more robust content syndication allowing for wide-ranging yet standardized transactions without modifying the core RSS specification. This can be achieved with an XML namespace which give names to concepts and relationships between those concepts. We can expect to see an increasing number of RSS 2.0 modules with established namespaces appearing in the near future such as Media RSS Module – RSS 2.0 Module.[11]

RSS is central to some of the leading companies such as Google, Yahoo and Microsoft.[12] Yahoo has stated that almost three out of ten Internet users consume RSS-syndicated content on personalized start pages without knowing that RSS is the enabling technology.[13] We expect that feed reading will become even easier than it is today, and should be incorporated into all kinds of connected devices especially mobile phones and home media units. We can expect to see it become more embedded into bit-torrent-based peer-to-peer applications where even now, feeds (also known as *Torrent/RSS-es* or *Torrentcasts*) allow client applications to download files automatically from the moment the RSS reader detects them. The term for this is broadcatching. News site such as the *Guardian* (*www.guardian.co.uk*) will continue to increasingly provide RSS feeds for a selection of news services and sites automatically updating as stories are added across the network, flagging up what is new as it breaks.[14]

We also expect to see diverse uses of RSS, such as the encoding of location in RSS as performed by georss.org. Here location is described in an interoperable manner so that applications can request, aggregate, share and map geographically tagged feeds. This site was created to promote a relatively small number of encodings that meet the needs of a wide range of communities in the hope that building these encodings on a common information model would result in an 'upwards-compatibility' across encodings.

Conclusion

Email suffers from an increasing number of problems as a medium for delivering information to the correct audience in a timely manner due to the volume of spam and viruses arriving in our inboxes on a hourly basis. RSS is a way of receiving constantly updated links to selected websites. Once a connection to a website is set up, a list of all the stories currently shown on a certain page or section of that site can be retrieved. There are several ways of receiving RSS feeds, but a common method is to download a program called a 'News Reader', which can then be set up to receive RSS information from websites offering it, and browse headlines and story summaries that link through to the full story on the website. Alternatively, newer web browsers offer similar functionality already built in, which will detect whether the website offers an RSS feed and will then let you create a constantly updated list of links in the 'bookmarks' menu. Perhaps the most compelling feature of RSS feeds is the ability to keep track of changes on the Web as it can be difficult to ascertain when sites make crucial changes. RSS feeds, however, provide us with the necessary aptitude to overcome such problems.

Notes

1. News feeds from the BBC. *http://news.bbc.co.uk/1/hi/help/3223484.stm*
2. Kerner, S. (2004) *The RSS Enclosure Exposure* – It's really simple stuff: audio feeds and the rise of RSS. Internet News – Realtime IT, *http://internetnews. com/xSP/article.php/3431901*
3. King, A.B. (2004) *Webref and the future of RSS, Introduction to RSS, WebRef and RSS, http://www.webreference.com/authoring/languages/xml/ rss/intro/3.html*
4. Oasis-open (2004) *Technology Reports, RDF Rich Site Summary (RSS), http://www.oasis-open.org/cover/rss.html*
5. *http://my.netscape.com*
6. Van der Vlist, E. (2001) *Building a Semantic Web Site.* XML.com.

7. Nilsson, M. (2001) *The semantic web: How RDF will change learning technology standards*. Center for User-Oriented IT-design, Royal Institute of Technology, Stockholm.

8. *http://en.wikipedia.org/wiki/Aggregator*

9. *http://www.nooked.com*

10. *http://www.userland.com*

11. MRSS (2007) Media RSS Module – RSS 2.0 Module. *http://search.yahoo.com/mrss*

12. Rubel, S. (2006) Trends to Watch Part III: "RSS Inside", Micropersuasion blog, December 2006, *http://www.micropersuasion.com/2005/12/2006_trends_to__1.html*

13. Hrastnik, R. (2005) *Analyzing the New Yahoo RSS* – Whitepaper for Marketers, RSS Statistics, *http://rssdiary.marketingstudies.net/content/analyzing_the_new_yahoo_rss_whitepaper_for_marketers.php*

14. *http://www.guardian.co.uk/webfeeds*

8

Javascript, XML, E4X and AJAX

Kevin Curran, Karen Lee and David McClenaghan

Asynchronous JavaScript and XML (AJAX) is a web development technique for creating interactive Web applications. The intent of AJAX is to make the Web experience interactive, faster and more user friendly; AJAX makes this possible by exchanging small amounts of data with the server behind the scenes, which results in the Web page on the client side not needing to be reloaded when a user makes a change, thus resulting in the once slow and painful Web application experience as one more similar to that of desktop applications.

Introduction

AJAX, which consists of XML, JavaScript technology, DHTML and document object model (DOM), is an approach that helps developers transform clunky Web interfaces into interactive AJAX applications. AJAX is also a key component of Web 2.0 applications such as Flickr, now part of Yahoo!, 37signals' applications basecamp and backpack, as well as other Google applications such as Gmail and Orkut.[1] Another definition of AJAX coined by Jesse James Garrett was that it was not just one technology but several, each flourishing in its own right, each coming together in powerful new ways. AJAX incorporates several technologies including standards-based presentation using XHTML and CSS, dynamic display and interaction using the document object model, data interchange and manipulation using XML and eXtensible StyleSheet Language Transformations (XSLT), asynchronous data retrieval using XMLHttpRequest and JavaScript binding everything together. The classic Web application works by a user triggering a HTTP request, which would

Figure 8.1 AJAX versus the classic web application model

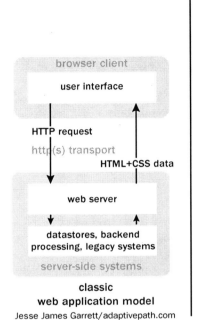
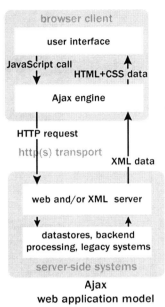

classic
web application model

Ajax
web application model

Jesse James Garrett/adaptivepath.com

be generated from the user's action. The user then waits while the server performs its processes, whether it be retrieving data, calculating numbers or talking to various legacy systems, and then returns an HTML page to the user. Figure 8.1 illustrates the classic Web application model and the AJAX Web application model. Although the AJAX model appears more technical, it offers a solution to what most users loath, namely having to wait during a Web session.

There is some initial wait for the AJAX engine to load up in a frame at the start, but once this period is over each AJAX site becomes speedier in response.

JavaScript and XML

Essentially taking each part of the acronym in isolation Asynchronous, means that when a request is sent, the user must wait for a response to come back but is free to do other things in the meantime. The response probably does not come back immediately, so the developer can set up a function that will wait for it to be sent by the server, and react to it once it happens. The next stage is JavaScript. This code is the core code running AJAX applications. It is used to make a request to the server. Once the response is returned by the server, the developer will generally use some additional JavaScript to modify the current page's DOM in some way to show the user that the submission went through successfully. JavaScript is the scripting language of the Web; it is used in millions of Web pages to improve the design, validate forms, detect browsers and create cookies; it is the most popular scripting language on the Internet and works in all major browsers, such as Internet Explorer, Mozilla, Firefox, Netscape and Opera. A major advantage for developers is that it is easy to learn.[2] JavaScript is a prototype-based scripting language with a syntax loosely based on C. Like C, the language has no input or output constructs of its own. Whereas C relies on standard input/output libraries, a JavaScript engine relies on a host environment into which it is embedded. There are many such host environment applications, of which Web technologies are the most well-known examples. One major use of Web-based JavaScript is to write functions that are embedded on or included from HTML pages and interact with the DOM of the page to perform tasks not possible in HTML alone. The final component in AJAX is XML. XML stands for eXtensible Markup Language, which is used as a way of describing data. An XML file can contain the data too, similar to that of a database. The primary purpose of XML is to facilitate the sharing of information across different systems, particular those connected to the Internet. AJAX passes data to servers packaged up as snippets of XML code, so that they can be easily processed with JavaScript. These data can be anything which is needed, and as long as required. It is not a new technology as this is already how the Web works, the only difference now being that these requests can be made from JavaScript. In short, a file is requested and a page is received in response.

The AJAX model

Ajax is not a technology but rather a family of technologies that have been available for years, each flourishing in their own right and coming together in significant new ways.[3] AJAX incorporates standards-based presentation using XHTML and CSS, the former being a stricter and cleaner version of HTML, which is used to build Web forms and identify fields for use in applications. CSS, which stands for cascading style sheets, define how to display HTML elements in a Web application. These standards are W3C recommendations which describe the communication protocols of HTML, XML and other building blocks of the Web.[3] Also incorporated in AJAX is dynamic display and interaction using the DOM, data interchange and manipulation using XML and XSLT, asynchronous data retrieval using XMLHttpRequest and JavaScript binding everything together, giving faster access, better support and acceptance as a data structure in a Web application. The preferred way to communicate with the server is by sending data as XML but other methods can be used. Although XML provides two enormous advantages as a data representation language, as it is text-based and is position-independent, it is not well suited to data interchange as it carries a lot of baggage, and it does not match the data model of most programming languages. However, there is another text notation that has all of the advantages of XML, but is much better suited to data interchange. That notation is JavaScript Object Notation (JSON). JSON is a lightweight computer data interchange format. It is a subset of the object literal notation of JavaScript but its use does not require Javascript. Its elegance and simplicity has resulted in its widespread use, especially as an alternative to XML in AJAX. One of the claimed advantages of JSON over XML as a data interchange format in this context is that it is much easier to write a JSON parser. JSON parses ten times quicker than XML, which is quite expensive to parse. In JavaScript itself, JSON can be parsed trivially using the eval( ) procedure. This was important for the acceptance of JSON within the AJAX programming community because of JavaScript's ubiquity among Web browsers.

For that reason JSON is typically used in environments where the size of the data stream between the client and the server is of paramount importance, hence its use by Google, Yahoo, etc., which serve millions of users, and the source of the data can be explicitly trusted, and where the loss of fact access to client-side XSLT processing for data manipulation or user interface (UI) generation is not a consideration. Although JSON is often positioned against XML, it is not uncommon to see both JSON and XML used in the same application. For example, a client-side application which integrates Google Maps data with Simple Object Access Protocol (SOAP) weather data requires support for both data formats. In comparing XML and JSON on attributes that are considered important, it is clear how simple JSON is; it has a much smaller grammar and maps more directly onto the data structures used in modern programming languages, and therefore less coding is required compared with XML. It is also easier for humans to read and for machines to read and write. Secondly, JSON is not extensible because it does not need to be. JSON is not a document mark-up language, so it is not necessary to define new tags or attributes to represent data in it. JSON has the same interoperability potential as XML and finally is at least as open as XML, perhaps more so because it is not in the centre of corporate/political standardisation struggles.[4] Whether XML or JSON is used, for developers to get the right look for an AJAX application, CSS is a crucial weapon in the AJAX developer's arsenal. CSS provides the mechanism for separating the style and design of an application from the content itself. Although CSS plays a prominent and important role in AJAX applications, it also tends to be one of the larger stumbling blocks in building cross-browser compatible applications as there are widely varying levels of support from different browser vendors.[5]

Therefore, the real complexity in JavaScript programming results from the incompatibility of Web browsers' support for varied technologies and standards. Building an application that runs on different browsers, for example Internet Explorer and Mozilla's Firefox, is extremely difficult. To that end, several commercial and open source AJAX JavaScript frameworks either generate JavaScript code based on server-side logic or tag libraries, or provide a client-side JavaScript library to facilitate cross-browser AJAX development. Some of the more popular frameworks include AJAX.Net, Backbase, Bitkraft, Django, DOJO, DWR, MochiKit, Prototype, Rico, Sajax, Sarissa and Script.aculo.us. The browser wars of a few years ago are still going on albeit on a much smaller scale, and one of the victims of this war relates to the XMLHttpRequest part of AJAX applications. Consequently, there are a few different things required to get an XMLHttpRequest object going. The key is to support all browsers. No developer wants to write an application that works just on Internet Explorer or an application that works just on non-Microsoft browsers. It is a poor answer to write an application twice, and therefore code should combine support for both Internet Explorer and non-Microsoft browsers in a multi-browser way. Modern browsers offer users the ability to change their security levels, and to turn off JavaScript technology, and disable any number of options in their browser. Therefore, developers need to handle the problems associated with these changes without letting the application fall over. Writing robust code is a challenge for AJAX developers.

E4X and JSON

The ECMA-357 standard specifies E4X, a language extension dealing with XML. E4X is basically an extension on the ECMAScript (JavaScript) that adds native XML support to the language, which in turn means that along with the types already useable in the ECMAScript, namely the number type, string type, Boolean type and object type, an XML type is also implementable for representing XML elements, attributes, comments, processing instructions and text nodes. There is also the added functionality of having an XMLList, which allows a list of XML objects. At present, there are two ECMAScript implementations that have been extended to implement E4X, the Mozilla Javascript engines Spidermonkey and Rhino. E4X is much simpler as an XML document can be declared an XML object and therefore it is easy to parse and manipulate XML. Without E4X an XML library or an XML component is necessary to work with XML. E4X does this by providing access to the XML document in a form that feels natural for ECMAScript programmers. The goal is to provide an alternative, simpler syntax for accessing XML documents than via DOM interfaces. Additionally, it offers a new way of visualizing XML. Until the release of E4X, XML was always accessed at an object level. E4X changes that, by defining XML as a primitive which provides faster access and better support.

JSON is a lightweight computer data interchange format. It is a subset of the object literal notation of JavaScript but its use does not require JavaScript. JSON is independent of other languages but uses conventions that are familiar to that in the C-family of languages. JSON is built on two structures, a collection of name/value pairs and an ordered list of values. The main benefit of JSON is not that it is smaller on the wire, but that it better represents the structure of the data and so requires less coding and processing. One of the most important advantages of JSON is that it bypasses JavaScript's same source policy, which is that JavaScript does not allow you to access documents sent from another server. However, with JSON you can import a JSON file as a new script tag. Another advantage is that JSON data are slightly simpler and slightly more in line with the rest of the JavaScript language than scripts for XML data. However, JSON can be difficult to read and each single comma, quote and bracket should be in the correct place. Although this is also true of XML, JSON's welter of complicated syntax, like the }}]} at the end of the data snippet, may frighten new users and make for complicated debugging. JSON is much younger than XML and of course needs time to grow. As the older kid on the block XML has wider support and offers more development tools on both the client side and the server side. However, client-side parsing for JSON is supported natively with JavaScript's eval( ) method.

Social interaction technologies and AJAX

The Amazon.com checkout sequence, Google search and the eBay selling sequence are common examples of the page-based approach. Although the screen- and page-based approaches have proven successful, each has drawbacks. AJAX, by contrast, marries the benefits of both screen- and paged-based approaches by allowing more sophisticated functionality using easier to implement Web standards. AJAX is a solid alternative for new interface development and experts have already affirmed the viability of the Web as a standalone software development platform. Its popularity is certainly helped with large companies such as Google creating amazing applications using the AJAX technology, for example Google Maps, Google Gmail and Google Suggest; another reason for its popularity is the continuing adoption of standards-compliant browsers that support AJAX technology, Firefox, Safari, Opera and Internet Explorer 6.[6] Most notably, Firefox supports Ajax software, e.g. ajaxWrite and ajaxTunes, which are all small, rich Web-based applications that run on a computer. These programs launch in 3–4 seconds and have all the interactivity of Writely or Microsoft Office applications. Ajax13[7] has just 6–8 servers and serves millions of people with their 'service from servers' Web-based applications. Their goal is to show all core applications from the Internet. They believe that consumers do not need to know anything about version compatibility with their existing computer or operating system.

ajaxOS[8] is a fully functional AJAX-aware operating system. Features in ajaxOS include the ability to store to a remote server, with full access to file navigation on this remote server as well as a computer's hard disk. As easily as documents on a local machine can be saved and opened, users will be able to do so on the company's secure servers. With the trend steering towards AJAX, it appears that this new approach to Web applications is here to stay; assisted by indispensable ubiquitous broadband, everything will soon be in the 'cloud'. With the simplicity of using AJAX applications coupled with the fact that they are built using nothing more than current Web standards, which makes them relatively easy to create, most Web designers familiar with building paged-based applications can migrate an interface to AJAX quickly. Also, enterprising AJAX developers have created easy-to-use building blocks that allow developers unfamiliar with the approach to migrate their applications without having to write code from scratch. There is also an abundance of articles in magazines, AJAX-related weblogs and AJAX tutorials on the Web for developers who want to start building these dynamic Web applications. As a result, AJAX is becoming a commonplace tool.

Conclusion

AJAX allows the user to interact with the current page with little or no communication with the server. The resources to enable AJAX to function are already available on all major browsers on most existing platforms. The most widely voiced concern regarding the usability of AJAX is that when a user selects the back button on their browser, they will not undo the recent AJAX-imposed change but that of the last page stored in the browser's history. Developers have tried to overcome this by using IFRAMES to store the status of a page at specific times. AJAX is currently being used by Google. Google groups, Google Suggest and Google maps are all based on AJAX, which proves not only that AJAX is technically sound but also that it is practical for real world application. The simplicity of JSON may lead to it replacing XML as first choice for sending data. E4X is a natural progression from the ECMA standard.

Notes

1. O'Reilly, T. (2005) What is Web 2.0 – Design patterns and business models for the next generation of software. *http://www.oreillynet.com/pub/a/oreilly/tim/news/2005/09/30/what-is-web-20.html*
2. W3Schools (2006) Ajax, Json & E4X tutorials. *http://www.w3schools.com/ajax/default.asp*
3. Garrett, J.J. (2005) Ajax: a new approach to web applications. Adaptive Path Publications. *http://www.adaptivepath.com/publications/essays/archives/000385.php*
4. Kelly, S. (2005) Speeding up AJAX with JSON, Developer.com. *http://www.developer.com/lang/jscript/article.php/10939_3596836_2*
5. Johnson, D. (2005) *Ajax: Dawn Of A New Developer* – The latest tools and technologies for AJAX developers, *Java World*. *http://www.javaworld.com/javaworld/jw-10-2005/jw-1017-ajax.html*
6. Porter, J. (2005) Using Ajax for Creating Web Applications. *Proceedings of User Interface 10 Conference*. Cambridge, MA: ACM.
7. *http://www.ajaxlaunch.com/*
8. *http://www.myajaxos.com/*

9

VoiceXML

Kevin Curran and Ashlean McNulty

Until recently, Internet applications have primarily been dependent on visual interfaces to provide access to information or services. Now advances in speech recognition technology are allowing the creation of voice applications; the user interacts with these applications by speaking to them through a telephone rather than by using traditional input devices. Driving this technology is Voice eXtensible Markup Language, or VoiceXML. VoiceXML is a standard language for building interfaces between voice recognition software and Web content. Just as HTML defines the display and delivery of text and images on the Internet, VoiceXML translates XML-tagged Web content into a format that speech recognition software can deliver by phone. With VoiceXML, users can create a new class of websites using audio interfaces, which are not really websites in the normal sense because they provide Internet access with a standard telephone. By allowing voice access to information anytime, anywhere and from any device, voice recognition can provide a more effective way for companies to communicate with customers, save money and facilitate those with disabilities.

Introduction

HTML is the original language used to power the Web. It has served its purpose and without it the Web would not be possible. However, due to the rapid growth and popularity of the Web, HTML has begun to experience limitations. These limitations are evident in the structuring and retrieval of data given that the number of Web documents have increased and are more diverse than before. A new approach was needed to overcome these limitations and hence XML was developed in 1998.[1] This meant that developers were able to create applications in the language and environment with which they are already familiar. XML is an industry standard; it is simple in that any computer can read it, simplifying communications with other systems in the Internet. The Internet was designed as an information medium but it is rapidly becoming a communications medium, providing the ability to talk to someone on the other side of the world via e-mail or even purchase a product from the comfort of your own home. However, voice recognition technology has proved to be a major drawback with regard to the development of the Internet. The Internet has raised public expectations, with people growing used to having information at their fingertips when they want it. VoiceXML (VXML) allows developers to bridge the gap between vast amounts of Web content and a purely voice interface. VXML converts human speech to data that are usable by applications and servers. The XML-based standard for voice browsing will significantly reduce the amount of time and effort needed to develop and deploy speech applications, because developers can use the same technology that they use for developing websites. One segment of the population that will benefit from the advances in this voice technology are those with disabilities, including the blind and visually impaired. Technology advances in hand-held devices and voice portals will reduce many barriers for these groups, leaving them to participate in society more fully.[2]

The importance of voice recognition

The emergence of voice recognition technology gives businesses a competitive edge and potentially higher operational efficiency. It will free the user from limited navigation and confusing touch-tone menus, resulting in greater customer satisfaction. Navigation is now given a new dimension, allowing the user to move in any direction and at a desired speed, all with the use of the most natural user interface – the voice. Since first being introduced in the late 1980s, voice recognition technology has become more efficient and less expensive, and the commercial market has expanded rapidly. The adoption of the standard voice scripting language, VXML, is expected to fuel voice portal services, just as HTML fuelled development of the Internet.

Computerised voice recognition provides opportunities, particularly for those with severe arthritis or those who are visually impaired or blind for communication. The capacity to communicate with and collect information from almost any point on the globe or from one's home has already expanded the ability of those with disabilities to participate in an information-orientated society more effectively than before. People with disabilities meet barriers of all types. However, computers are helping to lower many of these barriers through voice recognition. Voice output can be used to read screen text to blind and visually impaired computer users. Voice input provides another option for individuals with disabilities. Voice recognition systems allow users to control the menus on computers by speaking the specified words and letters. Sometimes different disabilities will require similar solutions. For instance, someone who is blind and someone who cannot use his/her hands both require full keyboard equivalents, as they both have difficulty using the keyboard and mouse but can use voice recognition software. Examples of barriers that the visually impaired may encounter on the Web include:

- Images that do not have alt text – a blind person cannot understand what the image is because it cannot be described in braille or read out by a text screen reader. The Alt Tag is important because it provides a description of the image which automated text readers can 'describe' to the visually impaired surfer.
- Complex images, for example graphs and charts, are usually not adequately described.
- Video that is not described in audio.
- Tables that do not make sense when read serially – in a cell-by-cell mode.
- Non-standard document formatting that can be difficult for a screen reader to interpret.

Examples of barriers that people with physical and motor disabilities affecting the hands and arms may encounter include:

- Time-limited response options on webpages – they will normally not be able to respond in the specified period.
- Browsers and authoring tools that do not support keyboard alternatives for mouse commands.
- Forms that cannot be tabbed through in order.

These barriers may be overcome if more websites were developed primarily in voice and where no visual aids such as images are needed. Voice recognition software and voice browsers make it possible for people to navigate the website by using their voice, some with both voice input and voice output, and some allowing telephone-based web access. This would eliminate many of these barriers; for example, filling in a form would be simple, with the voice-activated software asking the questions and presenting the specific options. The users can then simply choose the options that are most suited to their particular needs.

The W3C are working to expand access to the Web to allow people to interact with sites via spoken commands. This should allow any telephone to be used to access Web-based services, and will be a boon to people with visual impairments or needing Web access while keeping their hands and eyes free for other things.[3] The focus of the W3C has naturally been on auditory interfaces, and hence the work has had a positive impact on the user groups facing the severest access challenges on the visual Web today – namely the blind and those with reduced vision. Severe visual impairment is one of the rarest disabilities, affecting less than 1 per cent of the population and it is one of the most difficult to overcome when using information technology.[1] When the Internet became graphical it left blind people struggling to catch up. But voice recognition has helped to liberate blind and visually impaired users from specially designed keyboards and mice, which can be inconvenient. The Internet is more likely to improve the quality of life for adults with disability than adults without disabilities. According to a recent survey, 48 per cent of adults with some form of disability believe that the Internet has greatly improved their quality of life, compared with only 27 per cent of adults without disabilities. The Internet allows people with disabilities to be more informed and more connected to the world, and it also provides them with communication with people who have similar interests and experiences. If technology is designed to be useable by those with disabilities, it will increase their ability to participate in the workforce and lead independent lives.

VXML

VXML is a standard that has been defined by the VoiceXML Forum, an industry organisation founded by AT&T, IBM, Lucent Technologies and Motorola, and consisting of more than 300 companies. VoiceXML 1.0 is a specification of the VoiceXML Forum. It was released in March 2000, and was accepted by the W3C two months later as a standard for voice mark up on the Web. VXML is designed for creating dynamic, Interentpowered phone applications that feature synthesized speech, digitized audio, recognition of spoken DTMF (touch-tone) key input and telephone. Its major goal is to bring the advantages of Web-based development and content delivery to interactive voice response applications. VXML is a Web-based markup language based on XML. Its uses are somewhat similar to HTML, but whereas HTML assumes a Web browser such as Internet Explorer or Netscape, display screen, keyboard and mouse, VXML uses a voice browser with audio output [text to speech (TTS), or pre-recorded prompts]. XML is designed to represent arbitrary data and VXML describes grammars, prompts, event handlers and other data structures useful in describing voice interaction between a human and a computer. Until recently, the World Wide Web has relied exclusively on visual interfaces to deliver information and services to users via computers equipped with a monitor, keyboard and mouse. In doing so, a huge potential customer base has been ignored, for example those who due to location, time and disability do not have access to a computer. However, many of these individuals do have access to a telephone, so users will benefit from the convenience of using the mobile Internet for self-service transaction, while companies enjoy the Web's relatively low transaction costs.

VXML is similar to HTML in that it is a mark-up language for creating distributed voice applications, much as HTML is a mark-up language for creating visual applications. Just as HTML defines the display and delivery of text and images on the Internet, VXML translates any XML-tagged Web content into a format that speech recognition software can deliver by phone. With VXML, users can create a new class of website using audio interfaces which can access the Internet with a standard telephone. Phones are everywhere in the developed world, in far greater numbers than Internet-connected computers. They are more portable and accessible than computers. So with VXML, these common devices can be used for applications such as voice-activated weather forecasts, restaurant listings and other location-based services that are not feasible on computers. The best-suited applications for VXML are information retrieval, electronic commerce, personal services and unified messages. The value of moving applications and content to XML means that we are in a position to take advantage of VXML as it develops. It is apparent that basing VXML on the XML standard yields some important benefits. The most important is that it allows the re-use and easy retooling of existing tools for creating, transforming and parsing XML documents. VXML and XML are similar in that they both provide advances features such as local validation and processing, but VXML provides slightly more advanced features such as playback and recording, and support for context-specific and tapered help.

Voice applications are those in which the input/output are through a spoken rather than a graphical user interface. The application files can reside on the local system, an Intranet, or the Internet. A voice application is a collection of one or more VXML documents.[4] Each VXML document contains one or more dialogues describing a specific interaction with the user. These dialogues may present the user with information or prompt the user to provide information. When this is complete, they can redirect the flow of control to another dialogue in that document, to a dialogue in another document in the same application, or even to a dialogue in another application entirely. A user can then access the assembled applications anytime, anywhere and from any telephone-capable device. The designer can also design the application to restrict access only to those who are authorised to receive it. These voice applications provide a simple and novel way for users to surf or shop on the Internet – browsing by voice. Hence, there is no need for a keyboard/mouse, just voice.

As illustrated in Figure 9.1, a document server (e.g. a Web server) processes requests from a client application, the VXML interpreter, through the VXML interpreter context. The server produces VXML documents in reply, which are processed by the VXML interpreter. The VXML interpreter context may monitor user inputs in parallel with the VXML interpreter. For example, one VXML interpreter context may always listen for a special escape phrase that takes the user to a high-level personal assistant, and another may listen for escape phrases that alter user preferences such as volume or text-to-speech characteristics.

The implementation platform is controlled by the VXML interpreter context and by the VXML interpreter. For instance, in an interactive voice

Figure 9.1 Components of VoiceXML

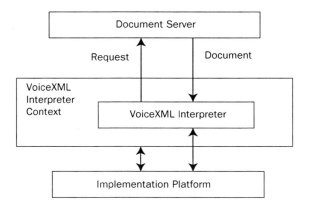

response application, the VXML interpreter context may be responsible for detecting an incoming call, acquiring the initial VXML document and answering the call, while the VXML interpreter conducts the dialogue after answer. The implementation platform generates events in response to user actions (e.g. spoken or character input received, disconnect) and system events (e.g. timer expiration). Some of these events are acted upon by the VXML interpreter itself, as specified by the VXML document, while others are acted upon by the VXML interpreter context.

VXML implements a client server paradigm, where a Web server provides VXML documents that contain dialogues to be interpreted and presented to the user; the users' responses are then submitted to the Web server, which responds by providing additional VXML documents, as appropriate. Unlike proprietary interactive voice response (IVR) systems, VXML provides an open application development environment that generates portable applications. This makes it a more cost-effective alternative for providing voice access services. Moreover, most IVR systems today accept input from the telephone keypad only, whereas VXML is designed predominantly to accept spoken input, but, if desired, can also accept telephone key pad (DTMF) input.[5] VXML supports local processing and validation of user input and playback of prerecorded audio files.

Conclusions

VXML is a standard language for building interfaces between voice recognition software and Web content. Just as HTML defines the display and delivery of text and images on the Internet, VXML translates XML-tagged Web content into a format that speech recognition software can deliver by phone. With VXML, users can create a new class of website by using audio interfaces, which are not really websites in the normal sense because they provide Internet access with a standard telephone. With voice recognition becoming more 'mainstream', significantly simpler to work with and less expensive, it is possible that users will become receptive to this technology and be willing to try it out. Voice command input can be more natural and much faster. People can speak in a natural voice to interact with their computers. Thus, combined with affordable pricing and increased consumer demand, VXML is leading to the evolution of transparent computing, where human/machine interaction is so natural that it is almost invisible.

Notes

1. Hocek, A. and Cuddihy, D. (2003) *Definitive VoiceXML*. New York: Prentice Hall.
2. Datamonitor (2008) VoiceXML tipped to become the dominant platform for IVR technology. *http://www.cbronline.com/article_feature.asp?guid=3AA03978-E715-49C2-A314-6D3AF5BE7703*
3. Shukla, C., Dass, A. and Gupta, V. (2002) *VoiceXML 2.0 Developer's Guide*. California: McGraw-Hill/Osborne.
4. Lucas, B. (2000) 'VoiceXML for Web-based distributed applications', *Communications of the ACM* 43, 53–7.
5. Phillips, L. (2000) 'VoiceXML: The new standard in Web Telephony', *Web Review Magazine*, *http://www.webreview.com*

10

Web services

Kevin Curran and Padraig O'Kane

The online community has been growing steadily year on year and with this escalation the number of services provided has increased in an attempt to meet the demands of a computer-literate audience. There has been a progression from a human-orientated use of the Web to an application-driven concept referred to as Web services. We discuss the factors leading to this development and the inspiration behind Web services. We detail the languages, platforms and systems involved in these services.

Introduction

The term 'Web services' was initially employed by Bill Gates, Chairman of Microsoft, at the Microsoft Professional Developers Conference in Orlando, Florida, on 12 July 2000. Fundamentally, the term refers to automated resources accessed via an Internet URL. However, a more comprehensive definition is that of the W3C,[1] which declares Web services as 'providing a standard means of interoperating between different software applications, running on a variety of platforms and/or frameworks.' An Internet connection allows retrieval of software-powered resources or functional components and is therefore regarded as an extension of the World Wide Web infrastructure. Web services represent the evolution of a human-orientated utilisation of the Web to a technology that is application driven. It attempts to replace human centric searches for information with searches that are primarily application based.

The primary elements associated with Web services are repositories (i.e. a location for storage) and messaging. Web service applications can perform a range of requests or processes yet several characteristics found are common throughout. All Web service applications connect over a network, i.e. a medium that allows users to share information and resources. The networks frequently associated with Web services are intranet (within an organisation), extranet (within an organisation including controlled outside partners) or the Internet (within the global community). Communication between the applications within the network is performed using a set of standardised protocols; those used include HTTP and the secure HTTP (HTTPS). Another common characteristic associated with Web services is that the connection between applications is standardised, yet it is independent of operating system and language so that disparate or varying systems can benefit. The principal language that conveys the information distributed across the network is XML and this language is expressed using simple object access protocol (SOAP) messaging. Web services are often called XML Web services to emphasise the importance of XML as the underlying language whilst distinguishing such services for other types commonly available on the Web. The interfaces of a Web service are often defined using the Web services description language (WSDL). It employs XML grammar in describing network services as collections of endpoints capable of exchanging messages. Through the use of WSDL, Web services can enable applications to use its services once they have found and interpreted its definition. Another common characteristic is that of universal description, discovery and integration (UDDI). Characteristics of a Web service including its existence, location and purpose can be published and discovered using UDDI Web service descriptions and the methods for publishing and discovering them are stored in a repository provided by UDDI.

History of Web services

Web services derived from the efforts of a number of businesses that shared a mutual interest in developing and maintaining an 'electronic marketplace'. In 1975, electronic data interchange (EDI) was launched and was deemed the first attempt to create a medium where businesses could communicate over a network. However, EDI was difficult to implement due to its complexity and cost constraints and in the more than 25 years since its introduction numerous efforts at a global business network technology have been introduced, for example the Distributed Component Object Model, UNIX Remote Procedure Call and Java Remote Method Invocation. Each of the applications failed to gain significant market status or enough momentum to succeed, although all of them exist today and are still useful. A combination of factors contributed to the failure of these previous technologies and it was imperative that software vendors accepted this and concentrated on implementing a technology where an 'electronic marketplace' was a realisation. Before the introduction of the Web, the possibility of ensuring that all major software vendors agreed on a transport protocol for communication across network application services was unrealistic. But when the Web was a reality, lower level transports for standardised communication were specified. The TCP/IP and HTTP standards were already integrated by the time the Web went global in 1994, all that was required was a messaging and data encapsulation standard, for which it was essential that software vendors cooperated fully.

The introduction of XML was instrumental in the rise of Web services. It officially became a recognised standard in February 1998 when the W3C announced that XML 1.0 was suitable for integration into software applications. XML is described as a 'widely heralded, platform independent standard for data description'.[2] It provided the means of communicating between standardised applications and by early 1998, a number of attempts where made at an XML protocol encouraging inter-process communication. One such protocol, SOAP, is regarded as the basis for Web services. It proved popular even though some individuals were at first dubious due to the fact that it was developed by Microsoft. SOAP was advantageous in that it was flexible, general purpose and its cross-platform compatibility meant that its acceptance was widespread. Surprisingly, IBM publicly backed Microsoft's SOAP and in March 2000 both companies began to develop SOAP 1.1. The two companies also began to work individually on protocols, which encouraged connectivity to a Web service. They emerged with IBM's network accessible service specification language and Microsoft's service description language and SOAP contract language. During the autumn of 2000, the protocol proposals were merged and WSDL was announced. Companies could now create and describe their Web services using SOAP and WSDL, yet a means of locating and advertising Web services was still required. IBM, Microsoft and now Ariba began working on a solution in March 2000, and their efforts produced the standard universal description, discovery and integration (UDDI), which was announced in September 2000. With SOAP, WSDL and UDDI in place it was apparent that the standards to create, locate and advertise Web services had arrived. However, software infrastructure vendors remained defiant and it was not until the end of 2000 that Oracle, HP, Sun, IBM and Microsoft revealed their intention to support and incorporate the standards into their products.

Web service technologies

Web services use a number of inter-related technologies and languages. However, we intend to focus on those that have aided the growth of Web services and those that were established in an effort to maximise its potential, namely XML, SOAP and WSDL.

XML

In order to understand XML[3] it is important to realise that it is an outgrowth of standard generalized mark-up language (SGML), which became a standard of the International Organization for Standardization (ISO) in 1986. SGML had its origins within IBM, which realised the importance of publishing content in a number of different ways. With a number of organisations struggling with similar problems, IBM seized the opportunity to create a standard for document mark-up. The resulting rich document mark-up language allowed authors to separate the logical content of a document from its presentation. This approach involved the introduction of metadata. Metadata describe the attributes of an information-bearing object (IBO), e.g. document, dataset, database and image. It is more commonly referred to as 'data about data'.[4] Another definition states: 'Metadata usually includes information about the intellectual content of the image, digital representation data and security or rights management information.'[5] With SGML, metadata were added to indicate the logical structure and to provide shared context. HTML is also a descendant of SGML. However, both HTML and SGML were lacking in terms of defining the requirements of metadata. Yet when companies began to develop a standard addressing the problems associated with these languages they naturally looked at SGML as a starting point. The W3C formed a working group to study the issue. Their primary goal was to establish a simplified subset of SGML suitable for use on the Web, as SGML is extremely complex and poses problems for automated processing of large volumes of Internet documents. A subset of SGML that would be simple enough for people to understand yet expressive enough to meet the need for shared context on the Internet was what was required. The resulting specification was XML 1.0. The XML approach to metadata and shared context is simple to grasp. Programmers add metadata through tags; the syntax is similar to that of HTML with angled brackets (<>) commonplace throughout (see Figure 10.1).

Figure 10.1 XML document detailing a letter regarding an order

```
<to>Padraig</to>
<from>Ruairi</from>
<re><customer-name>Joe Bloggs</customer-name>
    <customer-number>0101-0101-010</customer-number>
    <document-type-request>order form</document-type-request>
</re>
<p>Joe Bloggs wants to complain about his order. He feels he has been
overcharged.</p>
```

Document designers add shared context through document type definitions (DTDs). A DTD uses a collection of rules to specify the permitted order, structure and attributes of tags for a particular type of document; in simpler terms the DTD handles the mark-up language and therefore specifies what tags are valid. Using an Internet uniform resource locator (URL) a document can reference the DTD. XML offers a standard, flexible data format that is extensible and which therefore reduces the burden of organising a number of technologies needed to ensure Web services are a success. The XML syntax is an extremely important aspect, as are the concepts of the XML infoset, XML schema and XML namespaces. XML infoset is a formal set of information items and associated properties that provide an abstract description of an XML document. It attempts to define a set of terms that specifications can use to refer to information within an XML document. The concept of XML namespaces is extremely important in that it ensures XML documents remain recognisable and are free from 'collisions' that occur when other software packages use similar attribute or element naming conventions. The XML namespaces mechanism is a collection of names identified by a URL reference; they differ from other naming conventions in that the XML version has an internal structure and uses families of reserved attributes. The XML schema is a concept that allows machines to process work based on a series of rules developed by people. The structure and content of an XML document can be defined using such a schema.

SOAP

SOAP is a protocol based on XML messaging and is used to encode the information in Web service request and response messages before they can be sent over a network. SOAP is used to gain access to services, objects and servers in a standard way. Its main goal is to facilitate interoperability, i.e. the ability of software and hardware located in multiple machines to communicate. The messages are independent of any operating system and/or protocol and can be sent using a range of Internet protocols although the underlying communication protocol is that of HTTP. When SOAP was first introduced programmers/authors focused on accessing objects, a medium specific to technologies that recognised an object-orientated approach. Over time it was felt that SOAP was restricted and that a wider audience was required and therefore the specification moved away from an object-centric one to a generalized XML messaging framework. As mentioned, SOAP defines a method of transferring XML messages from one point to the next (see Figure 10.2).

The messaging framework carries out this transfer, as it is extensible, usable over a variety of underlying protocols and independent of programming models. The key to SOAP is its extensibility. Simplicity still remains one of SOAP's primary design goals, as is often witnessed with software. SOAP lacks in a number of various distributed system features such as security, routing and reliability, although such features can be added at later stages and with IBM, Microsoft and other software vendors working continually on SOAP extensions, developers remain optimistic. Secondly, SOAP can be used over any transport protocol such as TCP or HTTP, although a standard protocol was required in order to outline rules governing the environment. The SOAP specification encourages the definition of absolute protocols by providing such a flexible framework. The third characteristic of SOAP is that it does not conform to just one programming model. SOAP defines a model for processing individual, single-path messages, but it is possible to combine multiple messages into an overall message exchange, and SOAP therefore allows for any number of message exchange patterns. The SOAP messaging framework consists of a number of core elements: envelope,

Figure 10.2 Transfer of XML messages using SOAP

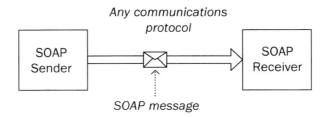

header, body and fault. The envelope element is always the root element of a SOAP message, making it easy for applications to identify a message by simply looking at the name of the root element. The version of SOAP being used can also be identified from information stated in the envelope element. The envelope element contains an optional header element, which is followed by a body element, which represents the majority of the message. The body element can contain varying numbers of elements from any namespace. The data that a user wants to send are placed within the body element. The fault element highlights errors within the body element in the event that something goes wrong. A standard error representation is paramount in that it ensures that applications cannot create their own, therefore making it impossible for the general infrastructure to differentiate between success and failure.[6]

WSDL

WSDL provides an XML grammar and supplies a means of grouping messages into operations and operations into interfaces. WSDL is essential to the Web services architecture as it describes the complete contract for application communication. WSDL is a machine-readable language and therefore tools and infrastructure can easily be built around it. Developments within this technology have ensured that programmers can use WSDL definitions to generate code that interacts with Web services precisely. Code generation like this encapsulates details concerned with the sending and receiving of SOAP messages over different protocols and makes Web services far more approachable. Regardless of the programming language in use, the classes generated from the same WSDL definition should be able to communicate with each other through the interfaces provided by WSDL. A WSDL definition contains several elements including types, messages, port type, binding and service (Figure 10.3), all of which come from the same namespace. It is therefore important when referencing something in a WSDL file that a qualified name is used.

The elements type, message, and port type are abstract definitions of the Web service interface. These three elements make up the programmatic interface that one interacts with. The final two elements (binding and service) describe the concrete details of how the interface translates messages onto the wire. The underlying infrastructure handles these details rather than the application code. Several editors are now available allowing the generation of WSDL and thus making the authoring of such definitions much easier.

Figure 10.3 Basic structure of a WSDL definition

```
<!-- WSDL definition structure -->
<definitions
        name="MathService"
        targetNamespace="http://example.org/math/"
xmlns=http://schemas.xmlsoap.org/wsdl/
>
        <!-- abstract definitions -->
        <types> ...
        <message> ...
        <portType> ...
        <!-- concrete definitions -->
        <binding> ...
        <service> ...
</definition>
```

Future of Web services

Web services have established themselves and have found a critical mass. In order to maintain this momentum, Web service standards need to progress quickly and efficiently and interoperability must be achieved. The choices evident within the world of Web services are extremely important, especially during such a formative period. The factors that will determine the success of Web services technology are those concerned with the variety of scales and whether the technology can be used with simple, small projects as well as more complex developments. Both SOAP and WSDL are complementary to projects of varying sizes and it is these technologies that will ensure continued support from businesses and organisations as these standards are now globally accepted. Integrated environments such as Microsoft's Visual Studio.NET already provide a framework to create and control Web services in a seamless fashion. Other Web service product developers such as IBM are extending their environments to encourage an easy-to-use development platform. It is predicted that as the number of businesses publishing Web services grows, such businesses will seek to provide service alternatives to guarantee 24/7 availability and aid the monitoring of Web services as well as validating service providers and offering one-stop shopping for Web services.

Conclusion

Since the introduction of XML in 1998, Web service technology has steadily gathered momentum. Both Microsoft and IBM were pioneering forces behind its implementation and their work together has seen a number of developments, most notably SOAP and WSDL, gain global status in an effort to establish Web services firmly as the key in developing an electronic marketplace. Companies are keen to exploit this solution, as highlighted by Systinet, Qwest and BizDex. However, it is imperative that companies, vendors and the W3C agree on standards and that the factors contributing to successful Web service growth are harnessed in order to ensure that the future for Web services is prosperous.

Notes

1. *www.webservices.org*
2. Levitt, J. (2001) 'From EDI to XML and UDDI: a brief history of web services', *Information Week*, October.
3. Goldfarb, C. and Prescod, P. (2006) *The XML Handbook*, 2nd edition. New York: Wiley Publishers.
4. Dick, K. (2001) *XML – A Manager's Guide*. London: Pearson Education.
5. *http://xml.coverpages.org*
6. Kotok, A. (2004) 'ebXML and web services to go the last mile', *BizDex Journal*, January.

11

Web 2.0

Kevin Curran, David Stephen Norrby and Martin Christian

Web 2.0 is a social phenomenon referring to an approach to creating and distributing Web content itself, and is characterised by open communication, decentralisation of authority, freedom to share and re-use, and 'the market as a conversation'. Web 2.0 is based on ensuring that users add value to a site as a side-effect of what they are actually using the site for. In effect, Web 2.0 makes use of the long tail of the Web, such as when Amazon collects user reviews of their products. Most of us are used to software being developed, packaged, picked up in a shop and kept updated through downloaded and installed patches. In the Web 2.0 world, applications are run online, with no installation, updates are constant and continuous, and access is instant from any computer with a browser. This chapter provides a clearer definition of Web 2.0 and the technologies and websites that utilise Web 2.0 principles.

Introduction

'Web 2.0' is a relatively new term. Most Web surfers will have come across the terms 'blog', 'wiki', 'podcast', 'RSS feed' and 'CSS and XHTML validated'. These are all associated with the umbrella term 'Web 2.0', although the actual definition of this term is still hotly debated. 'Web 2.0' was first used by O'Reilly Media as the name of a series of Web-development conferences[1] that started in 2004. Wikipedia defines Web 2.0 expression as referring to any of the following:

- The transition of websites from isolated information silos to sources of content and functionality, thus becoming a computer platform serving Web applications to end users.

- A social phenomenon referring to an approach to creating and distributing Web content itself, characterised by open communication, decentralisation of authority, freedom to share and re-use, and 'the market as a conversation'.

- A more organised and categorised content, with better developed deep linking Web architecture.

- A shift in the economic value of the Web, possibly surpassing that of the dot com boom of the late 1990s.

- A marketing term to differentiate new Web businesses from those of the dot com boom.

- The resurgence of excitement around the possibilities of innovative Web applications and services that gained considerable momentum around mid 2005.

Sub-categories of what Web 2.0 encapsulates include usability, economy, participation, convergence, design, standardisation and remixability. These are further broken down into, for example, blogs, audio, video, RSS, open application programming interfaces (APIs), wikis, social software and focus on simplicity. This chapter presents an overview of Web 2.0, including definitions, technologies involved and sites currently advocated as examples.

Web 2.0

Web 2.0 makes use of the network as a platform spanning all connected devices. Applications can then make the most of the intrinsic advantages of that platform by delivering software as a continually-updated service that gets better the more people use it, and remix data from multiple sources. Implicit in this also is that others can continue to remix, thereby creating network effects through an "architecture of participation," and going beyond the page metaphor of Web 1.0 to deliver rich user experiences.[2] Tim O'Reilly also posted the following figure to serve as a further explanation:[3]

Figure 11.1 is a diagram created at the Web 2.0 conference to describe the concept of Web 2.0 as not having a hard boundary, but rather a gravitational core. The Web is the platform for this concept, while the user gets to control his/her own data.

Figure 11.2 describes the evolution of services such as 'DoubleClick' and 'Britannica Online' into the Web 2.0 generation, the popularity of their Web 2.0 counterparts, 'Google AdSense' and 'Wikipedia',

Figure 11.1 Web 2.0 Meme Map

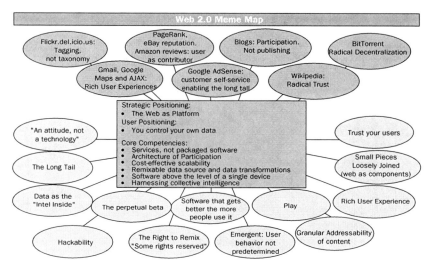

Reproduced, with permission, from *What Is Web 2.0: Design Patterns and Business Models for the Next Generation of Software*, by Tim O'Reilly, © O'Reilly Media, Inc. 2005. *http://oreilly.com/web2/archive/what-is-web-20.html*

Figure 11.2 What is Web 2.0

Web 1.0		Web 2.0
DoubleClick	-->	Google AdSense
Ofoto	-->	Flickr
Akamai	-->	BitTorrent
mp3.com	-->	Napster
Britannica Online	-->	Wikipedia
personal websites	-->	blogging
evite	-->	upcoming.org and EVDB
domain name speculation	-->	search engine optimization
page views	-->	cost per click
screen scraping	-->	web services
publishing	-->	participation
content management systems	-->	wikis
directories (taxonomy)	-->	tagging ("folksonomy")
stickiness	-->	syndication

respectively, having increased dramatically. A general comparison between Web 2.0 and Web 1.0 is provided in Table 11.1.

There are those who debate the validity of the term 'Web 2.0', claiming that Web 2.0 does not exist and that the term is merely a marketing slogan that is used to convince investors and the media that companies are 'creating something fundamentally new, rather than

Table 11.1 Difference between Web 1.0 and Web 2.0

	Web 1.0	Web 2.0
Mode of usage	Read	Write and contribute
Unit of content	Page	Record
State	Static	Dynamic
How content is viewed	Web browser	Browser, RSS readers, mobile devices, etc.
Creation of content	By website authors	By everyone

continuing to develop and use well-established technologies'.[4] Whatever the actual definition, the most widely accepted idea of what comprises a Web 2.0 website is the following set of criteria:

1. User-generated content, as opposed to content posted solely by the site author(s). One example of this would be the recently developed *www.newsvine.com*, which allows users to post their own news articles and maintain their own news columns.

2. Treats users as if they are co-developers of the site: the more people who use the service, the better it becomes. User contribution, by means of reviews, comments, etc., is encouraged.

3. Highly customisable content and interface. For example, allowing users to put their own news feeds on their homepage, as in *www.netvibes.com* (see Figure 11.3), rather than serving content that the user has little to no control over, as in the homepages of MSN, BBC or NBC.

4. The core application of the website runs through the browser and Web server, rather than on a desktop platform.

5. The incorporation of popular Internet trends such as 'blogging', 'tagging', 'podcasting', 'wikis', the sharing of media and content, and the use of Web standards such as validated XHTML and CSS.

6. Integration of emerging Web technologies such as AJAX, RSS and APIs.

Often, one can recognise a Web 2.0 site based on the following minor characteristics:

1. Clean interface with an extensive use of colour gradients, large fonts and CSS design.

Figure 11.3 Netvibes.com customisable homepage

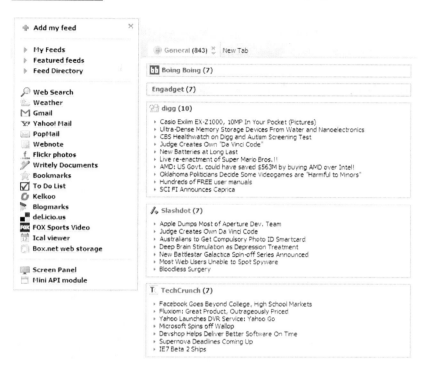

2. Contains a development wiki.

3. Separate RSS feeds for every part of the site.

4. Links to a 'meet the team' personal blog maintained by the site authors.

5. The company's name sounds like a character from *Star Wars* and/or at least one vowel appears to be missing, for example Renkoo, Gabbr, Meebo, Congoo, Flickr, Frappr, Tagyu, Goowy and Squidoo.

6. Box of 'tags' with varying font sizes (see Figure 11.4).

The use of hyper linking on Web pages underpins the 2.0 Web. The high level of connectivity between content on the Web has encouraged sustained growth as more and more users add new content. Users can then link to newly discovered sites in a way similar to dendrites forming links in the human brain. The success of Google is a result of 2.0 technologies. Google has created a business from linking users of one site

Figure 11.4 **Most popular tags on Flickr.com**

africa amsterdam animal animals april architecture art australia autumn baby
barcelona beach berlin birthday black blackandwhite blue boston building bw
california cameraphone camping canada canon car cat cats chicago
china christmas church city clouds color concert day dc december dog dogs
england europe fall family festival florida flower flowers food france
friends fun garden geotagged germany girl graffiti green halloween hawaii
holiday home honeymoon hongkong house india ireland island italy japan july kids
lake landscape light london losangeles macro march me mexico moblog mountain
mountains museum music nature new newyork newyorkcity newzealand night
nikon nyc ocean paris park party people photo portrait red river roadtrip rock
rome san sanfrancisco school scotland sea seattle show sky snow spain spring
street summer sun sunset sydney taiwan texas thailand tokyo toronto travel
tree trees trip uk urban usa vacation vancouver washington water
wedding white winter yellow york zoo

to the information or service provided by another. Google has none of
the trappings of software provider's products, namely the purchase cost
of the software, limited applications to a particular platform and the
product lifespan, where the next generation would involve the consumer
having to purchase an upgrade or a whole new software package. There
are no direct costs to the users of Google; all the business costs are met
by advertising and the placing of sponsored links in prominent positions.
Continuous upgrades are of very little significance to the end user as they
have no direct input either with time or resources. The key to Google's
success is the use of PageRank, which uses Web link structure as opposed
to the page content to rank search results. This open source operating
system would have been impossible to run with Web 1.0 technologies,
supporting the argument that Web 2.0 provides a platform where the
user has control of the information provided.[5] Although it is clear that
Web 2.0 has no clear and concise definition, one could argue that the
term is useful in that it allows non-technical users to the define the
complicated set of concepts and technologies that are constantly being
developed for use in new websites, and it allows companies to promote
their websites to the masses without having to explain the sophisticated
array of technologies used to create them.

Popular trends

A 'blog', short for 'web log', is a Web-based publication comprising individual articles that are posted periodically and are usually displayed in reverse chronological order. Blogs are often used to create online journals, and others may focus on one particular subject, such as technology or politics. Content submission to blogs is usually done on the Web server, rather than uploading manually, with templates automatically styling the newly created content to fit appropriately on the blog homepage. Most blog software allows readers to submit comments on each piece of content and it is customary, especially on professional blogs, to provide links to similar articles on different blogs. Blogs have become extremely popular over the past few years. technorati.com, a popular blog search engine, is 'currently tracking 36.7 million sites and 2.3 billion links' and, with free blog hosting sites such as *www.livejournal.com* and *www.blogger.com* allowing users to create a blog within minutes, that number is steadily increasing. Examples of popular blogs are engadget,[6] boingboing[7] and techcrunch.[8]

Syndication

Syndication involves the use of RSS and/or Atom feeds to allow users to view new site updates without having to visit the actual website, such as by using a news reader (e.g. Microsoft Outlook), downloading onto a mobile device or integrating the syndication feed into a desktop program (e.g. Google Desktop).

Podcasts

Podcasting is the use of syndication, RSS or Atom for the distribution of multimedia files such as audio recordings over the Internet for playback on mobile devices and PCs. The podcast is usually some from of show, such as a weekly radio programme.

Tagging

A tag is a word attached to a piece of content that acts as a category. Multiple tags can be assigned to the content and they allow content to be sorted according to category, in the same way that similar files can be located within one directory. The difference, however, is that sorting by tags is dynamic. Tags of a piece of content can be easily added, edited or removed with no hindrance to the sorting process as the sorting is done using software on the Web server. Tags are often used in Web 2.0 applications. For example, on *www.flickr.com*, users can assign their own tags to the photographs they have uploaded so that other users can see this when they are viewing photographs with similar tags. This method of open categorisation on the Internet is known as 'folksonomy'.

Mashups

A 'mashup' is a product that incorporates multiple technologies and information from different sources into one application by making use of APIs. One example would be the correlation of information with Google Maps, e.g. placing houses to buy and rent on the Google Maps interface, as used in *www.ononemap.com*.

Folksonomies

'Folksonomy' is a combination of the words 'folk' and 'taxonomy', literally 'people's classification management'. Folksonomies allow Internet users to categorize Web pages, photographs and links. This labelling process is called 'tagging' and the result is an improved quality of search results.

Web 2.0 is more interactive than its predecessor. Web pages are now described as 'user-dependent Web portals'. These portals require user input and feedback for success. eBay is an online business that depends on transactions conducted by its members to sustain growth. In a way similar to the Web, eBay is a supplier of content that supports user activities with continued market domination almost guaranteed due to its sheer scale of operation. Major high street retailers are now flexing their collective business muscle on the Web. Tesco.com provides all the facilities of their physical store online, enabling the customer to shop from home using JavaScript and secure Internet connections to facilitate transactions. And other businesses can now compete with large retail companies even if they are based solely online. Ryan Air provides agent-free bookings, removing the middle man and, more importantly for the consumer, agent fees from air travel. Web 2.0 applications have helped Ryan Air to grow as a company at a time when the general air industry is in recession.[9]

The way in which communities interact socially has changed with Web 2.0 innovations. No longer do people depend on written letters or telephone calls to communicate. Web 2.0 has helped to create online social networks for public use; some of them provide social software that members can use to connect with each other. Microsoft's MSN and Bebo.com are two of these online communities. Benefits to Web 2.0 include the fact that it holds collective intelligence. This makes the work on it collaborative. And because everything is updated instantly, using RSS feeds, there is instant gratification for users. They have a sense of ownership over the Web because it holds their work. This makes them much more passionate about using the Web and updating it regularly, meaning everyone who reads the information on the Web gets up-to-date information all the time. The early Web was primarily designed to provide information for users, whereas today a user can also now contribute to a website. Today's online tasks are more than surfing for information; they now include shopping, down- and uploading, blogging and sharing files with Web users both known and unknown to the user. There is no argument that there have been major developments in the way today's Web is run or in the applications and expectations end users now have of the Web. However, even given these developments, there still remains no direct evidence that Web 2.0 exists as an actual methodology or technology. It seems to be a phrase used to describe recent innovations in the natural development cycle, although some older technologies have been included under the Web 2.0 banner.[9]

Web 2.0 technology

The following is a brief overview of the technology and software used to create the Web 2.0 experience.

AJAX

AJAX stands for 'asynchronous JavaScript and XML'. It is a technique used to create interactive Web applications, where small parts of a website can be refreshed with new content without the need to reload the whole page to reflect any change made by the user. An example of AJAX in action can be viewed on *www.flickr.com*, where, when one wants to edit the title of a photograph, clicking on the title will automatically change it to an editable text-box and, when edited, the new title will be displayed in regular HTML. This is all done without ever reloading the page. The advantages of AJAX lie in its ability to present a large amount of interactivity to the user, and its portability, as the technique uses elements that are present in almost all modern browsers. There are a number of complaints concerning the use of

AJAX. One is that, if there are network latency issues, a user would not know if there is any information being processed or why there is a delay in the interface unless some sort of indication is given, much like the loading progress bar on Internet browsers when a page is being loaded. Another concern is that some browsers will not be able to support AJAX, either because the browser is too old or JavaScript is disabled. Internet Explorer 6 and earlier versions also require ActiveX to be enabled for proper use of the XMLHttpRequest object.[10]

RSS

RSS is a method used for Web syndication which delivers information in the form of an XML file.

Wiki

A 'wiki' is a type of website that allows the easy addition, removal and editing of all content. Wikis are ideal for the collaborative writing of articles, so it is no surprise that the most famous wiki is *www.wikipedia. org*, a large, free and up-to-date Web-based encyclopaedia. Wikis allow users with little to no knowledge of HTML to create neatly formatted articles, with pictures and links to other articles, by using a simple and extremely human-readable syntax. This also ensures that every article looks similar to the other articles contained on the site.

XML

XML allows us to create custom tags, which can transmit, validate and interpret data between applications but also require a DTD to describe the data that are going to be read. XML has a very descriptive filing system that allows you to label parts of the document relative to the content it holds. This is extremely beneficial when organising and searching for certain content.

XHTML

Put simply, XHTML is HTML done in XML. This means it has a much stricter syntax, and the document must be well formed with the proper use of tags. Stricter syntax encourages standardisation, so that the content is compatible with as many browsers, platforms and devices as possible.

CSS

The most common application of a cascading style sheet is to determine the style of documents created in HTML or XHTML. The primary advantage of CSS is that all the information about the presentation of a document's content is contained in one separate file, greatly increasing efficiency and flexibility when one wants to edit any aspect of the styling. This also means that the document will not be bloated with repetitive coding and countless '<font>', '<b>' and '<br>' tags, as the styling of individual HTML elements is determined only once in the CSS file. CSS has become very popular in the design of Web 2.0 websites as it allows for a neat, efficient and easily changeable interface design. Also, multiple style sheets can be used so that each user of the site can choose the look they want.

Popular Web 2.0 sites

Meebo (see Figure 11.5) enables users to chat using their AIM, ICQ, Yahoo! Messenger, Jabber, GTalk and MSN Messenger accounts through

Figure 11.5 Meebo.com

a neat AJAX interface. The AJAX interface allows the page to act much like a desktop where multiple chat windows can be open at once.

Flickr (see Figure 11.6) is an extremely popular photo-sharing site where users can browse photos according to user or category and upload their own photos. Photos are categorised using user-defined tags, and the site utilises an innovative AJAX interface to allow photo information to be easily edited without having to refresh the page.

Newsvine[11] (see Figure 11.7) is a site consisting of community-driven news. Users write articles and vote, comment and chat on articles created by both users and journalists. Extensive tagging is used to fully categorise every news article, and there are many RSS feeds available for the different news categories.

Gmail[12] is Google's answer to hotmail. It was launched in 2003 with a powerful adaptable interface and multiple functionality. Napster,[13] one of the most widely used music file-sharing networks, came to fame in 1999, but was forced to shut by lawsuits claiming the service was damaging the music industry unlawfully. It returned with a new release and pleasant XHTML/XML interface offering instant download and installation of the service. Del.icio.us[14] is a network of favourite Web resources, which

Figure 11.6   Flickr.com

Figure 11.7 Newsvine

allows the sharing of websites, articles, blogs and reviews with any individual who is registered. Wikipedia[15] is an online open-sourced encyclopaedia that allows users to add definitions for words, abbreviations and just about anything that is searchable. Users can add/edit/delete entries facilitated by a strict AJAX backend architecture and comprehensive content management system. Most of these websites do adhere to W3C standards due to the implementation of Strict DTD.. Although each of these services works across different browsers the closer we are to meeting W3C guidelines, the closer we are to a perfect Web.

Other examples include 30Boxes,[16] which is an online calendar and event planner. Using the AJAX-built interface, the whole calendar can be browsed without any page-refreshing, and users can easily add, edit and delete events in a pop-up box on the same page. Netvibes[17] is a start page similar to Google's personalised homepage. Netvibes supports RSS feeds, Google Mail, Webnotes, Web Search and Weather. It also allows users to integrate their photographs from their Flickr.com account, as well as their bookmarks from their del.icio.us account. AJAX is used to enable the user to dynamically edit the layout of the content that they add to their personalised homepage.

Conclusion

Making use of Web 2.0 is about ensuring that, as a side-effect to what the user is actually doing, they actually add value. In short, use of Web 2.0 principals involves use of the long tail of the Web. A common technique is simply to collect user reviews. Amazon was one of the pioneers of this strategies, and today the numbers of online stores that use this system has boomed. Google has revolutionised advertising by making it easy for small 'every day' websites (which make up the majority of sites on the net, i.e. the long tail) to put adverts on their sites without signing a large contract. Proponents speak of the Web as a new platform.

Notes

1. *http://www.web2con.com/*
2. *http://radar.oreilly.com/archives/2005/10/web_20_compact_definition.html*
3. *http://www.oreillynet.com/pub/a/oreilly/tim/news/2005/09/30/what-is-web-20.html*
4. Shaw, R. (2005) *Web 2.0? It doesn't exist.* ZDNet, December 2005, *http://blogs.zdnet.com/ip-telephony/?p=805*
5. McCormack, D. (2002) *Web 2.0: The Future of the Internet and Technology Economy and How Entrepreneurs, Investors, Executives & Consumers Can Take Ad (Execenablers).* Aspatore Books.
6. *www.engadget.com*
7. *www.boingboing.net*
8. *www.techcrunch.com*
9. MacManus, R. and Porter, J. (2005) 'Bootstrapping the social Web', *Digital Web Magazine*, May. *http://www.digital-web.com/articles/web_2_for_designers*
10. Gehtland, J., Almaer, D. and Galbraith, B. (2006) *Pragmatic Ajax: A Web 2.0 Primer.* Pragmatic Bookshelf.
11. *http://www.newsvine.com/*
12. *www.gmail.com*
13. *www.napster.com*
14. *http://delicious.com/*
15. *www.wikipedia.org*
16. *http://30boxes.com/*
17. *http://www.netvibes.com/*

Mobile social software

Kevin Curran, Jason Downey and Danny Otterson

Recent communications developments have created a new era in which online communities can share information and socialise in different ways. Communication information systems are closely linked to the strong emergence in social software. This chapter discusses the uses and applications of mobile social software and their risks and disadvantages.

Introduction

Mobile social software (MSS) supports user group interaction in online communities. It enables users to find one another, in a particular vicinity and time, for social or business networking. MSS has largely been targeted to cities, on the assumption that urban areas provide individuals at a sufficient density that users may serendipitously encounter as they go about their everyday lives.[1] Social software is defined by three characteristics, one or more of which need to be met:[2]

1. Support for conversational interaction between individuals or groups ranging from real-time instant messaging to asynchronous collaborative teamwork spaces. This category also includes collaborative commenting on and within blog spaces.

2. Support for social feedback, which allows a group to rate the contributions of others, perhaps implicitly, leading to the creation of a digital reputation.

3. Support for social networks to explicitly create and manage a digital expression of people's personal relationships, and to help them build new relationships.

Almost one in five people who log on to the Internet has signed up to a social networking site such as Facebook, Bebo or MySpace. In addition, the majority of teenagers today own a mobile phone. The merging of these trends has brought about the arrival of mobile social networking. Technology in mobile phones is advancing year on year. 3G uptake remains an expensive option but it has been predicted that by 2012 80% of phone users will in fact be 3G users.[3] With these technologies in place there will be opportunities for developers to design software to take advantage of the developments in social networking that exist.

E-mail was the first major online socialising network that allowed users to communicate with people they knew, but in this role it has now been superseded by instant messaging programs such as MSN Messenger and AIM and by online networks such Bebo and MySpace. MySpace was created by Tom Anderson in 2003 and was sold to News Corporation for $580 million in 2005. MySpace in January 2009 had 125 million users worldwide. MySpace is still number 1 in the US but trends suggest that by 2010, at current relative growth rates, Facebook will become the largest US social network.[4] MySpace, Facebook, Yahoo and Bebo are currently targeting all mobile phone users.

MSS providers

Slam (social, location, annotation, mobile)

Slam[5] supports real-time communication between groups of people. It works on the basis of people joining a group, which might be a person's friends, family, colleagues, classmates or even just a group of people with shared interests. The messages on each group discussion or chat are uploaded onto Web pages. When there has been a new posting on the page each member of the group will be alerted automatically.

Enpresence

Enpresence[6] is mobile phone software that uses Bluetooth technology. Personal information, likes, dislikes and hobbies are all requested by the software and this information is used to scan against other users of the software in a 100-metre radius using Bluetooth. When certain similarities are matched between users the phone informs the user. If the third party does not wish to reciprocate, then they discard that profile. If they do in fact want to send a message they can do so.

Dodgeball

Dodgeball[7] is popular mobile social software that is available in over 22 cities in America. Dodgeball aims to help users plot a social life. Friends are added to a user's list by visiting the website. Dodgeball Social allows users to find out if they have any friends within a ten-block radius. This feature is useful for finding people after a period apart and also could be helpful in the case of an emergency. The Dodgeball system works through sending a message to friends letting them know of the new location. A unique feature within Dodgeball is 'crushes', which allows each member to pick five people on Dodgeball and when they are in range, they receive an SMS message with details, picture and location, so they will have the choice of meeting the third party. The 'shout' feature of Dodgeball allows users to send all their friends a message and the 'check-in' feature allows users to let people know where they are. Dodgeball has recently been bought by Google.

Jambo Networks

Jambo Networks[8] is mobile social software used to match people with similar interests. Users need a wireless device (cell phone, PDA or laptop) with Jambo installed to get started. Next, they enter interests and social groups (school, a conference attended, etc.), upload pictures and Jambo will then notify them when people from their pre-defined network or similar interests are nearby so that they can meet.

Wavemarket

Wavemarket[9] is a suite of tools that can turn a mobile phone into an on-location broadcaster. Information and commentary about items such as restaurant reviews to safety tips can be added. One can find a buddy using the friend finder, which gives user information on where friends are located using interactive maps. The resource finder function can be used to track vehicles, look for a new house or check a child's location.

Peepsnation

Peepsnation[10] is social software used for interacting with groups at nearby locations. Filters can be activated to reduce the number of people one wishes to contact. Peepsnation provides groups that one can join such as those seeking friends, those seeking an activity partner and those looking for a date.

Risks of MSS

The Bluetooth/Wi-Fi hack is one of the most popular anti-mobile social software (MoSoSo) devices. Wi-Fi is not as secure as Bluetooth as it uses a fixed connection between the node and the network. Bluetooth is like a sonar connection between devices. Bluetooth can be attacked in four main areas:

1. *Bluesnarfing* – unauthorised access of information from a wireless device through a Bluetooth connection, often between mobile phones, desktops, laptops and PDAs. This allows access to a calendar, contact list, emails and text messages, and on some phones users can steal pictures and private videos. Currently available programs must allow a connection and to be 'paired' to another phone to steal content.

2. *Blue bugging* – this is when a hacker gains access to the Bluetooth device to use the function and features of the phone. A hacker can read personal texts and listen into phone calls.

3. *Blue jacking* – this is when a hacker gains access to a phone to send out offensive or abusive short messages.

4. *Denial of service* – this is when a hacker repeatedly sends an invite to the user's phone, therefore wasting the user's time and denying him or her from using other functions on the device.

The above misuses can be avoided by updating software frequently and keeping the mobile turned off when not in use. A problem with MoSoSo is that the location software allows people to see where a person is located in real time. Twenty-five per cent of 8–11 year olds who have Internet access have made a profile on social networking sites such as Bebo, MySpace and Face Book. Although the sites claim to have a minimum age of 13, the simple sign-up forms allow under 13s to sign up. Of 8–17 year olds, 41 per cent admit they do not use any privacy features, such as blocking everyone but friends from seeing their account. For children of such ages, having a social networking account could potentially be dangerous as many users post their address, date of birth and other private details that could be used fraudulently. The other problem with social networking sites is that users do not have to put in real details. Sites such as these can attract sexual predators; many of the sites have had issues with older men and women grooming children by pretending to be a child of the same age. A job advertising site call Craigslist was recently used to lure a victim to their death, when they went to meet their potential employer.

Conclusion

Mobile social network software seeks to facilitate social connection and coordination among friends in urban public spaces. With the expected upgrade of phones to 3G and 4G, mobile social network software will become more pervasive, allowing more and more websites to provide mobile software support. This will provide users with new contacts. One downside, however, are potential security issues associated with mobile social software and social networks.

Notes

1. Thom-Santelli, J. (2007) 'Mobile social software: facilitating serendipity or encouraging homogeneity?', *IEEE Pervasive Computing*, 6:3, 46–51.
2. *http://www.stoweboyd.com/*
3. Hirsch, T. and Henry, J. (2005) TXTmob: Text Messaging for Protest Swarms. *Extended Abstracts of SIGCHI Conference on Human Factors*, ACM Press, pp. 1455–8.
4. Arrington, M. (2009) Facebook Now Nearly Twice The Size Of MySpace Worldwide, Tech Crunch, 22 January 2009, *http://www.techcrunch.com/2009/01/22/facebook-now-nearly-twice-the-size-of-myspace-worldwide/*
4. *http://www.msslam.com/About.aspx*
5. *http://www.enpresence.com/*
6. *http://www.dodgeball.com/*
7. *http://www.jambo.net*
8. *http://www.wavemarket.com/news_press.php?newsid=18*
9. *http://www.peepsnation.com/*

13

The long tail

Kevin Curran, Danielle McCartney and Karen McClean

The long tail is the colloquial name for a well-known feature of statistical distributions. It is also known as 'heavy tails', 'power-law tails' or 'Pareto tails'. The long tail gets its name from the shape formed on a graph of, for example, number of plays (or sales) on the vertical axes against the rank (popularity) on the horizontal axis. Companies relying on the power of the long tail function according to three main 'rules': (1) make everything available, (2) cut the price in half and then lower it, and (3) help the user to find it. Google and eBay make most of their revenue from the long tail – Google from small advertisers and eBay from niche and collectible items. Their sites are easily accessed, easily browsed, and everything is well laid out, straightforward and, in the main, user-friendly. User-friendly in that someone who is not confident using the Web can search for and find something (Rule 3). Rule 1, however, is the main idea behind the long tail – make everything available. This chapter discusses the long-tail phenomenon.

Introduction

The long tail is the theory that customer buying trends and thus the economy are moving away from a small number of products widely available in offline stores towards a huge number of one-off and niche products that are only available online. When a graph of sales against products sold is plotted (Figure 13.1), it is clear that only a small number of products sell in large quantities ('the hits') and there are a large number of products which only sell in small quantities ('the misses'). These misses are the one-off and niche products that are not available in

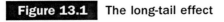

Figure 13.1 The long-tail effect

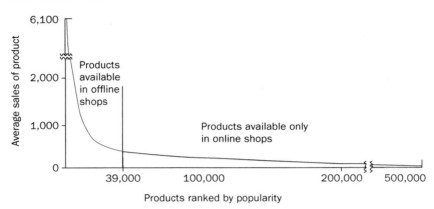

the high street due to the expense of shelf space and therefore form the long tail. The main reason that it has become possible for the long tail to become profitable is the fall in production and distribution costs through the Internet. Customers are now able to find products that are of special interest to them rather than the 'one-size-fits-all' products that are well marketed and available in most offline stores.

In 1988 a book by British mountaineer Joe Simpson, *Touching the Void*,[1] which did not initially sell well, was promoted by Amazon alongside a book written by Jon Krakauer, *Into Thin Air*,[2] released a decade later, which was also about a mountain-climbing tragedy. Amazon recommends products of similar interests to a customer when they are purchasing from the website, i.e. 'Other customers buying this product have also liked ...' This led to the great success of Simpson's book, which went on to outsell Krakauer's 1998 book two to one.[3] This was possible due to the public being able to leave positive feedback about the book, so that the consumer knew before they tried it how many other people had already found it interesting. This is not just true for online book stores, but also for online music and media centres. The long tail is also about online retailers making products available to the public that high-street stores or cinemas cannot do due to limited demand for the products. Anderson highlights this by stating that the average movie theatre will not screen a film unless it can attract at least 1500 people during a two-week run. This is basically the rent for a screen. Also, a typical record shop needs to sell at least two copies of a CD per year to make it worth carrying. This is equivalent to the rent for a half inch of shelf space. This model also applies to DVD rental shops, videogame stores, booksellers and newsstands.

The long tail and the Internet

Although many people have not yet heard of the long tail it is clear that many of the large Internet companies are already using this strategy in order to make their profits. For example, eBay uses the long tail by selling one-off and niche products through their auctions, which helps them to bring in new customers who are looking for a specific item, and cannot find it in the high street. This is profitable for eBay as they can make the same amount of money from the hit products as they do from the misses given that they are always paid for listing time regardless of the final price of the product. Google also makes a large percentage of its profits through small advertisers that want to advertise to as many people as possible but cannot afford to do so through the offline media such as newspapers and television. Three of the leading companies that use long-tail theory are Amazon, rhapsody and Netflix, who all make huge profits every year from selling long-tail products. Amazon offers its customers the choice of around 2.3 million books compared with the 130,000 'hit' books that are available in the average Waterstones store. Needless to say, Amazon makes a huge 57 per cent of its profits from selling books that are unavailable in any high-street store. The reason that they can do this is because if Waterstones were to stock books that only sold once a month they would be losing money due to the expense of shelf space whereas Amazon pays nothing to advertise an extra book on its site. Rhapsody offers its customers around 735,000 songs compared with around 30,000 by offline competitors. This, along with the fact that customers only have to buy the one or two tracks that they want, means that rhapsody can make huge profits, 22 per cent of which come from long-tail products. Rhapsody benefits because it costs them nothing to store old and niche music on a server somewhere so that it can be located when needed and does not take up necessary space when it is not in use.

Netflix offers customers the chance to rent or buy 25,000 DVDs, only 3,000 of which are available in the typical blockbuster store. This gives customers a chance to see films that perhaps never made it to a cinema near them or films that are of special interest to them. Twenty per cent of Netflix's profits come from products unavailable in offline stores. The fact that the company's customers can watch a short clip before purchasing and the low cost of delivery of products means that Netflix has also been successful. The companies that are setting the standards for long-tail products all follow three rules:

1. Make everything available.
2. Cut the price in half then lower it.
3. Help people to find what they want.

Some consider that it is not possible to survive in the long-tail market if all three of these rules are not carefully followed. If we look at Amazon, rhapsody and Netflix, we can see how they all fulfil the first rule by offering a larger number of products to their customers than offline shops. This helps to make them successful because if a customer is offered more choice they are more likely to find a product that they like and will therefore be more likely to become a repeat customer. The second rule was tested in an experiment by rhapsody in which they offered tracks at three different prices, and found that the cheapest tracks outsold the most expensive by 300 per cent although the company was making a loss on the cheaper tracks. This showed that they were able to attract more customers by lowering the prices of their products. Amazon and Netflix fulfil the second rule by having low overheads due to the fact that they sell their products on the Internet and therefore do not need to pay rent, heating or electricity costs. The second rule is important because everybody likes to think that they are getting a bargain and as these companies are selling a larger range of products they can afford to make less profit per unit sold and sell more products to make the same amount of profit.

The third rule is fulfilled by Amazon, rhapsody and Netflix in different ways. Netflix helps customers to find the products they want through recommendations of other customers. They do this by letting customers write reviews on the films that they have watched and then making these available when a customer wants to rent the film. This has proved to be successful for Netflix as they are selling a range of products that will appeal to groups of people with similar interests. Rhapsody uses human editors and genre guides in order to add links on their pages that will lead users to artists similar in style to the music that they like. Each page contains links to similar artists, followers and influences, leading users to music from different eras. This method helps customers to explore music that the may never have thought they would enjoy and leads them further down the long tail in search of their own style of music. This works well for Netflix but may not work for companies selling other products that are harder to categorise.

Amazon uses the information they gain from customer buying patterns in order to guide their customers to other products that they may enjoy. They do this by selecting a few products that have been purchased at the same time as the product a customer is going to buy and showing these at the checkout. They also provide reviews on their books in order to gain more sales. This works well as they are using a strong marketing tool that is also used in offline shops by leading the customer to make last-minute choices when they reach the checkout. Although these companies use different methods all three are successful in leading their customers to long-tail products, which are not advertised as widely and may never have appeared on the shelves of any highstreet shop. The above methods have become powerful marketing tools for the online market, although there is still strong emphasis on using the right method to suit the product that one is selling.

The future

One suggestion is that, due to the new powers that customers are gaining through being able to buy products considered to be of the long tail, large offline companies will be forced to offer more choice in their product range, although there are many problems that could arise from this. One of these is increased running costs resulting from additional products. This could have three effects. The first is that prices will increase to maintain profit margins, thereby lower demand for these products and returning the market to what it is now. The second effect is that the increase in price would lead many more customers to the Internet, cutting out many large offline companies except for necessity products such as food. Thirdly, large offline companies may keep long-tail products as loss leaders but increase the prices of their necessity products to maintain profitability.

A second suggestion is that owing to the large number of long-tail products now available to customers, the so-called 'hits' will end up being a thing of the past with top selling products only slightly out selling those at the bottom of the tail, as shown in Figure 13.2.

There is a possibility of this happening if customers decided to buy products that are to their own taste rather than following trends currently forced upon them by the large companies. Another suggestion is that with customers having so much choice in every product that they buy few will ever move down the tail and buy the one-off and niche items as they are happy to buy products that are heavily marketed in offline

Figure 13.2 A possible future sales pattern

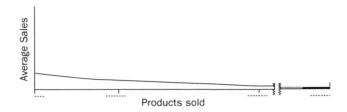

Possible Future Sales Pattern

shops, therefore keeping the market in its current state in which customers are divided equally between the long-tail businesses and those offline businesses that focus on 'hits' rather than long-tail products.

Conclusion

Companies currently making their profits using the long tail are set to continue to do so due to factors such as consumers favouring choice and the lower costs of running an online business. Consumers want more choice. The present generation of consumers is breaking boundaries by not simply putting up with the products forced upon them but rather selecting from niche products available to them online. This is why the long tail has taken off; customers are refusing to accept second best.[3]

Notes

1. Simpson, J. (1998) *Touching the Void*. London: Vintage Publishers.
2. Krakauer, J. (1998) *Into Thin Air*. British Columbia: Anchor Publishers.
3. Anderson, C. (2004) 'The long tail, *Wired Magazine*, 12:10, *http://www.wired. com/wired/archive/12.10/tail.html*

14

Podcasting, screencasting, blogging and videoblogging

Kevin Curran, David Pollock and Colleen Ferguson

Podcasting, blogging, videoblogging, and screencasting allow the uploading of personal content to the Web. Podcasting allows users to listen to music files from podcasting websites or indeed from any website. Unlike Internet radio, podcasting allows listeners to download the podcast so that they can listen to it later or store it on a mobile device. Screencasting has become popular with individual users who wish to document program bugs or oddities, as a visual demonstration showing how a program works can be much clearer than a verbal description. A blog is a website similar to an on-line diary where messages are posted describing items of interest to the blog author. A videoblog is a short video clip with sound posted on a website describing an event. This chapter discusses these new technologies.

Introduction

A podcast is a web feed containing audio and/or video files which is then placed on the Internet for anyone to download. What makes the podcast distinct from traditional media such as broadcasting and streaming is that the podcast file will arrive in archived form. A screencast is a digital recording of computer screen output, which contains audio narration. Screencasts are useful for demonstrating simple and complicated new software to others. It is a neat way to show off work, report bugs and show how a task can be accomplished. Screencasting is a term for recording a movie of a computer screen to a file that others can view. Screencasts are largely used for tutorials, overviews/tours, reviews and demonstrations. Screencasts may also be used as a way to enhance regular movie files. A weblog, or blog, is a website where the owner or user posts messages that others can read. Blogs often focus on one subject; for example, if the blogger is a computer programmer, then the topic of his or her messages is likely to be related to programming languages. However, many others are using blogs as online diaries where they post messages describing their daily news or how they feel about certain subjects. Videoblogging is a new form of blogging, which includes posting videos on the Web. It is a new paradigm for people to place aspects of their personal lives on the web. Videoblogging is rising in popularity partially due to the release of the Video iPod and the availability of videoblogs on iTunes. With the recent boom in iPod sales, videoblogs are likely to hit the computer industry by storm. The remainder of this chapter examines podcasting, screencasting, blogging and videoblogging.

Podcasting

A factor that is influencing the popularity of podcasting are cheap MP3 players such as the iPod. Podcasting allows users to keep up to date with items that interest them, for example local radio programmes, events in a city or region, sermons, technical talks or simply music.[1] RSS is a type of Web format that is widely used with podcasting. The Web feeds that the RSS provides simply link to the podcast. At present, there are is no clear revenue model related to podcasting, and only few podcasts actually make money via subscriptions. However, some podcasters are beginning to place advertisements in their podcasts. The other problem is also the sheer amount of junk placed online in podcast directories. Due to the nature of the very brief (or absent) podcast descriptions, it is generally necessary to download the podcast and listen to it to ascertain its actual relevance and quality.

Podcasting begain in 2004 when David Winer, a software developer, created a program from home to allow him to record broadcasts from Internet radio stations and play them on an iPod. He wanted to be able to save them to his computer so he could return to them later. He released the software online and eventually other software developers improved on the idea and podcasting gained momentum. 'Podcasting' derives from the 'iPod' and 'broadcasting'. The Internet caught onto podcasting quickly. For instance, in September 2004 a blogger and columnist,

Doc Searls, began keeping track of how many people searched Google for the word 'podcasts'. The first count was 24. A week later, it was 526, and after another 3 days, it was 2,750. It then doubled every couple of days, passing 100,000 on 18 October 2004. In October 2005 there were more than 100 million hits on the word 'podcasts' on Google.

Production of a podcast is not complex. Podcasters need a computer with access to the Internet along with a microphone to record sound and software to record the sounds to the computer. Fortunately, there is free software available for recording sounds and editing them. One popular package is gold wave.[3] Once a podcast has been recorded, it can be uploaded to a podcast directory. Many are free but some such as iTunes charge for adding content. Once uploaded to a directory or to a website, one must make sure that the file is accessible through an Internet address. In the next step the file provider then acknowledges the existence of that file by referencing it in another file known as the feed, which then reads the list of URLs and is published in RSS format that contains details of the file such as author, publication date, title and description. The third step is for the file provider to post the feed to a known and permanent location and make this feed URL known to the intended audience. A consumer then enters this feed into their desired software program (for example iTunes), which will then retrieve the data. This then allows the audience to do what they want with the file like any other computer file, listen, watch or archive.

In 2004, Musselburgh Grammar School in Scotland started handing out podcasts in class as revision aids for foreign language classes.[4] Church and religious groups are also broadcasting items ranging from church music to sermons, talks and prayers. The number of people who are using what the church would refer to as godcasts is growing. Many podcasters see it as a hobby. Many podcasts disappear over time as their creators rapidly find out that it takes a lot more time than initially expected to produce a weekly or daily show. Most of these podcasters do it simply to reach others on the Web about something they believe in passionately. They do not rely on ratings, which often allows them to talk about anything from how to cook an apple tart to just playing music all day long. Many of these podcasters take a liberal view on copyright issues.

Screencasting

Screencasting is where a video file of the running of a program is used to help people understand the functions of the program. It achieves this by using a narrator and capturing video of the program actually performing different functions. A narrator will talk through the process, describing operations mirrored on the video. This can be extremely helpful when training staff on a new system and can be more cost-effective than normal training. Another use is as a presentation, with the screencast explaining all the information, along with someone answering questions that the viewers may have about what they have just seen. This would be effective in marketing new products to a large audience at once.

The term screencasting was created in 2004 by Jon Udell, a columnist who wished to show his readers applications that he found interesting. Some caught onto the computer concepts immediately, but Jon wanted to transmit this knowledge to a less computer-literate audience as well. He had hoped that it would attract a wider, less technical audience and it worked. Screencasting, however, has been around since 1993 when Lotus introduced ScreenCam. This never gained popularity due to the size their limited features and indeed the size of the created files (pre-broadband). Modern screencasting produces compact files and possesses more advanced features that allow more detailed changes. For example, there was no sound available with ScreenCam and there were numerous problems with trying to locate and specify the location that the pointer should reside.

A popular program used for creating screencasts is Macromedia Flash MX. This provides editing features for manipulating even the smallest details on the screen. There are two main types of screencasting, screenshots and fluid movies. Screenshots are simply pictures of the screen every time the mouse has been clicked or key pressed. The images are produced by the screencasting tools, which save the location of the cursor and show the features of the programm through a series of screenshots. However, some programs offer the ability to press a hotkey to take you to a new screenshot. The problem with this is that it can be hard to capture images at the right times to make it resemble a smooth flowing movie. It often ends up as sequence of random screenshots like menus that seem to appear out of nowhere. Fluid movies work by capturing the desktop and audio at high rates. They are created by choosing an area of the screen, then recording a narrator's voice to accompany the recorded 'screencast'. When complete, a movie of actions can be edited and then published. The ability to record audio narrations and edit them in order to explain every move being made in the screencast is also desirable. How easy it is to remove screens, change cursor position and change audio will be essential for first-time users who have never created a screencast and need to edit constantly so that the output is to their standard. The ability of the software to record fast changes is an important feature. How well it handles occurrences of rapid screen changes is vital, because if this is a key feature for the user then he/she must consider it when buying the software. Interactive features, for example where users must click in places to continue, keep the user's attention and would be a useful feature. Smart automatic captioning is useful in software for novice computer users and most software has tools that can automatically add captions when you perform certain actions such as moving over the menu button. Some software packages that include all of these features include Camtasia Studio,[5] BB Flashback,[6] Macromedia Captivate[7] and ViewletCam.[8]

Figure 14.1 shows what a screencast might look like of an application being selected from the menu of a Windows XP desktop machine. The user gets the impression that the computer is running programs with no help from them. Screencasts are a powerful means of demonstrating an application's features. The saying 'a picture is worth a thousand words' could well be applied to screencasting.

People who screencast do it for similar reasons to those who blog and podcast. They simply have a message that they wish to communicate. Screencasting, however, allows one to speak it, show it and share it. Subscribers can then hear it, watch it and experience it. With a blog you can only write it and the reader can only read it. With a podcast you can only say it and the reader can only listen to it. Interestingly, each copy of Windows XP starts with a pop-up box asking the user if they wish to take

Figure 14.1 Screencast of a desktop

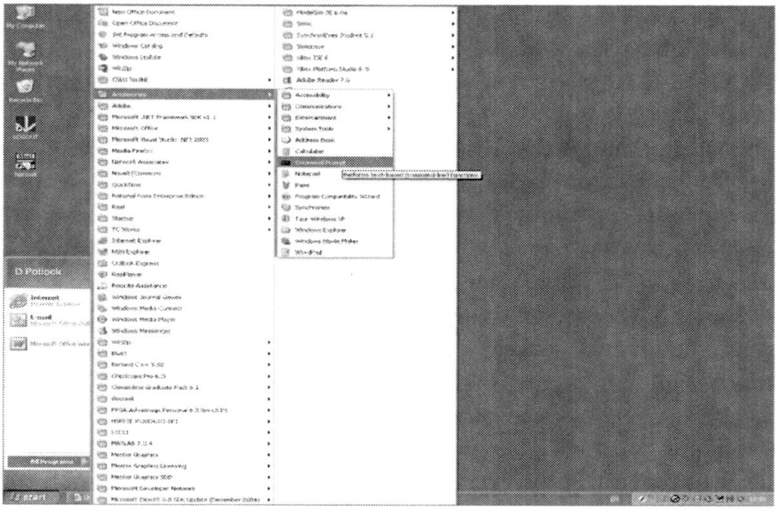

a tour. This is simply a screencast where one can watch the mouse run through features of Windows. Screencasting appeals to different groups of people. One group is software providers who want to make a demonstration movie. Screencasts allow the author to post on a website for potential buyers to guide them around the features and how to use the software appropriately and to its full potential. An example screencast is the animated whiteboard[9] by Troy Stein, product manager for Camtasia Studio, who made a screencast for the football team he coaches. This example comprises a picture of a football pitch with Stein taking you through the basics of football by explaining the rules through audio and drawing on the picture. It is well edited and easy to understand. Jon Udel has produced a screencast-enhanced video about a local flooding scene[10] from downtown Keene, New Hampshire, during October 2005. The screencast takes us through his hometown and visits the worst hit areas of the flood. It is largely video, with bits of screen animation interspersed to provide context.

Blogging

A weblog, or blog, is a website where the owner or user posts messages that others can log on and read. Blogs often focus on one subject, although some provide online diaries where the creator posts messages describing their latest thoughts usually in a fairly restricted domain although there is nothing to stop people from having blogs where they broadcast diverse musings on topics. The majority of blogs with large followings however tend to be focused on a particular subject. A person who has a blog is termed a blogger, and maintaining, adding to or reading other blogs is referred to as blogging.[11]

At the beginning of 2004, blogging began to make its mark, playing the role of a mainstream news service as bloggers began to provide nearly instantaneous commentary on televised events, instead of the more traditional online diary. An example is provided by the Boxing Day tsunami of 2004. Blogs such as Medecins Sans Frontieres were created, which used SMS text messaging to report from affected areas in Sri Lanka and southern India so that people could read about the extent of the damage. The term weblog was coined by Jorn Barger in 1997, and then shortened to blog by Peter Merholz in May 1999. Justin Hall, who began 11 years of personal blogging in 1994 while a student at Swarthmore College in Pennsylvania, is generally recognised as one of the first bloggers.

Blogging was preceded by several other similar communities such as Usenet, email lists and bulletin board systems. However, blogs evolved from online diaries, where people would keep a record of their personal lives; these first appeared in 1995. Most of the writers called themselves diarists or journalists. After a slow start, blogging rapidly became popular: the Xanga site, started in 1996, had only 100 diaries in 1997, but over 50 million by December 2005. It was the launch of Open Diaries in 1998 that helped blogging become more popular, as this was the first blog community where readers could add comments to other writers' entries. Others started blog communities including Pita.com, Diaryland, Blogger.com and Lifelog. The pioneer of weblogging tools is Dave Winer, who changed a blog from simply a website to a scene of frenzy within the computer world. One of his most significant contributions was setting up servers so that blogs could make sounds to indicate when it had been updated. In 2001 Andrew Sullivan's blog[12] and Ron Gunzburger's Politics1.com became one of the first broadly popular American blogs. These blog on US politics. User manuals also started to appear for novices. This helped the blog to become a modern phenomenon, as people who had no idea about out how to start their own could now do so. The blogging community gained rapid respect and importance, with journalism courses teaching about blogging. In 2002, Markos Moulitsas Zuniga started up DailyKos, which has had up to one million visits a day during peak events, and has now become one of the most trafficked blogs.[11]

When the war in Iraq began, it also started the first blog war. Iraqi bloggers started to read other blogs from America and their views on the war in Iraq, and then joined in to get their message across. One of the most memorable bloggers was Salam Pax, who published a book of his blog to give his views of the war and open the eyes of others. Blogs played an important role in describing the brutal facts of war. Blogs were also created by soldiers serving in the Iraq war. Such blogs were referred to as milblogs, and gave readers new perspectives on the realities of war, as well as often offering different viewpoints to those of official news sources.

There are many different types of blogs, from personal to educational. A personal blog is one in which the blogger uses it as an online diary, posting views on anything that they consider to be of interest. A career blog is one that is used to dictate a professional journey, demonstrate expertise or network with other professionals. It shows the blogger's career path, but has little or no ties to his/her employer. A paid blog is one in which a person is employed to blog for a living; this can be done to promote the company, log onto other blogs to tell others of the company, or to raise search engine relevancy so that the company becomes more well known. Cultural blogs allow the bloggers to discuss their preferred music, sports, theatre, arts and popular culture. These are among the most read blogs because people like to talk to others with the same interests and it is a great way to meet new people who have the same things in common, much like a chat room. Topical blogs focus on just one topic. An example of this is the Google blog which covers just news about Google. These types of blog need to keep the readers' attention and meet their needs so that numbers of readers and comments will increase. Business blogs can provide self-promotion as they are free and easy to maintain. The stock market is a popular subject for bloggers where both amateur and professional investors use blogs to share stock tips. A moblog or mobile blog, consists of content posted to the Internet from a mobile phone. This may require paticular software.

Collaborative blogs can be created by anyone or limited to a group of people. An example of a collaborative blog is Blogcritics, but this now considers itself to be an online magazine more than a blog. Educational blogs were created for students and teachers alike and are growing in popularity. Students can use blogs to record what they learn and teachers can use blogs to record what they teach. For example, a teacher can blog what homework students are required to carry out, including links to Internet resources, and recording each day what is taught. In this way, if a student is absent they can quickly catch-up, the teacher can use the blog as a course plan, and finally new teachers can refer to if the previous teacher is away or leaves. This type of blogging can motivate students to do more reading and encourage them to improve their writing style, due to the presence of potentially thousands of viewers. Spam blogs, often referred to as splogs, are a form of high-pressure advertising. They are generally like spam e-mails, often linked to each other to increase their Internet presence. Political blogs are among the most common forms of blogs. Most political blogs are news driven, and most political bloggers will link to articles from news websites so that they can add their own views on the subject. Other political blogs feature original commentary, with occasional hyperlinks to back up the blogger's talking points.[13]

Videoblogging

Videoblogging is similar to blogging, except that it presents the blog in a video format. A factor influencing the popularity of videoblogging is the video iPod, which is capable of playing video files. A videoblog is a video clip that includes sound for users to view much like podcasts.[14] Often, videoblogs contain text or captions to explain what is happening. Videoblogging has taken a while to gain followers, but with the uptake of broadband, it is becoming more ubiquitous.

Videoblogging increased in popularity around 2004. One of the main organisations to encourage its use was Yahoo! who started a videoblogging group. Users who were creating videoblogs moved to the Yahoo! service as it provided a larger audience where more people were able to view their blogs. In November 2000 Adrian Miles posted the first ever known video blog. It was not until 2004 that Steve Garfield (a videographer and video blogger) brought the concept to a much larger audience. The Yahoo Videoblogging Group was started by Peter Van Dijck and Jay Dedman.[15] They attracted a small group of people calling themselves vloggers. Video blogging then began to receive media attention from outlets such as the *New York Times*.[16] The first videoblogger conference was held in New York and classes teaching vlogging sprang up. VlogMap.org launched Google maps and Google earth so that they displayed vloggers throughout the entire world. By the end of 2005 the Yahoo Videoblogging Group had well over 1000 members and this number is rising rapidly.

Vloggercon is a site where vloggers can meet and swap information. Some of the video topics include communities, politics, journalism, music, iMovies, and technology. The site owner also has videoblogs about his shopping trips, family days out and work meetings. Chuck Olsen is a US documentary maker and video blogger. He is also the producer of the documentary film 'Blogumentary', which explores the impact of blogging on media and politics. BBC radio also hosts video blogs. There are video blogs on many subjects relating to entertainment.[17]

Conclusion

Podcasting, blogging, videoblogging, and screencasting allow users to upload personal content to the Web. Podcasting allows users to listen to music files from podcasting websites or indeed from any website. Files are generally in MP3 format but also WAV, WMA, QW or AU format. Unlike Internet radio podcasting allows listeners to download the podcast so that they can listen to it later or even store it on an MP3 player. Screencasting has also become popular with individual users who wish to document program bugs or oddities because a demonstration showing how a program functions can be more useful than a verbal description. A weblog, or blog, is a website where the owner posts messages so that others can log on and read them. Blogs often focus on one subject, although some individuals use blogs as online diaries where they post messages describing their daily news or how they feel about certain subjects. Since Apple released the video iPod, which allows videos to be viewed on the iPod, there has been an increase in videoblogging. Smartphones also allow the viewing of videoblogs and indeed their creation.

Notes

1. Farkas, B. (2005) *Secrets of Podcasting: Audio Blogging for the Masses.* Peachpit Press.
2. Morris, T. and Terro, E. (2005) *Podcasting for Dummies.* Hungry Minds Inc.
3. *www.goldwave.com*
4. *http://en.wikipedia.org/wiki/Musselburgh*
5. *www.techsmith.com/*
6. *www.bbsoftware.co.uk/BBFlashBack.aspx*
7. *www.adobe.com/products/captivate/*
8. *www.qarbon.com/presentation-software/vc/*
9. *http://www.techsmith.com/community/blog/movies/soccer3.html*
10. *http://weblog.infoworld.com/udell/gems/KeeneFlood.html*
11. Hill, B. (2005) *Blogging for Dummies.* Hungry Minds Inc.
12. *www.AndrewSullivan.com*
13. Holtz, S. and Demopoulos, T. (2006) *Blogging for Business: Everything You Need to Know and Why You Should Care.* Kaplan Professional.
14. Weynand, D., Hodson, R. and Verdi, M. (2006) *Secrets of Video Blogging.* Peachpit Press.
15. Dedman, J., Kinberg, J. and Paul, J. (2006) *Video Blogging.* Hungry Minds Inc.
16. Boxer, S. (2005) Watch me do this and that online, Critic Notebook Column, *New York Times*, 25 July.
17. Stolarz, D. and Felix, L. (2006) *Hands-On Guide to Video Blogging and Podcasting: Emerging Media Tools for Business Communication.* Focal Press.

Worldwide interoperability for microwave access (WiMAX)

Kevin Curran, Francis Doherty,
Conrad Deighan and Gerard Galway

WiMAX has signalled the arrival of the next wave of wireless data technologies. Unhampered by the short range and data orientations of wireless local area networks (WLANs) these technologies will see users having high-speed wireless on the road. WiMAX deployments are similar to that used in a WiFi network. WiMAX does not suffer from interference from, for example, mobile phone masts. Once in a residential setting the WiMAX base station beams a signal to the WiMAX receiver built into a desktop or notebook receiver. This is very similar to the process in a WiFi LAN. Developing countries will greatly benefit from deploying such networks. African countries are preparing to deploy WiMAX networks instead of cell-phone networks, WiMAX could also be utilised in disaster zones, giving them the ability to distribute crisis information quickly and cheaply. This chapter provides an overview of WiMAX.

Introduction

The success of Wi-Fi has served to encourage the development of WiMAX, which with the slow rollout of mobile 3G technologies has confirmed the emergence of mobile WiMAX has a viable alternative technology. WiMAX development has been driven by the WiMAX Forum, an industry-based consortium set-up to promote and certify the compatibility and interoperability of broadband wireless access equipment with conformance to the IEEE 802.16 set of standards. Particular attention is being given to mobile WiMAX or IEEE 802.16e, which in some quarters is seen as potentially the most important member of the IEE 802.16 group of standards. WiMAX transmits data from a single location within a city to multiple locations throughout that city or cities. WiMAX is a high-speed Internet wireless technology planned purposely for outsized IP networks, and provides superior coverage than its rival competitor Wi-Fi. WiMAX will be more cost-effective than other wireless technologies by ensuring compatibility between high-speed Internet wireless access equipment. WiMAX is available in two different standards, 802.16 for fixed networks and 802.16e is for mobile networks. The 802.16 standard is rigid, moveable and nomadic; 802.16 can be accessed via two different approaches, line of sight and non line of sight. 802.16 can reach frequency bands of 5.8 GHz. The 802.16e standard supports mobile access in frequency bands of up to 3.5 GHz. This chapter provides an overview of WiMAX, the history and evolution of wireless networking and current developments relating to WiMAX.

WiMAX is based on the IEEE 802.16 set of standards that have been developed from a need to have a standardized platform on which broadband wireless access could be introduced. The initial scope was that the technology would allow a standardisation of technology that was already in use by communications companies that were using the technology to connect between the communication end users and the telecommunications backbone. But these various vendors each had their own proprietary solutions which were not inter-operable. As a local in-house solution this was acceptable but limited acceptance and growth in the wider market. Areas of opportunity and growth outside the original remit were then realised and seen as markets to which the technology could be aimed. Fixed wireless access took a major lead, as this was seen as an opportunity to allow broadband access to areas that lacked digital subscriber line (DSL) or cable services. A major obstacle to the role of fixed line solutions such as DSL is the 'final mile',[1] i.e. the connection between the infrastructure backbone and the customer's home or place of work, and therefore an opportunity exists for WiMAX to exploit this in the marketplace.

The technology when used in these circumstances has a typical deployment area of between three and ten kilometres without direct line of sight to a base station, which if used in major towns and cities would allow full coverage from a small number of base stations; with this the need for expensive and high-maintenance fixed wire solutions would be negligible. This is seen as a large growth market in developing countries where current infrastructure is limited and the installation of new systems is prohibitively expensive. WiMAX technology is also advantageous in remote areas or where the terrain makes fixed solutions difficult to deploy; with a range of up to 50 kilometres from emitter to receiver the cost difference between wired and wireless solutions is significant.

The natural progression was then to investigate how the technology would be implemented in a truly wireless situation rather than a fixed wireless scenario, for which a different set of objectives were realised and the IEE 802.16e standards were published in December 2005. These standards allowed the technology to be developed to allow high-speed data access to be available to the mobile market. The mobile WiMAX market is seen as the most lucrative with possible earnings of up to US$45 billion per year from networking equipment only, compared with the fixed market with projected earnings of US$500 million per year.[2] The scope for mobile WiMAX encompasses different technologies, ranging from mobile telephones and laptops to PDAs. In the telecommunication market mobile WiMAX is seen as a viable competitor to 3G technologies, the rollout and take-up of which has been slower than expected due to high costs.

WiMAX can be used for a number of applications, including 'last mile' broadband connections, hotspot and cellular backhaul, and high-speed enterprise connectivity for businesses. Mobile WiMAX (802.16e) is part of a group of broadband wireless communications standards for metropolitan area networks developed by IEEE. It complements the earlier standard of 802.11 for WLANs. The earlier versions of 802.16a, b, c and d are only for fixed wireless connections whereas 802.16e enables connections for mobile devices. WiMAX uses microwaves to transfer data through the air at high speed for a number of miles. The earlier standard 802.11 uses channel to transmit and receive data and voice from a fixed width of the bandwidth spectrum. WiMAX 'condenses' these channels, narrowing the bandwidth and allowing more users to have access and to be served. The same width of the spectrum is used but more channels are available due to this 'narrowing' and more data are sent along the channels. The highway is divided into more lanes and more traffic is packed into each lane. The same core technology underpins both 802.11 and 802.16e but WiMAX coverage can extend to miles rather than metres. This means that you can maintain your broadband connection more easily. However, because the standard has only recently been ratified, commercialisation and true mobility will not be available for a few years. The 802.16e standard covers data rates from 1.5 to 70 Mbps over distances in excess of 20 miles, although the greater the distance the lower the data transfer rate. 802.16e is viewed as compatible with the 802.11 Wi-Fi LAN standards in that it can extend its range and support higher data transfer rates. WiMAX can be viewed at present as a complementary technology to 3G. However, the

WiMAX Forum and IEEE (both of which work to produce and test the standard) are keen to include greater interoperability in the standard. So when devices that are enabled for mobile WiMAX are actually produced commercially, different manufacturers' equipment and systems will be able to work together. Mobile WiMAX has clearly fixed its crosshairs on wireless data, which means it poses a potential threat to Wi-Fi, but it also is aiming to include wireless voice and as such is perceived by telecom operators as a threat to their monopolies, particularly with respect to the last mile. The last mile refers to the last leg in getting broadband technology to a user's home, which although is often a relatively short distance from the exchange becomes extremely expensive because of the costs involved in digging up roads, the cost of the equipment, etc., and return on investment is very low. With WiMAX the last mile does not present the same obstacles. Mobile WiMAX also alleviates the problems associated with 'backhaul', i.e. getting the network data on to the backbone so that it can be redistributed or routed to another location. The current explosion in Wi-Fi means that considerable investment has been put into deploying and promoting WLANs but one of the problems users of Wi-Fi run into is what is referred to as 'no-connection space'. This is where the user is 'out of coverage' for about five minutes on average in a metropolitan area network hotspot configuration. What WiMAX aims to achieve in the long term is for a nomadic user to get a connection anytime and anywhere and become a mobile user. The difference between the nomadic user and the mobile user is that the mobile user is connected at all times, whereas the nomadic user finds a hotspot, connects, disconnects, moves to another hotspot, connects and so on.[3]

The type of connection being referred to in the WiMAX specification is high-speed broadband connectivity to the internet or broadband wireless access (BWA). People who experience Internet access using broadband tend to leave their connection open, almost always remaining connected. WiMAX recognises that this could be a major selling point for the new technology; no matter where you are you will always be connected. There are obstacles to this and the standard must address such things as interoperability, network security and roaming. Interoperability is dealt with in 802.16e and addresses the problem quickly discovered by Wi-Fi operators when they attempted to extend their WLANs. Such users purchased equipment that was built to extend WLANs but found that it would not work with their particular brand of Wi-Fi equipment. The maximum transmission range for Wi-Fi is about 50 feet in an urban area, so a large number of access points are needed to provide reasonable coverage for the area and to meet customer expectations. The deployment of Wi-Fi tends to take on a mesh-like topology largely because the Wi-Fi chipsets are very inexpensive and are being built into more and more devices. WLANs are then deployed in close proximity to each other, each access point connecting to each other access point. This poses a smaller obstacle to WiMAX. Mobile WiMAX proponents need to convince manufacturers to install WiMAX components in their devices either alongside or in place of the Wi-Fi component. If this can be achieved it is certain to accelerate the rapid adoption of WiMAX-enabled products. This in turn will facilitate the spread of WiMAX. This ratification opens the door for the mass production of 802.16e-compatible technology, which will result in standard components that will enhance interoperability. WiMAX can deliver high-speed broadband Internet access over a wireless connection. It does not require line of sight between the source and the endpoint and this distance can range up to 50 kilometres, providing a shared data rate of up to 70 Mbps. This could provide high-speed Internet access of 2 Mbps for hundreds of homes on last-mile networks. Of course the service suffers from degradation the further away the endpoint is from the source. The source, a base station, which would probably be located in an elevated position, connects the users' devices, or subscriber stations, through their antenna, which may or may not be part of their device. This is then connected using a high-speed wired connection or microwave point-to-point link in to the backbone, which is the main pipe of the Internet. The WiMAX connection can also be routed or bridged into a standard LAN. Due to the absence of wires and cables, deployment of a WiMAX solution can be very fast.

WiMAX physical layers

IEEE 802.16 has been developed for point-to-multipoint broadband wireless, for use in the frequency range of sub-11 GHz and 10–66 GHz and covers the physical and media access control layers of the ISO model. The first standard was approved in December 2001 and was known as 802.16a. This was primarily developed for fixed broadband access. Further development was announced in June 2003 with the 802.16-2004 standard, which gave more support for customer support equipment. There has been a continual development and in December 2005 802.16-2005, commonly known as the 802.16e standard, was finalised. This is better known as the mobile WiMAX standard. The standard could now be better utilised and included mobility, the standard having primarily been developed for fixed operation.

During development of the standard a number of critical considerations were included in the requirements: the ability to use various physical types would allow for different operating environments to be utilised. Non-line of site conditions can be used in the sub 10 GHz frequencies compared with the higher frequencies in the 10–66 GHz range, which require line of sight; with this wide channels with high-capacity links can be set up. The WiMAX standard has been developed to use the same MAC (machine access control) layer for varying PHY (physical layers), allowing the technology to provide high inter-operability, with the hardware for different vendors being compatible. The standard uses a 256-point orthogonal frequency division multiplexed (OFDM) carrier rather than the 64-point OFDM used by the 802.11 technologies giving it a higher range. OFDM is a digital encoding and modulation technology that has been previously used in DSL and cable systems. Within WiMAX technologies it will allow for use in non-line-of-sight environments. Such environments have been addressed by use of OFDM, which allows the ability to deliver higher bandwidth and data transfer rate by using multiple overlapping carrier signals instead of one as with existing networks.

The recent ratification of 802.16e means that mobility is now included. The first 802.16 addressed spectrum ranges from 10 to 66 GHz, and focused on multipath line-of-sight issues that were tackled using OFDM techniques. It allowed for wide channels greater than 10 MHz in the licensed spectrum. Changes were made to the MAC layer and the PHY layer. The MAC layer uses point to multipoint as its foundation for the downlink from the base station to the subscriber station. That means all subscriber stations within a given frequency and antenna sector will receive the same transmissions. In other words, the downlink is broadcast to all unless modified otherwise. The MAC connection is geared towards quality of service and meeting and managing the services being used. This means, depending on the user's application, that the transmission can be continual as with voice over IP traffic or in bursts such as MPEG transmissions. When the subscriber station connects after satisfying a number of criteria based on the DOCSIS standard (data over cable service interface specifications) such downlink channel synchronisation, range and capability agreement, authentication, registration, and IP connectivity, bandwidth is allocated based upon the type of service. The base station can manage the allocation by resizing the amount of bandwidth needed by the service being used. In the mesh topology subscriber stations can communicate directly with each other without having to go through the base station. ARQ (automatic repeat request) processing maintains quality of service by retransmitting dropped or lost blocks. The scheduling service comprising the fast data scheduler, dynamic resource allocation and frequency-selective scheduling is designed to deliver the broadband services of data, video and voice efficiently and within quality-of-service parameters. Three handoff methods are supported: hard handoff, which is mandatory, fast base station switching and macro diversity handover. The delay of handover is kept to less than 50 milliseconds.

The PHY is defined for the 10–66 GHz licensed range of the spectrum and supports the 2 GHz band of licensed and unlicensed spectrum bands. The most significant modification to this layer allows the non-line-of-sight environment to send a signal by different routes. This was enabled by adding the OFDM modulation scheme. The data are transmitted in the signal with forward error correction in place, then using an inverse discrete Fourier transform applied to the data the frequency domain is converted, filtered and modulated up to the carrier frequency using time division multiplexing on the downlink and time division multiple access on the uplink. 802.16e is based on the Orthogonal Frequency-Division Multiple Access (OFDMA) system. In this system the signal can be divided into many sub-channels that run at lower speeds. This increases the resistance to interference that would be experienced on the non-line-of-sight multipath routes. As noted previously, depending on the distance and services being accessed by the user the allocation of sub-channels is dynamically assigned. When the location is in close proximity to the base station, QAM (quadrature amplitude modulation) can be used for higher bandwidth across several channels. When the distance from the base station is great the number of channels being used drops but the power per channel increases ensuring that even if the data rate goes down the user stays connected. OFDM technology uses fast Fourier transform (FFT) algorithms to get the frequencies perpendicular (orthogonal) to each other so that the sub-channels can overlap without causing interference to one another. This method fully utilises the available spectrum. FFT is a formula that uses a variable N, where N can be 512 bytes, 1K, 2K, 4K, etc., and the FFT is extremely useful in analysing unsteady measurements, because the frequency spectrum from an FFT provides information about the frequency content of the signal. So by using this technique, OFDMA in the PHY layer dynamically corrects and stabilises the multipath spectrum used by Mobile WiMAX. It is important to note that OFDMA and OFDM are two different modes that have much in common. Both support high data transfer rates, utilising multipath methods to increase signal quality in non-line-of-sight environments and the ability to split channels into many subchannels. Both also support time division duplex (TDD) and frequency division duplex (FDD) in the modulation scheme to dynamically shift the allocation depending on capacity and proximity. OFDMA is also scalable, which means it can adapt to the different channel frequencies in different countries, and can use a variety of FFT versions. Deciding on the type of architecture to deploy is dependent on whether to use TDD or FDD. TDD will only transmit or receive at a specified time, reducing interference because the transmitter is off when the receiver is on. However this can create problems when switching modes and reduce throughput, thereby curtailing the number of users supported. It is economical due to the reuse of the local oscillator to generate the frequency, which saves space, costs and components. FDD can be employed in both the base station and the subscriber stations; it uses two different frequencies to transmit and receive at the same time. This method uses a considerable amount of the spectrum bandwidth but does provide higher throughput and can support many more users. All these factors come into play when approving the standard. At least three manufacturers have to agree to provide a basis for interoperability. The choice will affect the mobility and speed of handoff (going from one cell to another), the spectrum range and size of channels available.

A phrase that is commonly associated with WiMAX technologies but not necessarily mobile WiMAX is 'the last mile', the Holy Grail in communications infrastructures, and needs to be explained to understand the demand for this new technology. With the development and rollout of broadband services, a bottleneck worldwide has been the connection between the infrastructure backbone and the end user, whether he or she is domestic or commercial. In the developed world the telecommunications network has been established and in place for many years and is totally unsuitable to use with the new technologies; the cost of replacing this has been high with a large financial outlay to the companies that have gone ahead with the upgrade. In the developing world the cost of installing this technology is prohibitively high. It is also seen that major telecommunication companies own and manage the network infrastructure and are therefore in an advantageous position to implement broadband technologies, to allow for more competition by means of allowing more service providers to enter the market, thereby giving the customer more choice. The wireless networks supplied by WiMAX will allow for low-cost installation and maintenance of the network, for both provider and customer.

WiMAX versus 3G and Wi-Fi

WiMAX does provide significant advantages over Wi-Fi. WiMAX has a superior range and provides more bandwidth. WiMAX could eventually replace most of the cabled networks that connect to the Internet as it can

Table 15.1 WiMAX statistics

Wireless communication standard	Maximum data rate (Mbps)	Maximum range
Wide Area Network		
802.16d Fixed WiMAX	75	6 Miles
802.16e Mobile WiMAX	30	3 Miles
Local Area Network		
802.11a/g WIFI	54	300 Feet
802.11b WIFI	11	300 Feet

provide connectivity to entire towns and cities. WiMAX could even replace the Wi-Fi receivers that are built into laptops as WiMAX was built for outdoor mobility. The main challenge now for WiMAX developers is to get more chips (WiMAX receivers) into laptops and PCs.

At present, mobile WiMAX is the biggest threat to 3G and the technologies are competing to offer the better wireless connectivity. WiMAX proponents are still trying to market the technology and 'experts' believe that the longer it takes to get such products to the market the better chance for 3G. Intel state that 3G is excellent for voice and WiMAX will take over the market for mobile data services. For providers to stay competitive they may have to start to offer WiMAX and 3G. Table 15.1 illustrates the distance range and data transfer rate that each standardisation provides. WiMAX is superior to Wi-Fi in terms of data transfer and the range that it provides.

Conclusion

WiMAX promises cost-effective service for both consumer and manufacturers as it has all the key components to supply a wider area with high-speed Internet access compared with wired broadband. WiMAX sends the wireless frequencies directly to the customer, avoiding the need for underground cabling. WiMAX is most certainly a promising next-generation wireless technology with high data transfer rates (peak 20 Mbps) over vast distances, removing the necessity of having to find a Wi-Fi hotspot. Telecoms have spent small fortunes upgrading their mobile network but are limited to transfer speeds of approximately 400–700 kbps per user. WiMAX can operate at environmentally friendly frequencies below 11 GHz. Higher frequencies do require line of sight. There are concerns, however, regarding the 'battery life' for WiMAX and it appears that portable competition from 3G and 4G networks will provide the main competition.

Notes

1. Marks, R. (2003) IEEE Standard 802.16 for Global Broadband Wireless Access, *http://ieee802.org/16/docs/03/C80216-03_14.pdf*
2. Cisco Systems, Inc. (2006) *Cisco Position paper on WiMAX and Related Technologies for Mobile Operators*. San Jose, CA. *http://whitepapers. techrepublic.com.com/abstract.aspx?docid=106932*
3. Barry, A., Daly, C., Johnson, J. and Skehill, R. (2005) Overview of WiMAX 802.16e. *Proceedings of 5th Annual International Conference on Information Telecommunications and Technology*. Cork: Cork University.

16

Hybrid Web applications

Karen Lee, Joan Condell and Kevin Curran

To date there has been a distinct difference in the way applications are delivered. Applications tend to be either desktop or Internet-based. This has worked for the most part. However, since the widespread deployment of wireless technology, there is a greater need to offer end users increased functionality that will allow them to work seamlessly with an application whether it has a connection to a network or happens to be intermittently disconnected. Google Gears is a new open-source JavaScript application programming interface (API) that allows the building of offline Web applications which can meet the demand for 'dual' applications. Adding Google Gears support to an application enables it to offer functionality offline and provide an experience similar to a native client-side application.

Introduction

Applications tend to be either desktop- or Internet-based. Users are currently looking for more functionality especially since the widespread deployment of wireless technology. This has led to research into and the evolutionary growth of hybrid Web–desktop applications. The hybrid Web–desktop terminology used simply describes applications which can run seamlessly offline as well as online. When in offline mode, users have exactly the same functionality as online users. They will be able to enter and edit data as if online. This is particularly useful when there is a loss of connectivity or travelling by car or air, allowing users to manage their time and plan ahead. The application will automatically update the new data once a connection is re-established, therefore allowing more effectiveness among users.

Desktop applications typically use thick client architecture as this provides users with more features, graphics and choices, making the applications more customisable. Thick clients do not rely on a central processing server because the processing is done locally on the user's system. In addition, the server is accessed primarily for storage purposes, providing the user with more functionality hence making the PC more useful. Desktop applications became popular in the 1970s for home use with the revolutionary spreadsheet application VisiCalc, which then spread to business users. VisiCalc was soon superseded by Lotus and Microsoft Excel, the latter remaining one of the most powerful desktop applications. These applications are technically more robust, allowing for a greater uptime. An important feature is ability of such programs to integrate with other products, e.g. when a user needs to exchange data with Word or Excel. Automation such as this is easy to achieve with a desktop application, but is not as easy with a browser-based interface. Making the integration process between applications sufficiently generic to work across all browsers is difficult. Fewer server requirements are needed as a thick client server does not require as high a level of performance as a thin client server because thick clients generally do much of the application processing. This may result in cheaper servers although in practice many thin client servers are actually equivalent to file servers in specification but with additional memory. Performance is generally quicker on a desktop because the screen is drawn only once and only the data change.[1] This prevents a lot of screen data coming from the server to the client, which increases the time taken to display the data.[2] A feature common in today's desktop applications is better multimedia performance especially in the field of video gaming as thick clients have advantages in multimedia-rich applications that would be bandwidth intensive if fully served. Games applications also typically need to interact directly with the video card on the user's PC, which is much simpler to do than through a browser. Additionally, desktop applications are suitable for poor network connections and it may also be possible to work offline with a thick client, although the network-orientated manner in which many people work today means that thick client usage can still be curtailed if the network is down. From the software developer's point of view, desktop applications can be difficult to deploy, as they usually come on a CD or are downloaded from a website and installed directly on any computer. This involves problems such as compatibility, i.e. an application is not backward compatible etc. Desktop applications may use the Internet to download updates, but the code that runs these applications resides on the desktop. Desktop applications are usually quite fast as they are running on a computer, and therefore Internet connection speed is not an issue, and they have great graphical user interfaces which usually interact with the operating system. Desktop applications are extremely interactive – they can be clicked, pointed and typed. Additions such as pull-up menus and sub-menus can be played used, with almost no waiting. Microsoft remains strong, with market share based on revenue of at least 95% in 2007 according to research firm International Data Corp. However, Google is distributing Sun Microsystems' StarOffice 8, a rival productivity software suite. Google also have a Web-based Google Docs and spreadsheets application. Another competitor is Apple's iWork application suite; Apple have also introduced a new spreadsheet application called Numbers which could compete with Excel. There is also OpenOffice, an open-source suite built on the same code as Sun's StarOffice, along with several Web-based applications such as ThinkFree and Zoho, which have been gaining ground from Microsoft.

In the early days of the Web, websites consisted of static pages, which severely limited interaction with the user. Web portals started to become popular and were the opening point for people surfing the internet. In the early 1990s, the limitation with static pages was removed when Web servers were modified to allow communication with server-side custom scripts. No longer were applications just static brochure-ware, edited only by those who knew HTML, and with this single change, normal users could interact with the application for the first time. Web applications have an advantage in that they make use of ubiquitous Web browser software. The first of these were Netscape Navigator and Microsoft Internet Explorer, with Explorer taking the lead in 1999 as a result of its distribution advantage. Web browsers do not make large demands on the client-side infrastructure as use of a Web application does not usually require any configuration or installation of client-side software.[3] Web-based applications have one large advantage over the desktop application in that they have far more reasonable demands on end-user random access memory (RAM) than locally installed programs. They reside and run off the provider's servers, and therefore these Web-based applications use in most cases the memory of the computers they run on, leaving more space for running multiple applications at the same time without incurring frustrating performance hits. By contrast, traditional Web applications provide limited user interfaces hampered by the stateless nature of HTML applications. A user can interact with one Web page at a time, entering information on the page, sending information to the Web server, then waiting for a new page as the result. From a developer's point of view they are unable to make use of the more sophisticated user interface capabilities users expect from everyday desktop applications. However, these Web-based applications are less prone to crashing and creating technical problems due to software or hardware conflicts with other existing applications, protocols or internal custom software. Software updates, hot fixes and upgrades can all be dealt with efficiently, allowing no user impact. Data are safer than on a desktop application as there are no hard disk storage issues. Today companies such as Google can take over the storage of user data, with highly reliable redundant data storage farms such as Gdata[4] becoming the norm rather than the exception, and users will have much less risk of losing their data due to an unforeseen disk crash or computer virus. Increasingly companies providing Web-based applications are providing extensive back-up services either as an integral part of their basic service or as a paid option. Web-based applications do not require the distribution, technical support and marketing infrastructure required by traditional downloadable software. This therefore allows online applications to cost a fraction of their downloadable counterparts if not being altogether free, while offering additional components and premium services as an option. Web applications are adaptable and can be written in any language using any Web technology. Web-based applications do not have to be downloaded, installed and configured. A further development is the rich internet application (RIA),[5] which can provide be run on common browser software while at the same time delivering a user interface on a par with that expected from a thick client.

An RIA is an entirely new kind of Web experience that is engaging, interactive, lightweight and flexible. RIAs offer the flexibility and ease of use of an intelligent desktop application and add the broad reach of traditional Web applications. Traditional Web applications centred all activity around a client–server architecture with a thin client. Under this system all processing is done on the server, and the client is only used to display static content. A drawback with this system is that all interaction with the application must pass through the server, which requires data to be sent to the server, the server to respond, and the page to be reloaded on the client with the response. However, it needs only to retrieve the data that are needed, making the interface behaviours typically much more responsive than those of a standard Web browser, which must always interact with a remote server. As with traditional Web applications, a broadband connection is a requirement for these Web applications. Even the most sophisticated Web applications need Internet access for users to log on and use the application. This causes inconvenience to users who may be travelling or moving in and out of hot-spot areas.

This advance is linked to the perceived Web 2.0 approach. The concept of 'Web 2.0' began with a conference brainstorming session between O'Reilly[6] and MediaLive International in early 2004, and there has since been a huge amount of disagreement as to what defines Web 2.0. It is clear that the Web has changed since the dot.com era.

AJAX (asynchronous JavaScript and XML) evolved and is injected into Web applications to make them look and feel like a desktop application with the added advantage of convenience. When these technologies are combined in the AJAX model,[7] Web applications are able to make quick, incremental updates to the user interface without reloading the entire browser page. Where a computer has an Internet connection, these 'new' applications can be accessed typically with a username and password. Google is most certainly the standard bearer for AJAX RIAs as they have invested a considerable amount of time and money researching and developing AJAX applications, most notably the free Web-based Google Docs, Google Reader and Google Maps. Reducing the maintenance burden further is another Web 2.0 concept which can be integrated in RIAs. RSS (really simple syndication or rich site summary) is an XML-based format that allows the syndication of lists of hyperlinks, along with other information, or metadata, which then helps viewers decide whether they want to follow the link. The technique reads the summary of the site for general information and presents the key points to the user. Google, Yahoo and Microsoft have been developing RSS readers which add a richer user experience to these new Web applications. RSS can also be attributed to the success of podcasting and videocasting. It is the RSS feed with audio or video enclosures that makes a podcast visible to search engine spiders. SEO (search engine optimisation) then increases the number of visitors to a website by giving it a high ranking in the search results of a search engine. The higher a website ranks in the results of a search, the greater the chance that that site will be visited by a user. Google along with other major 2.0 Web presences, e.g. Adobe, Microsoft, Java and Amazon, have been developing a new technology that could revolutionise the way business-to-business and business-to-consumer services are provided. The definition peer-to-peer Web services describes a standardised way of integrating rich Web-based applications using the XML, SOAP (simple object access protocol), WSDL (web services description language) and UDDI (universal description, discovery and integration) open standards over an Internet protocol backbone. No longer does each application need to copy and maintain external data sources. The user can request and get information in real time, and transform it to their particular format. Individualised software and services can then be delivered, which saves time and money as the maintenance burden is reduced. Amazon, del.icio.us and Flickr[8] offer their information free via a representational state transfer (REST) API. This can be seen as direct and indirect advertising as this service opens access to the majority of items in Amazon's product catalogue. The API is quite rich and allows manipulation of users, wish lists and shopping carts. However, its essence is the ability to lookup Amazon's products. Most applications that build on top of this service drive traffic back to Amazon, boosting sales of the fantastic E-Commerce application. These Web applications rely on the use of mash-ups, as they overlay traffic data from one source on the Internet for example, over maps from Yahoo, Microsoft, Google or any content provider. This ability to mix and match data and applications from multiple sources into one dynamic entity is considered by many to represent the promise of a Web service standard, which is also referred to as on-demand computing.

Mobile computing is a term describing the ability to use technology 'untethered', i.e. not physically connected to a local area network. In practice mobile computing is often connected wirelessly to and through the Internet or to and through a private network. This connection ties the mobile device to centrally located information and/or application software through the use of battery-powered, portable, wireless computing and communication devices. Mobile computing can include laptops, mobile phones, PDAs and other mobile devices. Connectivity can include Wi-Fi, bluetooth, general packet radio service (GPRS) or occasional physical connection. As computers have increased in popularity so too have mobile devices such as mobile phones and PDAs. In just 35 years, almost the same amount of time as the PC and nearly one-quarter that of the landline phone, mobile device penetration has surpassed the PC and landline phone combined, reaching 2.7 billion mobile subscriptions in 2006. In fact, in some developed areas of the world, penetration is at 100%. According to a study conducted in January 2007 by Telephia and comScore, two leading research firms for mobile media and Internet metrics, respectively, 5.7 million people in the UK used a mobile device to access the Web compared with 30 million who accessed the web from a PC.

Web-based applications have been applauded for their richness, simplicity and elegant user experience, but only while an Internet connection is available. There are numerous occasions when a connection is lost due to a fault on the line, moving house and having to wait for broadband installations, air travel or maintenance issues, etc. This is disruptive as users are immediately impacted due to the loss of service from their connection. Today, with applications such as Google Docs and Google Spreadsheets, this is indeed the case. If the user is creating a document and experiences a sudden loss in connectivity, not only will they lose access to Google's word processing logic, they will not be able to save their document or open up others. This could also depend on how the browser responds to a loss of connectivity – the user may lose any work done since the last 'save' took place. Users will not be able to access work or emails and will have to wait for the connection to be re-established. This could take time, leaving users frustrated and dissatisfied. Business companies will be losing revenue and reputation if users cannot access their portals. The US-based customer relationship management giant Salesforce.com were plagued by major outages last year and minor outages this year, which resulted in the company losing millions in revenue, disappointing their customers and damaging their reputation. The company is currently working with Google to develop a beta version of the application with some offline capabilities, preventing the reoccurrence of outages. Developers appreciate that although the Internet is pervasive it is still not truly everywhere and in an offline world desktop applications still have supremacy. Therefore, making offline Web applications a reality is a vision which many see as the future. Critics of Web applications like those served up by Web giants Google, Yahoo and Salesforce.com have argued that those applications can never replace their desktop counterparts because of the so-called 'off-line problem'.

Hybrid webified applications

More and more applications these days are being 'webified' in that they are made to operate on the Web using a browser or made to function in a similar manner. The reason for this is that the Internet is capable of significantly augmenting human interaction, with its decentralised system of ubiquitous data accessibility. Webaroo is a free software service that gives you the power to search and browse the Web on the go. Webaroo's advanced technology enables the user to search Web content offline on your laptop, PDA or smartphone. As the Web becomes increasingly interconnected and applications continue to blur the distinction between the desktop and Web, we should expect to see more applications that allow Web/desktop synchronization. This will happen with the increasing development of Web services that enable applications to work equally well across Web and desktop clients. Applications such as the Microsoft Windows Live suite supplement the traditional desktop applications with Web-based software and services. Google is very browser-centric so their offerings tend to be online only and are heavily tied to the 'cloud'. Microsoft has years of desktop experience and is leveraging all of that in their RIA push. They see many benefits in keeping a majority of the processing power and storage on the desktop but providing the flexibility and freedom that comes with the Web through a number of different online services. By tying those online services such as Office Live Workspace and some of the other Windows Live products to their desktop counterparts, a workflow that transitions reasonably seamlessly between Web and desktop is accomplished. Adobe, by contrast, have taken a balance approach. They have made money on their desktop software but have always had a presence on the web with, for example, Flash, PDF and server software such as ColdFusion. Current browser–desktop hybrid solutions such as Adobe Integrated Runtime (AIR) are representative of that involvement and a hybrid approach appears to be a successful way to go. The future is hybrid, where desktop and Web-based software and services become intertwined to the point at which users will not know the difference between the two. There is a greater need to offer end users increased functionality which will allow them to work seamlessly on a desktop and on the Internet using a hybrid application that can be developed to be accessed anytime and anywhere regardless of Internet connectivity. Internet applications simply cannot compete at a user interface level with a desktop application, so with these limits and the offline limitation the next step will be to create other Web-centric features to bridge the gap. Currently there are a handful of applications that can be accessed regardless of Internet connection. 'Remember the Milk', the popular online to-do list application was the first popular non-Google Web application to go offline with Gears technology. Anything that is possible online with 'Remember the Milk' now works offline too. Not only can the user access their lists, but they can add new tasks and notes, edit existing tasks, and complete, postpone, prioritise, tag and change due dates without Internet access.

Google's own application Google Reader is a decidedly simple yet very usable and quite comprehensive Web-based RSS feed reader.[9] Google began experimenting with offline capabilities and Reader became the first Google application to benefit. Due to high demand for this functionality Google announced in April 2008 that Google Docs has become available with the same offline functionality as Reader. Competitors such as Zoho Writer, the online word processor, launched a new version in August 2007 that lets users work on their documents offline.[10] On 26 November 2007 they added read and write offline functionality, pushing the boundary of what online office applications now mean. The Read/WriteWeb notes are a large leap forward from what other office RIAs are providing in that users can work on the document offline and, when reconnected to the Internet, the synchronisation will take place for initially sharing files and much more is promised from this application.

With the movement of Web applications onto the desktop, Adobe Air[11] lets developers use their existing Web development skills in HTML, AJAX, Flash and Flex to build and deploy rich Internet applications to the desktop. It is an out of browser application which uses ActionScript 3 but with all of the traits and features that make for a rich Internet application. What AIR has over a purely Web-based RIA depends on what it is required for. Local access to the file structure and the local windowing system is enabled, allowing the developer to save and open files in the native window. Drag and drop plus a SQLite-embedded database add to the overall feeling of permanence. Among other benefits, applications developed with AIR will be independent of the operating system.[12]

Mozilla recognise that personal computing is currently in a state of transition and while traditionally users have interacted mostly with desktop applications, increasingly they are using web applications. As a result the latter often fit awkwardly into the document-centric interface of Web browsers. Consequently, Mozilla Labs are launching a series of experiments to bridge the divide in the user experience between Web and desktop applications. The first release is Prism, the new name for WebRunner. Prism allows developers to create desktop-like applications out of individual websites. Prism will enable greater desktop functionality much like AIR. Prism also lets users split Web applications out of their browser and run them directly on their desktop.[13]

Flex is a cross-platform development framework for creating RIAs. Flex enables the user to create expressive, high-performance applications that run identically on all major browsers and operating systems. Adobe Flex is a collection of technologies released by Adobe Systems for the development and deployment of cross-platform, rich Internet applications based on the proprietary Adobe Flash platform. Flex is the first and most complete solution for accessible RIAs. It combines the responsiveness and interactivity of desktop applications with the broad reach and ease of distribution of Web applications, while still creating an experience that all users find accessible, regardless of ability. It includes 23 accessible components that accelerate application development and create a consistent, usable experience for users with disabilities. Using these key components, developers can create RIAs quickly and easily while ensuring a high level of accessibility.[14]

A major competitor to AIR is JavaFX. The demand continues to grow for secure, interactive content, applications and services that run on a variety of clients. To simplify and speed the creation and deployment of high-impact content for a wide range of devices, Sun has introduced JavaFX, a new family of products based on Java technology designed to enable consistent user experiences, from desktop to mobile device to set-top box to blu-ray disc. The JavaFX family of products comprises a set of runtime environments, widgets, development tools and scripting environments. The widespread deployment of Sun hardware and a highly polished developer network make it a strong contender to expand Sun's horizons in this field. Sun also currently has plans to make it open source, which will also have an impact. Sun's motto, 'write once, run anywhere', promises to create highly interactive and animated content running on computers, digital TVs, regular TVs and mobile devices, and have the content look the same across all platforms and behave the same way.[15] The JavaFX product family uses the Java FX Script tool to create content for Web and Web 2.0-orientated applications. FX Script is designed for content authoring of Web and network-facing applications. Developers will be able to access and use all of the Java SE/ME (standard edition/micro edition) applications and libraries. Therefore, unnecessary bridging to libraries will no longer be a problem as Java FX will handle that efficiently. It also offers features for safer use. It does not rely on a constant connection such as JavaScript in the AJAX model. Java FX will need only one new library to be installed along with the standard SE or ME runtime. By having locally installed SE/ME files working with Java FX it has potential to take the Google applications offline and work on them.

Microsoft Silverlight is a cross-browser, cross-platform plugin for delivering next-generation media experiences and RIAs for the Web. Silverlight offers a flexible programming model that supports JavaScript, Visual C#, Visual Basic and other languages. Silverlight directly competes with Adobe's Flash and was developed to compete with RIAs, with Internet users seeking out better experiences both in the browser and outside it, and both online and offline. Microsoft and Adobe are battling it out in the 'richer' products – which either extend the browser or utilise the desktop. Silverlight is an impressive package with a seemingly endless array of compatibilities. A full .NET framework means that any .NET languages can be executed, alongside multimedia and text-based content from WMV (Windows media file format), MP3 (media player3), XML and JavaScript.[2]

Prior to the arrival of Google Gears, there were other approaches to the same problem. One involved a Java-based database that is referred to as the Derby Project by the Apache Foundation (also called JavaDB). However, neither the Apache Foundation nor Sun saw the need to drive Derby/JavaDB into the market as a solution to the so-called offline problem. Francois Orsini, a talented engineer at Sun, saw the potential for JavaDB to take Web applications offline and proved this with some self-built prototypes. At that time solving the offline problem for Web applications was not one of Sun Microsystems' priorities and hence the project ended without any further considerations by Sun.[15] Dojo Offline is an open-source toolkit that makes it easy to create sophisticated, offline Web applications.[16] It sits on top of Google Gears, which helps extend Web browsers with new functionality. Dojo Offline makes working with Google Gears easier, extends it with important functionality, creates a higher-level API than Google Gears provides, and provides developer productivity features.

Google is also partnering with Norway's Opera Software AIR, maker of the Web browser popular with mobile phone users, and Mozilla, the group behind Firefox, the largest alternative to Microsoft's Internet Explorer browser. Firefox has currently added offline support to Zimbra, a Web-based open source server and client software for messaging and collaboration, email, group calendaring, contacts, Web document management and authoring, therefore delivering end users increased productivity, flexibility and choice. Firefox has developed their own Greasemonkey extension which works with Gears to customise the way Web pages look and function. Firefox has named their mix GearsMonkey and they are advocating that all developers inject Gear code so that all Web applications can be used offline.[17] Phyton with Django are also developing the DjangoKit framework which will take a Django application and turn it into a stand-alone MacOS application with a local database and media files to bring offline functionality. The 'not yet released' Ruby on Rails product, Joyent Slingshot, is a new technology developed by Joyent and Magnetk which provides a Windows and OS X client for designing Rails applications. The advantage with Joyent is that the application looks more like a desktop application than other Web applications with online/offline functionality.[12]

Google Gears

Google has a vision of creating Web software that runs online and offline to let users work remotely from planes and trains, over slow dial-up connections or even from the most remote locations. The technology, called Google Gears, allows users of computers, phones and other devices to manipulate Web services such as e-mail, online calendars or news readers whether online, intermittently connected to the Web or completely offline. By bridging the gap between new Web services and the older world of desktop software, where any data changes are stored locally on users' machines, Google is pushing the Web into whole new spheres of activity and posing a challenge to rival Microsoft, the market leader in the desktop software era.[12] With the release of the open source code, Google Gears JavaScript APIs allow the building of offline Web applications that can meet the demand for 'dual' applications. This open source browser extension installs six Google APIs for employment on the user's browser. The first API is a LocalServer which handles the creation of data objects to store application information locally, the second is an SQLite relational database[18] for searching the data, and the third, the WorkerPool, will enable asynchronous JavaScript so applications can synchronise data in the background without overburdening the browser. The HttpRequest API module implements a subset of the W3C XmlHttpRequest specification, and makes it available in both workers and the main HTML page (the WorkerPool API allows web applications to run JavaScript code in the background, without blocking the main page's script execution). The Timer module implements HTML 5 Timer specification, and makes it available in both workers and the main HTML page. This is the same timer API that is traditionally available in browsers on the window object. Finally, the Factory module uses the Factory class to instantiate all other Google Gears objects. In addition to making the user's transition from online to offline seamless, this platform has the potential to improve Web page performance by allowing larger portions of the computationally intensive tasks such as animation, video and complex calculations to be passed onto the local computer. In recent years, we have seen the Web and desktop move closer to each other, with Web-based versions of desktop software such as the previously mentioned Google applications. Many applications developed using the above technologies will take this direction one step further, falling somewhere between desktop applications and websites but offering the unique offline functionality. Google reported at the Gears launch that not every application would be suitable to have an offline option. Applications such as a stock pricing ticker or a chat application could not have an offline option as these applications need to retrieve the live data every second from the online server. That said, general applications such as online word processing, email and calendaring applications would be suitable to have an offline option and would be useful for frequent travellers or when a network or Internet connection is unavailable. Then once connected to the Internet, the data will automatically synchronise, making the application real time for all users. Applications such as a Web portal that offers staff the option to query a company database, issue sales orders or invoices would also be suitable to have an offline option. Google's push into the world of Web services has given it a much wider reach than its core search business and the rationale behind Google Gears is that they can see there is a demand for Google applications to run without its servers.

Security is a key issue with Google Gears offline functionality as the user's privacy can be breached. In most cases the offline feature is only safe for use on the user's own PC, laptop or PDA, where they are sure that no one else has access as the information resides on the local computer. Google Gears data files are protected with the user's operating system login credentials although two people could theoretically access each other's Gears data files. Therefore, working on a public or shared computer should be avoided at all times, thus eliminating the possibility of identity fraud or corruption of the users' files. To protect users in general, Google Gears shows a warning dialogue when a site first attempts to use the Google Gears API, as user opt-in is important. Users can then grant or deny access for each security origin. When a user grants access to Gears from a particular origin, Gears remembers this decision for the future. Denying access to users is only remembered until the page is reloaded.

Another key issue for users planning to use Google Gears on more than one computer is that each computer synchronises offline separately and for that reason each computer must be synchronised with the offline data, as synchronised changes on one computer will not be reflected on another. Conflict resolution for situations such as when two users are working on the same offline data and synchronise it at different times requires workarounds not currently available for Gears. Circumstances like these could lead to inaccuracy and confusion for the user, resulting in lost data and negative acceptance of the application. In addition, each browser synchronises offline data separately, i.e. Firefox 1.5 and Internet Explorer, and therefore if a user plans to use Google Gears on more than one browser, they must also remember to synchronise each browser and be aware that uninstalling Google Gears will not clear any offline information the user currently has on their system. These data are not encrypted as Google stores all the data in plain text in the database or local server. Files cannot be password protected either. This would be a major issue if the system was maliciously attacked. It would also be an issue if the user wished to sell or recycle the computer in the future. Synchronisation of the data will also make the browser slow in response as it uses extra memory to start the process.[19]

Conclusion

To date, the greatest limitation to using a Web application is the need for a constant connection to the Internet. When an Internet connection is disrupted or is unavailable, a Web application is inaccessible to the many users who now use and depend on them for business or personal use. There is now more than ever a greater need to offer end users increased functionality that will allow them to work seamlessly on a desktop or a mobile device using a hybrid application that can be developed to be accessed anytime and anywhere regardless of Internet connectivity. Google has recognised this and are helping to bridge the gap between desktop applications and Web-based applications with their set of new APIs which ultimately attempt to ease the pain of developing offline/online synchronisation for hybrid Web applications.

Notes

1. Microsoft (2002) *NET Development (General) Technical Articles, Designing for Web or Desktop?*
2. Microsoft (2007) *Application Device Overview.*
3. Teamquest (2008) *http://www.teamquest.com/solutions-products/products/technical-details/rich-web-applications/*
4. Google data APIs provide a simple standard protocol for reading and writing data on the Web.
5. W3, Rich Web Application Backplane, *W3C Coordination Group Note,* 16 November 2006.
6. O'Reilly, T. (2005) What is Web 2.0? *http://www.oreillynet.com/pub/a/oreilly/tim/news/2005/09/30/what-is-web-20.html#mememap*
7. Garrett, J.J. (2005) *Ajax: A New Approach to Web Applications.* *http://adaptivepath.com/ideas/essays/archives/000385.php*
8. ProgrammableWeb, API Dashboard, 2007. *http://www.programmableweb.com/apis*
9. Google Reader is a Web-based aggregator, capable of reading Atom and RSS feeds online or offline. It was released by Google on 7 October 2005. Google Reader was the first application to make use of Google Gears
10. Zoho Writer is a tool to access, edit and share documents from anywhere.
11. Adobe Air, also known as Adobe Integrated Runtime, codenamed Apollo, is a cross OS runtime environment for building rich internet applications (RIAs).
12. Google (2007) 'Take your web applications offline with Google's Gears', *Web Designer,* 138, 26–8.
13. Mozilla Labs (2007) *http://labs.mozilla.com/2007/10/prism/*
14. Adobe Labs (2007) Adobe Integrated Runtime. *http://labs.adobe.com/technologies/flex/*
15. Sun (2007) *http://java.sun.com/javafx/faqs.jsp#1*
16. Neuberg B. (2007) Creating offline web applications with Dojo Offline. *http://docs.google.com/View?docid=dhkhksk4_8gdp9gr&pli=1*
17. Mozilla (2007) *http://www.mozilla-europe.org/en/products/firefox/*
18. SQLite is an in-process library that implements a self-contained, serverless, zero-configuration, transactional SQL database engine.
19. Googlegears (2008) *http://code.google.com/apis/gears/api_workerpool.html*

Designing for the mobile Web

Kevin Curran and Winston Huang

Mobile communications is a continually growing sector in industry and a wide variety of visual services such as video-on-demand have been created that are limited by low-bandwidth network infrastructures. The distinction between mobile phones and PDAs has already become blurred with pervasive computing being the term coined to describe the tendency to integrate computing and communication into everyday life. This chapter outlines the peculiarities of designing sites for visitors who will be browsing via mobile devices.

Introduction

In ubiquitous computing, software is used by roaming users interacting with the electronic world through a collection of devices ranging from PDAs (Figure 17.1) and mobile phones (Figure 17.2) to personal computers (Figure 17.3) and laptops (Figure 17.4). The heterogeneity added by modern smart devices is also characterised by an additional property, which is that many of these devices are typically tailored to distinct purposes. Therefore, not only do memory and storage capabilities differ widely but so too do local device capabilities, in addition to changes in the availability of resources.

The mobile Web refers to the World Wide Web accessible to cell phones, PDAs and other mobile devices connected to a public network. Accessing the mobile Web does not require a desktop computer and as it can be accessed with a number of mobile devices, the Internet can be accessed in remote places that were previously unconnected. For example, medical information could be sent by a mountaineer in difficulty and received by rescuers. Currently, mobile visitors browsing the Web via

Figure 17.1 PDAs

Figure 17.2 Mobiles

Figure 17.3 Desktops

Figure 17.4 Laptops

wireless mobile devices such as PDAs and Smartphones are the fastest growing community of web users. According to market data released by market advisory firm IDC, in the opening quarter of 2005, the European handheld devices market (including smartphones and PDAs) grew by 55%, with shipments reaching 2.5 million units compared with 1.6 million in the corresponding quarter of 2004.[1] A large proportion of mobile devices sold today connect to the Internet either through WiFi or Third Generation (3G) connections. Mobile devices are not the same as their desktop counterparts; instead they can be limited by slow text input facilities, the environment of the user, low bandwidth, small storage capacity, limited battery life and slow CPU speed. Scripting or plug-ins are often not supported by mobile browsers and therefore the range of content supported is limited. Other limitations include:

- *Environment of the user.* A computer user will generally be in a specially designed office environment and can devote their attention to the screen. Conversely, a mobile device user may be in a noisy, distracting environment and only devoting some time to the device. The content and interface therefore need to be designed for quick and easy reading, without too much detail.

- *Limited keyboard.* The O2 Mini S and O2-Xda-Exec have a small QWERTY keyboard; other portable devices may have only a few keys and touchscreen. As such, the first factor to be considered should be to place the significant content of the Web page in an obvious area so that the user sees it without the need to scroll.

- *Limited memory.* The memory of a typical desktop computer is around 4 GB; by contrast, that of a mobile device is less than 512 MB. In other words, a mobile device typically only has one-fifth the memory of an Internet-enabled desktop computer. Any solution that attempts to deliver Internet content onto a mobile phone must therefore be very space efficient.

- *Limited power.* Handheld devices do not have a limitless supply of electrical power. Great strides have been made in recent years to increase the amount of so-called standby time that cellular phones can make use of. This allows the modern mobile phone to wait for long periods (often as long as several weeks) to receive a call. Unfortunately, this ability to exist in standby mode for weeks at a time does not help when you are connected to the Internet. For all intents and purposes, a connection to the Internet from modern mobile phones is the same thing as a telephone call. If a user can expect an hour's talking time on a single battery with their current phone, then her or she can expect about the same period of Internet connectivity. Compared with a laptop where the battery enables access to the Internet for 5 hours or more, the battery of a mobile device allows less than 1 hour on average.[2] Other limitations such as display quality, processor speed, available bandwidth and supported protocols are also significant.

- *Limited display screens.* Compared with a conventional PC, smartphones, PDAs and Ultra-Mobiles all have limited screen area. A smartphone may have a screen of only 2.5 inches, a PDA of 4 inches and Ultra-Mobile PC 7 inches, with resolutions from QVGA (240 × 320 pixels) to 800 × 480 or greater for an Ultra-Mobile PC. Web page design therefore needs to be able to adapt to different sizes and shapes of screens.

Screen size limitations require special attention because this directly affects the interaction between users and Web pages. Studies have shown that when browsing on small screens, users follow links less frequently than those with larger displays.[3] As shown in Figure 17.5, a traditional Web page can be hard to read on a small screen device, such as a PDA.

Figure 17.5 shows that viewing a page designed for the desktop on a small screen device requires users to scroll not only vertically but also horizontally.[4] Figure 17.6 shows the homepage of the University of Ulster viewed on both a Sony Ericsson and a Nokia N70. The page has been distorted so that browsing is not a pleasant experience.

Figure 17.5   Original layout on mobile devices

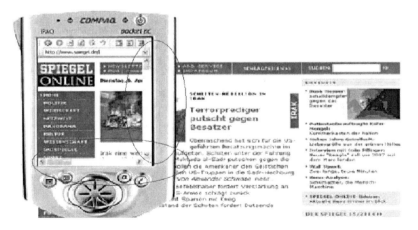

Figure 17.6 K750i and Nokia N70 showing the University of Ulster homepage

There are a number of methods for adapting traditional Web pages for smaller screens. One solution is to present Web pages in full form on a mobile screen but this approach is problematic given battery and bandwidth limitations, even with compression. Furthermore, the full-form view results in excessive scrolling requirements in vertical and horizontal dimensions. Some approaches use single-column views to facilitate the reading process, although they generate a large amount of vertical scrolling, instead of horizontal scrolling.[5]

To avoid excessive vertical and horizontal scrolling, a miniature version of the page can be presented to users, and thumbnails and summarized versions of the page can be displayed. Overviews provide users with visual context, and allow one to zoom in on content. However, as shown on the left of Figure 17.7, due to the inherent limitation of small screens, users find that the content is reduced and the actual screen is unable to show which titles hold the relevant information due to space restrictions.[4] The collapse-to-zoom technique addresses the above problems by offering an alternative exploration strategy. It allows users to collapse areas deemed irrelevant, such as advertising and archive material. Un-collapsed content will need to be redrawn in more detail. The full-size view is then switched, and the page size reduced significantly, so that users can view the remaining relevant content with little scrolling (Figure 17.7b). Unfortunately, the collapse-to-zoom technique requires mobile devices to be equipped with touchscreens.

Figure 17.7 (a) Thumbnail view on PDAs, (b) collapse-to-zoom view

thumbnail view (a) about to collapse column (b)

Other popular approaches are to concentrate on minimising the amount of content on pages and only sending the relevant piece of content to the mobile device. Filtering methods can be divided into those based on the structure of the HTML page,[6,7] and those based on the user's preferences.[8,9] Without specific metadata in the HTML code, however, the relevant content from a page is difficult to be rendered properly by these filtering methods.

The Tate Modern in London launched an interactive audio-visual tour of its Museum for handheld devices. It is provided to visitors when they visit and users can see video and still images on the display. Thalys[10] provides leisure and business travellers with a high-speed European network that provides the information they need via mobile phones. The site offers train schedules and fares information for the mobile users in four languages with up-to-the-minute traffic information. The University of Alaska Anchorage (UAA) Campus has a guided tour on a PDA using an Avantgo Web channel. The Avantgo service makes the content maintainable and enables the information to be viewed on most PDAs. Tags in the Avantgo help to minimise the impact to the host server by utilising server caching and helps the website to customise PDA-appropriate content and graphics. The system enables any individual with a PDA to be able to download and conduct the self-guided tour themselves. It provides both visual and textual content, and is constructed to allow users to start their guide anywhere and go in any direction they want.

Mobile Web-enabling technologies

HDML (handheld device mark-up language) was one of the first popular standards to target the mobile Web. HDML contained features to program a mobile phone User Interface (UI) (e.g. soft keys, numeric keyboard) and make the best use of scarce wireless bandwidth (client-side variable, deck/card metaphor). Since 1999, WML can be seen as the first global wireless mark-up language. It retained almost all the features of HDML along with additional features such timers. HTML 2.0, HTML 3.2 and HTML 4.0 (1997) were defined as the proper formalisation of what was just current practice. By the time of the development of HTML 4.0, XML and XML hype were created and the 'xmlification' of HTM became the logical next step. XHTML 1.0 was introduced in 2000.

XHTML

Extensible hypertext markup language (XHTML) has the expressive possibilities of HTML but with a stricter, more particular syntax. It is considered to be the current or latest version of HTML. XHTML 1.1, XHTML 1.0 and HTML 4.01 are recommended for Web publishing by W3C. HTML is a flexible markup language but is a limited subset of SGML, an application of XML. HTML requires a relatively complicated and custom parser. XHTML can be considered as the intersection of HTML and XML, as it is a reformulation of HTML in XML. Although the XML suitable for data conversion is likely to replace HTML, it is too soon to adopt XML as the key language in designing the Web as thousands of HTML-based websites already exist. For this reason, XHTML as an extension of XML has been developed. The goal of XHTML is to provide a smooth transition between HTML and XML. Its extensibility and flexibility make it suitable for mobile Web applications. XHTML Mobile Profile 1.0 (XHTML MP) is the official mark-up language of WAP 2.0 created by the Open Mobile Alliance (OMA) (formerly the WAPForum) for wireless devices. XHTML MP adds styling information [style attribute and tag plus Wireless Cascading Style Sheets (WCSS)] in addition to a handful of style tags belonging to other XHTML 1.0 modules such as b, i, big, hr, big and small. Cascading style sheets (CSS) are another mechanism for adding style (such as colours and spacing) to Web documents.

XML

Extensible markup language (XML) is a simple, flexible text format derived from SGML. It is a subset of SGML and supports a wide variety of applications. Its goal is to enable generic SGML to be served, received and processed on the Web in the same way now possible with HTML. Originally, its primary purpose was to meet the challenges of large-scale electronic publishing. XML is also playing an increasingly important role in the exchange of a wide variety of data on the Web and elsewhere. It has been designed for ease of implementation and for interoperability with both SGML and HTML. Now, its primary goal is to facilitate the sharing of data across different information systems, particularly those connected via the Internet. Compared with HTML, XML is a small subset of the SGML standard, allowing the powerful features and convenience of HTML to be used on the Web. Maintaining its extensible feature, XML is quite different from the HTML. It allows us to define many tags to describe the information in a document, rather remain restricted to fixed tags which may not provide us with the descriptive power needed. In other words, HTML is a general method to display Web data whereas XML provides a general method to deal with Web data directly. HTML focuses on the display format of a Web page whereas XML focuses on the content.

Mobile device HCI

When technology reaches the point that meets user requirements, consumers no longer seek the best technology, but rather the most convenient one, the one with the most satisfactory user experience, the lowest cost, and the greatest reliability.[11] Human–computer interaction (HCI) as a discipline is concerned with the design, evaluation and implementation of interactive computing systems for human use and with the study of major phenomena surrounding them. HCI aims to produce usable, multifunctional, safe systems. Namely, the goal is to develop or improve the safety, utility, effectiveness, efficiency and usability of systems that include computers. Here, the 'system' refers not only to the software and hardware but also to the entire environment. 'Usability', a key concept in HCI, is concerned with making systems easy to learn and use. Poorly designed computer systems can be extremely annoying to users. HCI draws from the knowledge and methods of many different disciplines, chiefly computer science, cognitive psychology, social science and the ergonomics of human factors. Websites may be accessed by people for multitudes of tasks, so making a site friendlier and more responsive is a problem for HCI design. The key principles are thus that HCI design should be user-centred, integrate knowledge from different disciplines and be highly iterative. In order to produce computer systems with good usability, developers must attempt to:

- understand the factors that determine how people use technology and systems,

- develop tools and techniques to enable building suitable systems, and

- achieve efficient, effective and safe interaction and put people first.[11]

In summary, the key principle in designing HCI is understanding how users will interact with them and what approaches will lead to more effective usability. User-centred design methods and processes improve the usability of systems.[12] However, designers often overlook important HCI factors, even with conventional interactive systems. In the case of mobile Web technology, designers in the past have developed many devices with little regard to well-known HCI factors. In fact, applying known HCI guidelines can improve the experience of users on such devices, owing to the limitations already mentioned. The first factor that should be considered is the impact of reduced screen size on reading rate, interaction and comprehension. For example, navigation needs rethinking for small screen situations to provide systematic, direct access mechanisms. In addition, designers should pay attention to past usability experiences but should not assume that everything will transfer effectively from the desktop to the handheld environment. The distinction between mobile device and conventional PCs also should be considered carefully within design. User-centred design focuses on placing users at the centre of web design and development. Developers are encouraged to talk directly to the users about the main aspects of site design to ensure that the final site meets their requirements. The most important aspects here are that user-centred design requires particular attention. It is important to be able to anticipate how users would like to navigate so that efficient site navigation can be provided.

When designing mobile sites, it is recommended that a menu be structured in a shallow fashion in order to reduce the cognitive burden, rather than creating a deep hierarchy.[13] This means fewer levels but more choices per level. Placing a brief summary with key information on a page can enable users to better understand a body of content that is spread over separate pages. In addition, partitioning information into separate pages will decrease scrolling while reading the separate pages.

Customisation is defined as the ability of a website to tailor itself or to be tailored by users, namely personalisation and tailoring. It requires designers to filter unnecessary information to minimise the constraints of a small screen. Due to the limited display in viewing Web pages, users still often feel frustrated and it is recommended that a brief site map is inserted to identify the locations and icons placed linking to the start page.[13] Account should be taken of the capabilities of the requesting device, such as designing suitable Web pages for various mobile screens, and presenting the most important information first at the top of the hierarchy. There are also other limitations such as visible navigation bars being impractical along with mouse over type techniques.

Standard Web pages are generally unsuitable for mobile devices, which vary considerably in their capabilities. Mobile-specific content is a more suitable approach to developing mobile Web content. There are three main categories of mobile Web authoring techniques: multiple authoring, single authoring and flexible authoring.[14] Multiple authoring and flexible authoring are approaches to developing different versions for different devices. The associated development and maintenance costs are usually considered prohibitive, although it provides authors with complete control over the user experience on each device. Authoring, which is an adaptation solution that translates the single authored content into a form appropriate to a wide range of mobile devices, is the most suitable for a mobile Web portal.

The objectives of authoring can be categorised into several aspects, and different authoring techniques can be applied to different aspects. For example, structure refers to the relationship between parts of the delivered page and the subsequently delivered page. Navigation allows users to move from the currently perceived unit to some related unit, with the minimum of effort. Content is intended to convey information to users by the raw text and other media resources from the delivered content. In addition, style, layout and application interaction are also parts of the authoring process, and each of these aspects can be addressed by different authoring techniques.[14]

Well-known structures are often used to represent content in mobile Web development. Linear structure, hierarchy and mesh have different influence on content navigation. Linear structure has many problems such as users having to browse a single page each time. For instance, Figure 17.8 shows a typical 'hierarchy' Web page structure. Here the site is represented by nodes that make up an ordered collection of one or more item (such as N.1, which comprises N.1.1 and N.1.2 in Figure 17.8), and items which may be a piece of content or a node (such as N.5.1 in Figure 17.8).

Figure 17.8 Website map

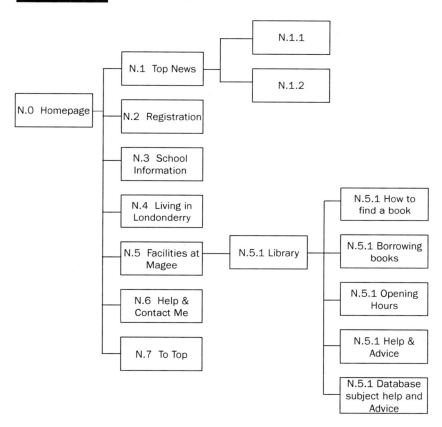

As shown in Figure 17.8, a hierarchical structure can be applied to a mobile site with a simple drill-down architecture nesting content into labelled categories. To cater for small screens, information has to be spread out into multiple pages rather than placed on a single page. Providing a well-designed click stream requires particular attention. This is an effective approach to show what actions users will probably take to reach the content needed. However, to avoid users become disorientated as they go deeper into a site, the levels should be limited as far as possible. Only three levels are presented on this portal. In the simple site map (Figure 17.8), the 1st level is the homepage (N.0), and the nodes from N.1 to N.7 are presented on level 2; level 3 contains nodes, for example, from N.5.1 to N.5.3. One factor during design is to limit links per page. Navigation enables users to browse the page in the order intended by the designer, and locate any necessary content. Given the limited screen size and navigation capability constraints of mobile devices (for example, some devices do not support script and are not equipped with desktop inputs such as a mouse), it can be difficult to navigate Web pages. A preferred and common method of creating mobile navigation schemes is to employ a simple vertical list of menus. As shown on the right of Figure 17.9, the 'body' area lists all the main topics in a simple vertical list of menus from 1 to 7. Following those topic links, users can reach each sub-topic. For instance, using *Accesskey* in the code, an attribute of XHTML enables users to quickly navigate to areas of the pages via the numerical keypad. Assigning a vertical list of menus on one page creates less disorientation for users as they browse pages. It might also be a consideration to place a link 'Go to the Top' on the bottom of each page to allow navigation to the top of the page.

To help users to judge where they are, a 'top guideline' can also be placed on each Web page. This provides escape points to the parent page, homepage or both. As shown in Figure 17.10, a path is presented on each page except the homepage. Node N1 is the parent node of N1.1, and they are both linked to a corresponding page.

Figure 17.9   'Go to top' link action

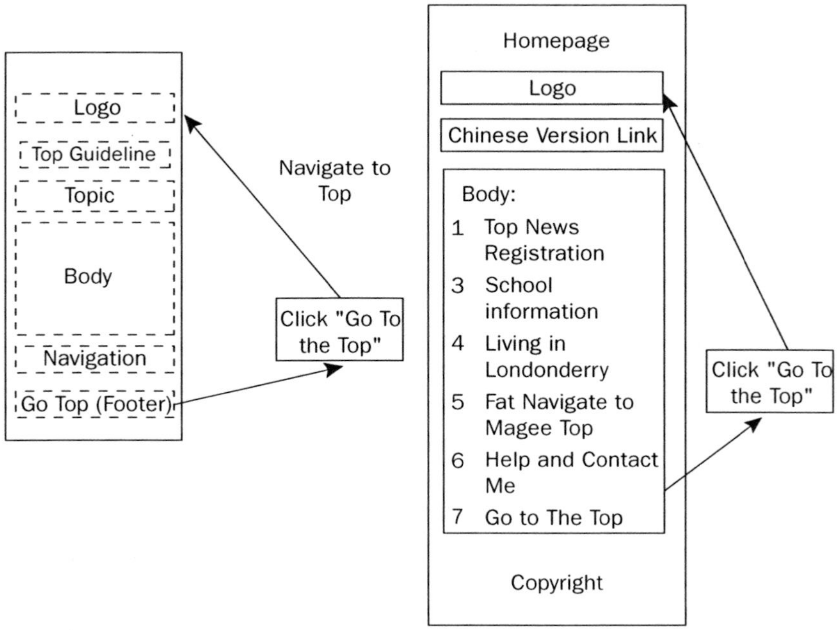

Figure 17.10 Top guideline

Node 1 >> Node 1.1 >> Node 1.1.2

On each page, a series of navigation bars should also be provided to link to the nodes on the same level. Rather than browsing mobile pages, users in a mobile context are often seeking a particular piece of information. Designers need consider what content users are seeking and offer appropriate information. Clear and simple language is essential to enable users to reach the information effectively. Limited content should also be offered to ensure that users pay less for the experience. Pages should be divided into usable but limited size portions. In addition, due to the memory limitations of devices, authors should ensure that the overall size of a page is appropriate so that an appropriate balance between page portion and scrolling is achieved. Scrolling sometimes cannot be avoided (such as with maps), so scrolling should be limited to one direction only. Frames are not supported by all mobile devices so use of frames should be avoided.

Mobile browsers identify and treat a document by the HTTP servers sent by MIME types. Incorrect MIME types within a document may cause the browser to incorrectly interpret and fail to render the document. Also, many mobile devices do not support objects and scripts, and therefore their use should be avoided. In addition, due to the limited bandwidth and high latency often experience by users of 2G devices, it is useful to provide caching of information where possible to reduce the need to reload data such as style sheets, pages and images, thus improving performance and lowering cost of use. This helps in particular with resources such as logos or stylesheets; for instance, to set an expiry time of '200' under the title in the code as follows:

```
<meta http-equiv="Cache-Control" content="max-age=200"/>.
```

Emulator testing, which uses one or more mobile device emulators, is a common method to test a site designed for the mobile Web. Typically, it will mimic the device experience for a particular device or class of devices via a desktop or Web-hosted application. Emulators can offer quick verification of how code performs without actually loading it on a device. DotMobi provides a tool[15] that adheres to industry standards set by the W3C. The tool simulates mobile devices such as the Sony Ericsson K750i and the Nokia N70. Output from the tool provides assessment scores for websites ranging from 1 (least mobile ready) to 5 (most mobile ready).

A rating of 5, for example, suggests that a mobile site 'will probably display very well on a mobile phone'. A more detailed output is presented in Figure 17.11. The readiness score is also calculated to reach 4.55/5.0. This means that the majority of mobile users can access and view pages effectively and efficiently. Page size is a significant aspect in the test as it would directly relate to whether a device can download the page successfully within its limited memory and network bandwidth. Figure 17.12 illustrates that the page tested here is only 12.96k. The size is much lower than the recommended minimum size by W3C, of 20k per page. Download time is also a major concern in creating a website, due to users not waiting longer than about 30 seconds for a page to download. Currently, GPRS, 3G and WiFi are the common methods to access the Internet for mobile devices. The homepage being assessed here took 4.14 s to access via GPRS, and 1.22 s via 3G. The fastest method of access is by WiFi where the page only took 0.53 s to load.

Figure 17.11 Site overall result

Figure 17.12 Readiness, size, time and cost

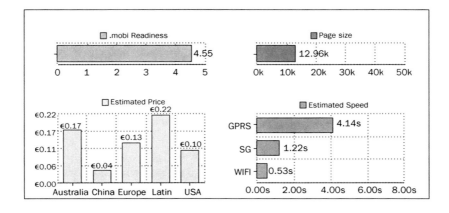

Figure 17.13 DotMobi compliance tests

Mobile data transfer can be expensive so it is good practice to provide only relevant information. Figure 17.12 shows that loading the sample page costs only €0.13 in Europe and €0.04 in China. It is €0.17 in Australia, €0.22 in Latin America and €0.10 in the USA.

Three key tests for these devices are for XHTML Mobile Profile, Valid Markup and no frames. Frames are not supported by most mobiles and therefore it is recommended that they be omitted (see Figure 17.13). The tests suggest that the site should use XHTML-MP as the default markup to ensure pages work on multiple mobile devices as well as standard browsers. Non-validating markup might not display correctly or efficiently on mobile devices. In some cases, particularly on older mobile devices, it will cause error messages in the browser when failing to render. There are other tests that should be performed as well such as compatibility checking for image maps, measures, use of style sheets, objects or scripts, and large graphics and tables for layout.

Conclusion

The content provided on websites designed for an audience using mobile devices must try to meet all the standards of mobile Web design given their inherent limitations. Small screens bring not only convenience but also limitations when viewing sites. Thus, logical website structure and page layout will directly influence the interaction between users and mobile devices. Navigation becomes more important and it is important to note that images, frames and scripts are not recommended as bandwidth is limited and many mobile devices do not support scripts or frames. The development of successful mobile websites involves a balance between satisfying the wishes of users and ensuring designs conform to the limitations of the devices.

Notes

1. Tilak, J. (2005) European mobile devices market grew 55% in Q1, DMEurope, 13 May, *http://www.dmeurope.com/default.asp?ArticleID=7838*
2. Ferguson, D. (2002) *Mobile.NET*. New York: Springer.
3. Jones, M. and Marsden, G. (1997) 'From the large screen to the small screen – retaining the designer's design for effective user interaction', *IEEE Colloquium on Issues for Networked Interpersonal Communicators*, 139(3): 1–4.
4. Baudisch, P., Xie, X., Wang, C. and Ma, W. (2004). Collapse-to-zoom: viewing web pages on small screen devices by interactively removing irrelevant content. *Proceedings of the 17th annual ACM symposium on User interface: software and technology*. Fort Lauderdale, Fla.: ACM Press, pp. 91–4.
5. Buyukkokten, O. (2000) Power browser: efficient web browsing for PDAs. *Proceedings of the Conference on Human Factors in Computing Systems*. Fort Lauderdale, Fla.: ACM Publishers, pp. 21–32.
6. Roto, V. and Kaikkonen, A. (2003) Navigating in a mobile XHTML application. *Proceedings of the SIGCHI conference on Human factors in computing systems*. Fort Lauderdale, Fla.: ACM Publishers, pp. 329–336.
7. Kaljuvee, O., Buyukkokten, O., Garcia-molina, H. and Paepcke, A. (2001) Efficient web form entry on PDAs, *Proceedings of 10th World Wide Web Conference*, pp. 663–72.
8. Anderson, C., Domingos, P. and Weld, D. (2001) Personalizing web sites for mobile users. *Proceedings of the 10th international conference on World Wide Web*. Fort Lauderdale, Fla.: ACM Press, pp. 565–75.
9. Kaikkonen, A. and Roto, V. (2003) Perception of narrow web pages on a mobile phone. *Proceedings of the 19th International Symposium on Human Factors in Telecommunication*. Berlin: HFT Publishers, pp. 205–12.
10. Thalys.mobi
11. Preece, J. (1994) *Human Computer Interaction*. New York: Addison Wesley.
12. Jones, M., Buchanan, G., Marsden, G. and Thimbleby, H. (2000) User interfaces for mobile web devices. *WWW9 Mobile Workshop Position Paper, 9th International World Wide Web Conference*. Fort Lauderdale, Fla.: ACM Press
13. Lee, Y.E. and Benbasat, I. (2003) Interface design for mobile commerce. *Commun. ACM* 46:12, 48–52. DOI= http://doi.acm.org/10.1145/953460.953487
14. Hanrahan, R. and Merrick, R. (2004) Authoring techniques for device independence. W3C Working Group Note, *http://www.w3.org/TR/di-atdi/*
15. *http://ready.mobi*

18

Adaptive mobile applications

Conrad Deighan, Joan Condell and Kevin Curran

The area of computing incorporates a vast range of devices with different capabilities in terms of battery life, network connectivity, processing power and disk management. An endless battery life and flawless connectivity to multiple wireless access points are increasingly essential for the mobile device user. Nevertheless, battery life and the ability to connect to wireless networks vary greatly between devices. Portable multimedia devices such as PDAs and Smartphones with restricted memory will also vary greatly; however, users of these devices will expect optimal multimedia delivery. Therefore, there is need for an intelligent middleware application that will take a critical role in the coordination between hardware and software so that the user can get the full potential from the mobile device. This chapter outlines attempts to provide mobile devices with the ability to detect and respond appropriately to changes in network connectivity, network connection quality and power consumption.

Introduction

Mobile devices such as ultra mobile personal computers (UMPCs), laptops, PDAs and Smartphones are becoming an increasingly frequent element of any IT-orientated business. Business users need their applications to work just as well while on the road as they do when they are in the office. This means that developers of mobile applications face complex tasks of extending existing or developing a new range of mobile applications that target multiple platforms to meet the requirements of users in the mobile environment.[1] The Intel Mobile Software Development Kit (SDK) is an open source library which enables the creation of context-aware applications by taking advantage of the mobile features on UMPCs, notebooks and PDAs. It also allows the creation of applications with the platform and the environment in mind by leveraging information about the platform's configuration and context. This means that developers can provide more expressive interactions and better user experience for applications, especially on mobile platforms where intermittent connectivity and limited power are common issues. For instance, if applications could be aware of the platform they are running on and the environment, then they could leverage multi-core power to provide more immersive user interfaces, postpone certain tasks during low power situations, avoid network traffic over low-bandwidth/high-latency connections and delay saving files back to network drives while not connected to the network.

Currently, there are various versions of media players available for consumer use, on both mobile- and PC-based environments. Popular media players include Windows Media Player, QuickTime and Real Player. Although these media players carry out their intended functionality, playing audio and video, they lack the ability of being aware of their context. For example, they do not have the ability to inform the user if they try to retrieve a media file from an unavailable location or if they have disconnected from the power supply. The mobile environment has very limited resources compared with the traditional desktop computing environment. Applications for mobile devices have lacked innovation due to the fact that the device in which they are installed has strict limitations in terms of memory capacity, processing power and battery power compared with the desktop computer. Screen size is a challenging area for developers as most devices vary in size, therefore resulting in the need of an application being re-designed and re-coded to suit the target device. Most mobile users will use their device frequently but only for a brief amount of time and will have a different usage paradigm, i.e. for input, output, e-mail and calendar scheduling. Mobile applications must be dynamic and adapt to changes in the environment in which they exist. The application must therefore be self-organising and able to accommodate new sets of requirements and functionality when it is deployed in the context that it will exist. Mobile device users are expecting much more as technology increases. Instead of the device working for a limited time scale in restricted environments, users are now expecting developers to come up with applications that will enable them to:

- manage connections
- balance power and performance

- work offline and
- work across multiple platforms.

Users want their connections to be managed transparently where their main focal point is the task in hand without having to worry about managing a connection to one or more networks. They expect to get optimal performance from their available battery life where there is no available power source. When they are outside the range of a network or server they want to be able to locally store their data and information so they can continue to work with clients and then synchronise their data with the server when they re-connect to the network.[1] Working across multiple platforms is essential for users as they can then choose a device that suits them rather than having to use a device that they are unfamiliar with just because it has the relevant software installed.[2] When developers are either creating or extending mobile applications they face two important obstacles:

- Creating applications that are aware of platform context and resources that can efficiently adapt when changes occur. This is a new paradigm, and not well supported by current software solutions.
- Developing cross-platform and runtime solutions to enable applications to be deployed over multiple clients is challenging, given that there is no standard way to implement this functionality across a wide range of mobile devices.

Unfortunately, most people do not take into consideration the fact that the three types of devices use different software and have different screen sizes. Here developers run into problems as they need to change a great deal of code to transfer from one device to another. Therefore, a method for developing software that is aware of which device it is being implemented on would make the re-design and re-coding process significantly easier. The application would know how to adapt to the environment on which it has been implemented. Each mobile phone, PDA or Smartphone that is available to consumers has an emulator released so that applications can be developed for that device. So in order to develop a mobile application, the developer has to design and code each application to target each emulator's specification. This means developers need a common development interface with consistent naming criteria, parameters and object model so that they can minimise extensive re-coding in order to get an application operational on a range of devices.

Heterogeneity is a major problem for those developing any type of application regardless of whether it is for the mobile or desktop environment. For example, if an application was developed on a Windows platform, there could be runtime and compatibility issues if deployed into a Linux-based environment. The interoperability of current devices remains largely untapped due to the fact that heterogeneity exists. This means that devices with different contexts cannot operate and communicate effectively and efficiently with each other. In order for these devices to interoperate with each other, developers must come up with a solution that will make this possible. A middleware layer primarily hides the underlying complexity of the environment by insulating the applications from explicit protocol handling, disjoint memories, data replication, network faults and parallelism. Moreover, it masks the heterogeneity of computer architectures, operating systems, programming languages and networking technologies to facilitate application programming and management.[3] Previous middleware projects include Gaia,[4] M3 system[5] and Aura[6] for efficient ubiquitous computing. The Gaia project aims to make physical spaces such as homes and buildings intelligent. The M3 system uses a component-based modelling paradigm and employs an event-based mechanism that provides significant flexibility in dynamic system configuration and adaptation. The Aura project aims to provide the user with a distraction-free computing environment and minimise intrusion of systems. CORBA (Common Object Request Broker Architecture) enables applications to dynamically select the components that best met their requirements and to verify that the requirements are appropriate for the services that are in use. CORBA is a trading service to support dynamic component selection. An extensive monitoring facility within CORBA supports the use of dynamically defined requirements.

The fact that a mobile device must be aware of its power and network connectivity status is no secret to developers and users of these devices. This chapter documents an adaptable middleware architecture that allows high flexibility by probing a platform's configuration, e.g. display, storage and processor, and its context, e.g. bandwidth, connectivity, power and location, within a mobile application. A challenge in distributed system design is to cope with the dynamic nature of the execution environment. If mobile applications could be made aware of the platform they are running on and the environment they exist within then they could detect and respond appropriately to changes in network connectivity, network connection quality and power consumption optimisation and more easily handle intermittent connectivity. Middleware applications stress modularity, which encourages decoupling of applications into modules. By incorporating these runtime and libraries into mobile applications will still enable them to have minimal footprint and small impact on system resources, which is a must if they are to be implemented onto PDAs and Smartphones.

Dynamic mobile applications

We have become accustomed to a computation model in which applications require only a single or a small number of devices. One distinct characteristic of ubiquitous computing, however, is the attempt to break away from the traditional desktop interaction paradigm, making computational power available to the end-user whenever and wherever possible. Furthermore, ubiquitous computing involves a wide range of devices of different capabilities in terms of processing power, screen display, input facilities, middleware, and network connectivity of various wired and wireless links. Among them, middleware takes a crucial role, consisting of remote procedure call, file service and directory service, reflecting dramatic advances in hardware technology, fast networking, and workstation systems. A middleware layer primarily hides the underlying sophistication of the environment by insulating the applications. Recently, applications (desktop- and web-based) have been moving from the static environment to a more dynamic adaptive one. An adaptive application has the ability to predict changes in context and automatically handle these changes in a runtime environment without the need for a programmer. It would be classed as a component-based middleware, where the middleware can reorganise components by insulating the application. Non-adaptive software can also be described as 'fragile', if it is used outside the context in which it was developed. One of the key factors with developing software is that it can be an expensive and a time-consuming process. This is the main objective behind dynamic applications as the software can adapt to the non-functional requirements of their components and reconfigure in real-time. With this objective met, an application can be re-used and not require any time-consuming re-write to meet a new set of requirements.

If an application has not been specifically designed for the mobile environment the mobile user may be disappointed. An example of this would be excessive power that the system needs when running on a battery power source. This will decrease the length of time that a device can be used in between battery charges. Another example is long running or power-hungry operations such as writing to a CD or DVD when power is low. By using intelligent adaptation in applications, we could, for instance, suspend non-critical operations or processes whenever the device is running on a battery power supply. The main problem with applications is that they are not developed to save system power and suspend non-critical processes when running on battery power and then continue the operation when the device is connected to an AC power supply. In order to add this functionality into the application without asking the operating system for power connection status we need to bypass the operating system.

Managing resources such as runtime and platform state changes is vital on mobile devices. Therefore, we need to efficiently manage these resources and adapt applications to act on these changes. With the use of some kind of intelligent middleware these programs can become aware of their context and adapt elegantly to the change. For example, if a mobile application was developed specifically for a mobile device then in order to get the application fully functional on other devices there would be a need for re-coding of the application. The need to re-design and re-code the application would be necessary as these two devices are not similar in terms of screen size, memory, processing speed and battery power. This would result in the user not getting the full functionality and potential from the application. This is why developers need to access information regarding the target device so that it can elegantly adapt to the context of the device. Developers need a common environment to develop applications that can self-manage and adapt effectively to changes in platform context and take advantage of the capabilities of the runtime platform.

Screen size can vary from device to device; therefore, if mobile applications are not aware of the device that they are going to be deployed on, the user's application may become unusable because the application does not complement the display of the target device. Incorporating tools from the Intel Mobile SDK will enable an application to retrieve the target device's screen information, process that information and then adapt the application to meet that size of display.[7]

Modern mobile systems such as laptops and UMPCs are equipped with multi-core processors. Processing power has thus doubled, so in turn we need applications that can take advantage of the extra cores. This is why developers would need to access information regarding the processor of the target device so that the application can adapt to the processor that is available (i.e. single core, dual core and quad core). Intelligent middleware between device and application can redesign the application to take advantage of the extra available cores. For example, if an application was developed for a single core processor and then deployed onto a multi-core processing device, it would only take advantage of one of the available cores. In this case, the middleware would redesign the application and take advantage of the multiple cores and result in processing time being decreased.

There is also a need for applications to be designed specifically for the mobile environment as most mobile applications require a steady connection to remote resources to access information. This is where there is a clear need for network connections to be managed seamlessly. If applications are not designed for the mobile world then the user will have to manually manage their network connections in order for their application to run. Some applications may require a 'restart' in order to become functional again if these connections are not managed.

Energy-aware processors are now being manufactured that can tackle the problem of power consumption; these processors will be designed to consume much less power than that of a normal processor. Intel's XScale[8] architecture has been designed to optimise on low power consumption; XScale has become a major building block of Intel's PCA architecture. SpeedStep is a technology that enables the processor to drop to a lower frequency and voltage while still maintaining a high level of performance, resulting in the conserving of battery life.[9] Software application techniques are becoming more significant for power management on mobile devices. Ellis states that the gains from a high-level power management level are significant at the application level as well as at the operating system level.[10] With the advancements of these energy-aware processors developers can enhance their applications to take advantage of the power-saving techniques included. This will result in the hardware and software becoming power aware and giving a longer battery life to the mobile device.

Managing resources such as battery power, screen size, hard disk and connectivity is essential on mobile devices as each has a unique specifications. This can result in the need for applications to be re-designed and re-coded to manage resources differently. As mobile devices have certain limitations compared with the desktop PC, there is a need for their resources to be managed far more efficiently. This is where the application must monitor the resources and change state when necessary in order to get the full potential from the device. In order for more mobile applications to become aware of their context and available resources there must be some sort of active middleware to communicate efficiently between the application and the device. The Intel Mobile SDK will play a major role in the development of new applications as it can effectively manage and adapt applications where necessary.

Intel Mobile SDK

The Intel Mobile SDK version 1.2 is a free open-source library which enables the development of applications which attempt to overcome the mobile features of mobile devices. The Intel SDK comprises multiple libraries and runtime components with a built-in interface which is familiar to programmers across various supported platforms. The Intel Mobile SDK would also be similar to object-orientated languages as its main aim is to maximise code reuse with the feature of mobility in mind. When developing applications for mobile devices, developers must take connectivity into consideration. In theory, users want 100% connectivity. Unfortunately, this is unrealistic in the real world, and therefore applications must have the ability to determine the current status of connectivity and make a decision based on any change in circumstances.[11]

The most significant feature of the Intel Mobile SDK is that it facilitates software functionality with mobile devices. Mobile device users expect their applications to adapt whenever they leave the office in order to get the same type of performance and power combined as they would whilst in the office. The effective balance of power and performance, the ability to work across multiple platforms, the adaptation of screen types and the ability to manage network connectivity and bandwidth within mobile devices and applications are major areas in which developers must tap into.[7]

Figure 18.1 demonstrates the context awareness area of the mobile device that Intel Mobile SDK provides and manages. The Intel Mobile SDK supports the development of context-aware mobile applications via the use a of multi-platform and multi-runtime development kit. The Intel SDK supports three different object-orientated development languages: C++, C#.NET and Java. With the addition of the Intel Mobile SDK libraries incorporated into one of these development environments, developers have the ability to develop context-aware mobile applications without the burden of having to gain knowledge of a new development environment.

Figure 18.2 demonstrates where the middleware layer is situated between the application programming interface and the platform interface so that applications can communicate with each platform's interface. With the availability of the Intel Mobile SDK developers can include an active middleware into a new range of applications to combat the heterogeneity aspects of the mobile environment. To run the Intel

Figure 18.1 Overview of the Intel SDK

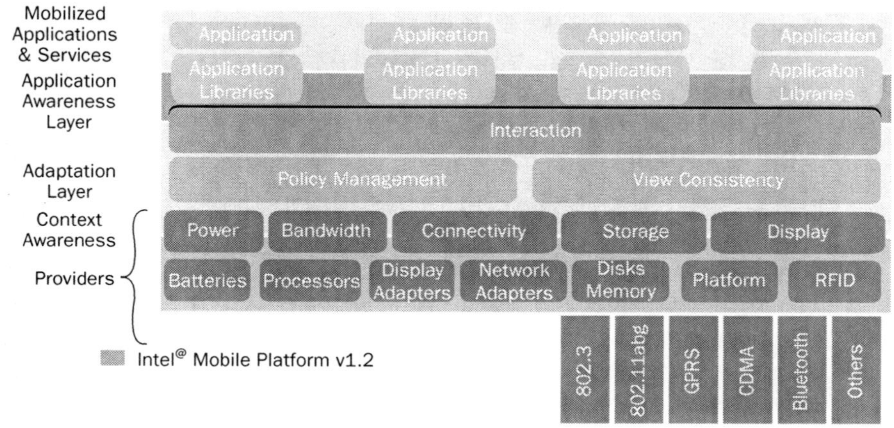

Mobilized Applications & Services

Application Awareness Layer

Adaptation Layer

Context Awareness

Providers

Application

Application Libraries

Interaction

Policy Management

View Consistency

Power   Bandwidth   Connectivity   Storage   Display

Batteries   Processors   Display Adapters   Network Adapters   Disks Memory   Platform   RFID

Intel® Mobile Platform v1.2

802.3   802.11abg   GPRS   CDMA   Bluetooth   Others

(softwarecommunity.intel.com/articles/eng/1164.htm)

Figure 18.2 Use of Middleware

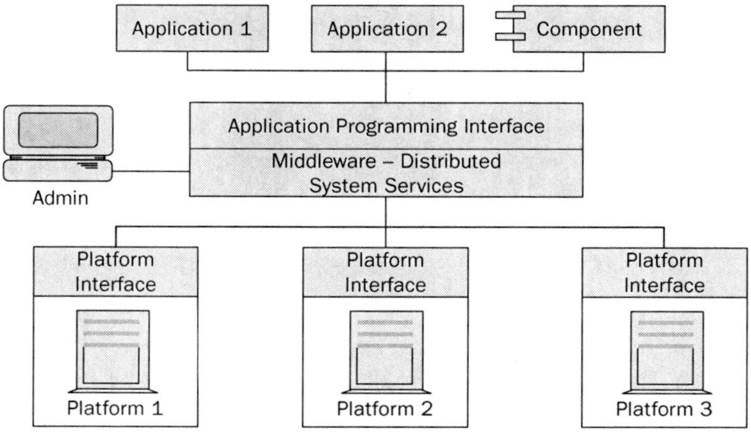

Application 1   Application 2   Component

Admin

Application Programming Interface

Middleware – Distributed System Services

Platform Interface   Platform Interface   Platform Interface

Platform 1   Platform 2   Platform 3

(softwarecommunity.intel.com/articles/eng/1164.htm)

SDK system, laptops and UMPCs need additional software such as the .NET Framework and the Intel Mobile Platform SDK. PDAs and Smartphones will need the .NET Compact Framework and the Intel Mobile Platform SDK installed. There is generally a two-tier architecture approach to developing the system which identifies each layer with its own distinct properties and functionality.

- *Client.* Users will use the windows-based application and be able to select from available media.

- *Application.* The middle layer will provide a service that will enable the mobile device to reach its full potential of battery life and connectivity status.

Conclusion

With technological advancements in the world of computing, mobile devices are becoming smaller, faster and more powerful; they are also becoming increasingly popular. There is consequently a gap in the market for a new range of mobile applications – applications built with mobility as the main objective. There are, at present, few development environments available to build this new range of applications needed for the mobile world. We have documented here the Intel Mobile SDK, which can save power and dynamically allow applications to adapt themselves to deal seamlessly with the context in which they exist. If these features can be targeted and dealt with appropriately, mobile devices can be just as powerful as, if not more powerful than, the traditional desktop computer. Applications on mobile platforms are becoming more popular and are being used more frequently used with mobile device users. However, if the applications are not correctly managed and aware of the environment in which they exist, this can lead to problems where intermittent connectivity and power sources are limited to the user. In order for developers to resolve this problem they must use a common application–program interface that can monitor the device and applications so that it can address these problems and deal with them efficiently.

Notes

1. Intel (2007) Making applications aware of their mobile contexts using the Intel® Mobile Platform SDK, *http://softwarecommunity.intel.com/articles/eng/1457.htm*
2. ISN – Intel Software Network (2005) Introducing the Intel Mobile Platform Software Development Kit (Intel Mobile Platform), *http://cache-www.intel.com/cd/00/00/20/47/204798_204798.pdf*
3. Bernstein Philip, A. (1996) Middleware: a model for distributed services. *Communications of the ACM* 39:2, 86–97. *http://www.sei.cmu.edu/str/descriptions/middleware.html*

4. Román, M., Hess, C., Cerqueira, R., Ranganathan, A., Campbell, R. and Nahrstedt, K. (2002) 'A middleware infrastructure for active spaces', *IEEE Pervasive Computing*, 1:4, 74–83.

5. BEA (1998) BEA begins shipping BEA M3 middleware on schedule to enterprise customers worldwide, *http://www.bea.com/framework.jsp? CNT=pr00137.htm&FP=/content/news_events/press_releases/1998*

6. Harkes, A. (2000) Real time distributed objects for interactive multimedia, *http://www.cs.cmu.edu/~auraRT/*

7. ISN - Intel Software Network (2007) Mobile Platform Software Development Kit – an open source project for Windows and Linux, *http://softwarecommunity. intel.com/articles/eng/1331.htm*

8. IST (2000) Intel XScale Technology, *http://www.intel.com/design/intelxscale*

9. Intel PCA (2008) Intel PCA Developer Network, *http://www.intel.com/ support/processors/sb/cs-028855.htm*

10. Ellis, C., Lebeck, A. and Vahdat, A. (1999) *System support for energy management in mobile and embedded workloads: A white paper*. Tech. rep., Duke University, Department of Computer Science.

11. Chabukswar, R. (2007) Intel® Mobile Platform SDK: monitor connectivity status, *http://softwarecommunity.intel.com/articles/eng/1111.htm*

19

Cryptography

Kevin Curran, Niall Smyth and Brian McGrory

One of the main methods of security is cryptography – encrypting data so that only a person with the right key can decrypt and make sense of the data. There are many forms of encryption, some more effective than others. This chapter discusses a little of the history of cryptography, some popular encryption methods and also some of the issues regarding encryption, such as government restrictions.

Introduction

The history of cryptography dates back to the early twentieth century, when various devices and aids where used for encryption. During World War II, several mechanical devices were invented for performing encryption, including rotor machines, most notably the Enigma cipher. The ciphers implemented by these machines brought about a significant increase in the complexity of cryptanalysis. The art of cryptography, however, can be traced back as far as 1900 BC when an Egyptian scribe used a derivation of hieroglyphics to communicate. Through history many people have been responsible for the growth of cryptography. Julius Caesar used a method based on a simple substitution of characters. Another historical figure who used and changed cryptography was Thomas Jefferson. He developed a wheel cipher in 1790, and this was then used to create the Strip cipher, which was used by the US Navy during World War II. Encryption methods have historically been divided into two categories: substitution ciphers and transposition ciphers. Substitution ciphers preserve the order of the plaintext symbols but disguise them. Transposition ciphers, in contrast, reorder the letters but do not disguise them.[1] Plaintext is the common term for the original text of a message before it has been encrypted. What is possibly the earliest encryption method was developed by a Greek historian of the 2nd century BC named Polybius, and is a type of substitution cipher.[2] This method worked with the idea of a translation table containing the letters of the Greek alphabet. Figure 19.1 shows an example of such a table using English letters.

This was used for sending messages by torch telegraphy. The sender would have ten torches, five for each hand. He would send the message letter by letter, holding the number of torches representing the row of the letter in his left hand, and the number of torches representing the column of the letter in his right hand. For example, in the case of the letter 'x', the sender would hold three torches in his left hand and four in his right hand. Polybius wrote that 'this method was invented by Cleoxenus and Democritus but it was enhanced by me.'[3] This method, although simple, was an effective way of encrypting telegraphic messages. The table could easily be changed without changing the method, so as long as both the sender and the receiver were using the same table and no one else had the table they could send messages that anyone could see being sent but which would only be understood by the intended recipient. This is a form of private key encryption – where both the sender and the recipient share the key to the encrypted messages. In this case the key is the letter table.

Another type of substitution cipher is the Caesar cipher, which is attributed to Julius Caesar.[1] In this method, the alphabet is shifted by a certain number of letters, this number being represented by k. For example, where k is 3, the letter A would be replaced with D, B would be replaced with E, Z would be replaced with C, etc. This is also a form of private key encryption, where the value of k must be known to decrypt the message. This simple form of encryption is clearly not difficult to

Figure 19.1 Translation table containing the letters of the Greek alphabet

	1	2	3	4	5
1	S	Y	D	W	Z
2	R	I	P	U	L
3	H	C	A	X	F
4	T	N	O	G	E
5	B	K	M	Q	

crack, with only 26 possible values of k; it is only a matter of shifting the encrypted message with values of k until you get a comprehensible decrypted message. There are also more complex methods of cracking such encryption, such as using letter frequency statistics to work out likely letters from the message – for example, 'e' is the most commonly used letter in the English language, so the most common letter in the encrypted message is likely to be 'e'. Replacing the most common letters in the encrypted message with the most commonly used letters of the language may help to make sense of some words. Once a word is partially decrypted, it may be easy to guess what the word is, which will then allow more letters to be substituted with their decrypted versions. For example if 'e' and 't' had been used to replace the most common letters and one of the partially decrypted words is 'tXe', then the X is likely to be h forming the word 'the', so replacing all occurrences of 'X' in the message with 'h' may provide additional words which can be guessed easily.

Cryptanalysis is the study of methods to obtain the plaintext of encrypted information without access to the key that is usually required to decrypt. In layman's terms it is the practice of code breaking or cracking code. Cryptanalysis is defined as the analysis and deciphering of cryptographic writings/systems, or the branch of cryptography concerned with decoding encrypted messages. Cryptanalysts are the natural adversary of cryptographers, in that a cryptographer works to protect or secure information and a cryptanalyst works to read data that have been encrypted. However, they also complement each other; without cryptanalysts or an understanding of the cryptanalysis process it would be very difficult to create secure cryptography. So when designing a new cryptogram it is common to use cryptanalysis in order to find and correct any weaknesses in the algorithm. Most cryptanalysis techniques exploit patterns found in the plaintext code in order to crack the cipher; however, compression of the data can reduce these patterns and hence improve resistance to cryptanalysis.

Popular encryption methods

Cryptography works by taking the original information and converting it via ciphertext, which encrypts the information to an unreadable form. To decrypt the information we simply do the opposite and decipher the unreadable information back into plaintext. This enciphering and deciphering of information is done using an algorithm called a cipher. A cipher is, put simply, a secret code, but the main difference between using a secret code and a cipher is that a secret code will only work at a level of meaning. This basically means that the secret code could be made up with the same letters and words but just rearranged to mean something else. Ciphers work differently; they can target individual bits or individual letters and design a totally unrecognisable representation of the original document. Another interesting thing about ciphers is that they are usually accompanied by the use of a key. Depending on the type of key, different forms of encryption can be carried out; without the key the cipher would be unable to encrypt or decrypt.[4]

One-time pads

The traditional forms of encryption discussed above can be broken by someone who knows what to look for, but there is another method known as the one-time pad that can create unbreakable encrypted messages. One time pads (OTP) are unconditionally secure encryption systems. This means that one cannot break them with any amount of compute time. One of the reasons, however, that they are not used more widely is that in order to use a OTP, pads have to be traded with each person and the system will critically depend on the randomness of the pad and on keeping the pad secret. A random bit string is used as the key and the message to be encrypted is then converted into a bit string, for example by using codes for each character in the message. Then the EXCLUSIVE OR of these two strings is calculated, bit by bit. For example, take the key to be '0100010' and the message to be 'A'. The ASCII code for 'A' is 1000001. The resulting one-time pad would be '1100011'.

A one-time padded message cannot be broken, because every possible plaintext message is an equally probably candidate.[1] The message can only be decrypted by someone who knows the correct key. There are certain disadvantages to this. First, the key must be at least as long as the bit string to be encrypted. As the key will be a long random bit string, it would be very difficult to memorise, so both the sender and the receiver will need written copies of the key, and having written copies of keys is a security risk if there is any chance of the key falling into the wrong hands. Also, if the sender and the recipient both have a previously agreed key to use, the sender will be limited as they will not be able to send a message too long for the key. With computer systems, the one-time pad method is more useful, as the key can be stored digitally on, for example, a CD and can therefore be extremely long and relatively easy to disguise.

DES

IBM developed a method of encryption known as the data encryption standard (DES), which was adopted by the US Government as its official standard for unclassified information in 1977. The standard 'is no longer secure in its original form, but in a modified form it is still useful.'[1] When IBM originally developed DES, they called it Lucifer, and it used a 128-bit key. The NSA (National Security Agency) discussed the system with IBM, and after these discussions IBM reduced the key from 128 bits to 56 bits before the government adopted the standard. Many people suspected that the key was reduced so that the NSA would be able to break DES on encrypted data that they wished to view, but organisations with smaller budgets would not be able to.[1] It was also suspected that IBM kept the design of DES secret to hide a trapdoor which could make it even easier for the NSA to break DES.[5]

As with all forms of encryption, it is possible to break DES encryption by means of a brute-force approach, where a computer is used to attempt to decrypt the data using possible keys one after the other until the correct key is found. Owing to the constant increase in computer processing power, it becomes faster to break DES encryption with every passing year. The key size of DES is no longer large enough for it to stand up to brute-force attacks long enough to make the attacks pointless, so in its original form DES is no longer safe for use. Many other encryption methods which work on similar principles to DES have since been proposed, including IDEA (international data encryption algorithm), which uses a 128-bit key and is still safe from brute-force attacks due to the length of time required to find the correct key from the huge key space.

All of the encryption methods discussed so far have been private key methods – they depend on data being encrypted with a key known both to the sender and to the recipient. This means that an unencrypted key must somehow be transferred between the sender and the recipient, and finding a secure method of doing that can present a problem in many situations. For example, there is no point in encrypting an email to a business partner, and then emailing him the encryption key, as this defeats the purpose of making the original email secure. Next we discuss another type of encryption which solves this problem – known as public key encryption.

Public key encryption

The idea of public key cryptography was first presented by Martin Hellman, Ralph Merkle and Whitfield Diffie at Stanford University in

1976.[2] They proposed a method in which the encryption and decryption keys were different, and in which the decryption key could not be determined using the encryption key. Using such a system, the encryption key could be given out publicly, as only the intended recipient would have the decryption key to make sense of it. A common use of this system is for a person to give out a public key to anyone who wishes to send them private information, keeping their private key to themselves. Of course, the encryption algorithm will also need to be public. There are three important requirements for a public key encryption method:

1. When the decryption process is applied to the encrypted message, the result must be the same as the original message before it was encrypted.

2. It must be exceedingly difficult (ideally impossible) to deduce the decryption (private) key from the encryption (public) key.

3. The encryption must not be able to be broken by a plaintext attack. As the encryption and decryption algorithms and the encryption key will be public, people attempting to break the encryption will be able to experiment with the algorithms to attempt to find any flaws in the system.

The RSA algorithm

One popular method for public key encryption was discovered by a group at MIT in 1978, and was named after the initials of the three members of the group: Ron Rivest, Adi Shamir and Leonard Adleman.[1] Shortly before the details of RSA encryption were to be published, the US government reportedly 'asked' the inventors to cancel the publication. However, copies of the article had already reached the public – A. K. Dewdney of *Scientific American* had a photocopy of the document explaining the algorithm, and more photocopies of this quickly spread. The RSA algorithm was patented by MIT, and this patent was then handed over to a company in California called Public Key Partners (PKP). PKP hold the exclusive commercial licence to sell and to sub-license the RSA public key cryptosystem. They also hold other patents which cover other public key cryptography algorithms. This gives them absolute control over who may legally use public key cryptography in the US and Canada.[6] Since the RSA patent was not applied for until after publication of the algorithm, the patents are only valid within the US and Canada.

There is a recognised method of breaking RSA encryption based on factoring numbers involved, although this can be safely ignored due to the huge amount of time required to factor large numbers. Unfortunately, RSA is too slow for encrypting large amounts of data, so it is often used for encrypting the key used in a private key method, such as IDEA. This key can then be transferred in public securely, resolving the key security problem for IDEA.

The knapsack algorithm

This algorithm was invented by Merkle and Hellman, who first proposed the idea of public key encryption, in 1978. The idea is that someone owns a large number of objects, each with a different weight. The owner encodes the message by secretly selecting a subset of the objects and placing them in the knapsack. The total weight of the objects in the knapsack is made public, as is the list of all possible objects. The list of objects in the knapsack is kept secret. With certain additional restrictions, the problem of figuring out a possible list of objects with the given weight was thought to be computationally infeasible, and formed the basis of the public key algorithm.[1] It was subsequently found not to be computationally infeasible, as when Merkle offered a $100 reward to anyone who could break the encryption, Adi Shamir (one of the inventors of RSA) did so and collected the reward. After strengthening the algorithm, Merkle offered a $1000 reward to anyone who could break this, and Ron Rivest (another of the inventors of RSA) did so and also collected the reward. Merkle offered no further rewards. Although the algorithm was strengthened again, it is not regarded as secure and is not used widely.

Pretty good privacy

Published for free on the Internet in 1991, PGP (pretty good privacy) was a public key email encryption software package. It was originally designed by Philip R. Zimmermann as a human rights tool, allowing human rights activists to protect sensitive information from prying eyes.[7] At the time of its development there were laws against the export of cryptography software from the US, so when PGP spread worldwide after its release on the Internet, Zimmermann came under criminal investigation. Despite this, PGP spread to become the most widely used email encryption software in the world. PGP used a combination of IDEA and RSA encryption to allow emails to be transferred securely under public key encryption. There were, however, some disputes over patent issues. As mentioned earlier, PKP were the patent holders for the

RSA algorithms. PKP, however, avoided legal action – they did threaten Zimmermann, but did not actually take action. They did refuse to license RSA for use in PGP, until MIT (the original patent holders) forced them to license MIT PGP 2.6. Another US company named ViaCrypt licensed the RSA algorithm from PKP, and were then able to sell a fully legal version of PGP using RSA. MIT later released their own version of PGP, and PKP threatened them with a lawsuit, but MIT refused to give in, and later distributed a legal freeware version of the program.[6] Eventually in 1996 the US government dropped its case against Zimmermann, and he then founded PGP Inc. to continue development of the software. PGP Inc. bought ViaCrypt and began to publish new versions of PGP. PGP Corp. carries on the tradition of publishing the source code of their software for peer review so that customers and cryptography experts may validate the integrity of the products, and satisfy themselves that there are no back doors in the software allowing easy decryption.[8]

Conclusion

Cryptography is a powerful tool, both for keeping important information private and, when in the wrong hands, for keeping illegal activities hidden from government agencies. As computers grow faster and methods for breaking encryption become more viable, encryption algorithms will need to be constantly strengthened to stop them becoming insecure. There is little that can be done about the usage of cryptography to keep illegal activities hidden – short of making all forms of strong encryption illegal, which would create outrage in Western countries used to freedom in such matters, and would still not guarantee that usage of strong encryption would stop. It is a problem that may become increasingly pertinent; with more criminal and terrorist groups making use of encryption, no easy solution is currently visible.

Notes

1. Tannenbaum, A. (1996) *Computer Networks*, 3rd edn. New York: Prentice Hall.
2. Burgess, J., Pattison, E. and Goksel, M. (2000) Public Key Cryptography. Stanford University. *http://cse.stanford.edu/classes/sophomore-college/projects-97/cryptography/history.html*

3. Dénes, T. (2002) Cardan and cryptography – The mathematics of encryption grids. Hungary. *http://www.komal.hu/lap/2002-ang/cardano.e.shtml*

4. *http://en.wikipedia.org/wiki/Cryptography#Terminology*

5. Denning, D. (1996) Comments on the NRC Cryptography Report. *http://www.cs.georgetown.edu/~denning/crypto/NRC.txt*

6. Menage, M. (1994) Pretty Good Privacy – Legal Issues. *http://193.125.152.107/pub/msdos/crypto/pgp/pgp-legal/*

7. PGP Corporation. (2005) PGP Corporation Source Code. Silicon Valley, California. *http://www.pgp.com/downloads/sourcecode/index.html*

8. Zimmermann, P. (2004) Philip Zimmermann – Creator of PGP. Silicon Valley, California. *http://www.philzimmermann.*

20

Honeynets

Kevin Curran and Mairead Feeney

Worms, viruses, denial of service and many other varieties of attacks are an everyday occurrence that are putting pressure on today's security professional to prevent or minimise their impact. There is a requirement for real-time systems to analyse the data we receive and examine the contents for possible malware contents. The possibility of using such a function would aid an organisation in detecting inconsistencies in data and function as a potential early-warning system that an attack could be imminent. A honeypot provides one such solution. It is a enticing server that lures the hacker under the pretence of infiltrating a susceptible server, but instead of the hacker gathering the spoils the 'queen bee' gathers 'honey' in the form of information from the hacker. It is this information that provides the vital clues as to what services, ports and potential security holes the hacker is attacking and in doing so allows security personnel to ring-fence those areas in the production environment.

Introduction

Law enforcers are being confronted with the increased need to investigate crime perpetrated through the use of the Internet or some other electronic media. The need to be able to access, trace, interrogate and retrieve information from any electronic device has become a sought after expertise by both law enforcers and commercial organisations alike as both are keen to build up a portfolio of evidence to help either solve crimes that have been committed or pre-empt potential crimes or identify weaknesses before they occur. Intrusion is any action that attempts to compromise the integrity, confidentiality or availability of a resource.[1]

Intrusion can be caused by individuals from both outside and inside an organisation. We commonly assume when in conversation that intruder means outsider but in fact the intruder from within the organisation poses a much greater threat. They may have access to confidential security data such as passwords or be aware of known vulnerabilities that exist within the computer systems. To this end they can land more deadly blows. Intruder knowledge and sophistication each year is expanding, thanks in part to the large number of tools at their disposal. All organisations have security policies in place to help combat intruders, such as logical access, audit trails, firewalls, authentication, and the use of encryption and decryption. These techniques are not enough, however, and with the new release of every computer application there will always be bugs and vulnerabilities that will give hackers the back door means of entry to our systems. For many years, intrusion detection systems have been employed by organisations but these systems have limitations as will be discussed below. It is only in medium to large organisations that we can find dedicated security administrators. In most companies, security may be just one of many tasks on a person's work schedule. As a result, administrators may find themselves consistently playing catch up with the hacker who has only one task. Many organisations are turning to honeynet technology to supplement or help fortify their computer systems by providing the means to be proactive in restraining the intruder rather than reacting to the consequences of the attacker's actions.

The history of honeynets

Honeynets are the brain child of the Honeynet project.[2] This organisation is a not-for-profit, dedicated volunteer research body, whose aim is to raise awareness and gain insight into Internet computer security through research into the threats and vulnerabilities. The Honeynet project was originally founded by 30 US-based security professionals and today is a worldwide organisation with honey project groups in all five continents. All of these groups share the same goals of raising awareness, providing accurate and timely information and providing open source tools to help organisations and individuals better protect their computer environment. In Ireland a Honeynet project was founded in March 2002 and is sponsored by Deloitte and Espion Ltd. The purpose of this venture was to track and analyse the behaviour of hackers in Ireland and those from other countries. Armed with this information they can keep the Irish

Internet community aware of the tools, techniques and advances of the hacker community and in response better prepare individuals when hackers try and strike.

A honeynet is a network of honeypots. A honeypot is a system that is purposely built to attract hackers and analyse how they try to compromise computer systems. A honeypot can provide any systems administrator with alerts to potential vulnerabilities or misconfigurations within their computer systems. A honeypot is an information systems resource whose value lies in unauthorised or illicit use of that resource.[3] When a computer system is attacked, the user jumps into reactive mode, trying to minimise the amount of damage that could potentially be done. The user does not have time to analyse the system to investigate how this attack was instigated. Using a honeypot allows us watch or monitor any advances towards our systems from hackers and patch any vulnerabilities they may find before our production machines are compromised. A honeypot is like a mousetrap – anything you catch in it is a problem.[4] A honeynet can replicate any type of system, which helps to fool the hacker into believing they are accessing a live production area. A honeypot can be anything you want it to be; it can be a decoy to attract a hacker's attention away from your production system or it can be a learning tool which will allow you analyse the motives of a hacker and use this information to better protect the systems of the future.

Intrusion detection systems (IDSs) provide a common method of vetting whether a computer system has been compromised. These systems work in two ways. First, anomaly-based IDSs compare current behaviour against what was observed in the past and noted as usual activity. If there are any anomalies between the two an alert it raised to notify whoever is in charge of a possible attack in progress. This functionality can lead to many false positives. The second main type of IDS is a signature-based system, where rules are setup and allow identification of known attacks. The problem here is that we then can only recognise an attack if we have a signature to identify it. Honeynets are not seen as a replacement for IDSs but a supplement to help boost their defences. A honeynet sits, scans and logs all traffic coming past its door. The honeynet is only used for this purpose so any activity on the honeynet can immediately be treated as suspicious. In a production environment there can be a vast amount of data traffic moving across a network at any one moment, making it nearly impossible to sort manually the good from the bad. Honeynets can serve to make threats more visible, to act as an early alarm system, giving a company a more proactive approach to security. We need to be able to close the door before any unwelcome guests arrive.

Intrusion detection systems

IDSs are computer-based programs that are designed to scan computer systems for evidence of intrusion. False positives are the main limitation of IDSs. Owing to their very nature IDSs tend to raise many false alarms. If systems are weakened to reduce the number of false positives this in turn opens up systems to a greater number of attacks. IDSs do not provide not a 100% infallible means of detection. Attacks can still occur undetected. These are called false negatives. IDSs are required to monitor and analyse traffic in real time. If there is a large amount of traffic this can lead to systems performance levels being lowered and packets being dropped.

The use of IDSs has provided the traditional approach to detect unwelcome guests on a computer system and there are many different models or schemas that can be used. Such systems can be rule based, signature based or just based on trying to detect behaviour that can be observed or categorised as not normal. Using this method alone can lead to a few red herrings and too little caviar. Honeynets add a new dimension to the area of intrusion detection; they are not a replacement technology for traditional methods but rather a supplement, an extra layer of security, a little bit of honey on the toast. Honeynets are a proactive step that aim to highlight potential threats before they strike. A honeynet or honeypot can bring extra beneficial information to computer systems personnel. The amount of traffic that traverses a network cannot feasibly be monitored by IT personnel in the hope of spotting malicious content or activity. A honeypot can watch, listen and report anything dubious to the security administrator, leaving them free to carry out other important tasks. A security administrator can put firewalls in place or close certain ports to eliminate or severely hamper the chance of an attack. This may stop the attack from happening but what does the systems administrator learn? They do not know the reason for a potential attack or what the intent of the attacker was or what methods they used and how they failed to gain admittance. A honeypot can carry out all of these actions. A honeypot can be sent on a reconnaissance mission to infiltrate the enemy and bring back intelligence.

Honeypots can be classified into two categories, namely those that are set up purely to aid research and gain intelligence and those that are sitting on a live network surrounded by many other production servers. The concept of a honeypot was borne to aid research and, among many others, this is still the main objective. Here the focus is on intelligence gathering and learning the technology and methods used by hackers. Production honeypots are used for a duel purpose, first as an early warning system that an attack may be imminent or that suspect traffic as been encountered, and second as bait to distract the hacker from the production system – lure the hacker to the honeypot where information can be collected and in parallel keep the hacker away from the real production machines. Depending on the purpose of the honeypot deployment, research or production, different levels can be used. If placed in a production environment, a high interaction honeypot is used. If research is of primary interest, a low interaction honeypot will serve instead.

Botnets

Malware is one of the biggest problems facing the Internet community today, especially if it has been constructed specifically to destroy. Hackers are even more interested in gaining access to computer systems using back doors and by controlling systems from a distance. A network of nodes controlled by a hacker is called a botnet. A botnet is a set of machines networked together using programs using a common Command and Control infrastructure.[5] Attackers scan networks, especially Class B (128–191 address range) networks, for vulnerabilities in applications such as Internet Explorer, misconfigured or vulnerabilities in the firewall or non-updated security patches. Once a machine is located they install an IRC (Internet relay chat) bot on the machine. This allows for real-time communication with the machine.[6] Various forms of IRC bots are in existence and they are becoming ever more complex. The bot opens a link with a specified IRC channel on an IRC server and awaits commands to be issued by the hacker. Hackers can join many and distributed bots together to form a botnet. As a consequence of the potential of hackers to form huge botnets, this could pose serious threats, such as distributed denial of service attacks (DDos). According to the Alliance Research paper, even if a botnet comprises only 1000 bots (1000 home PCs with an average upstream of 128 kb can offer more than 100 Mb) their combined bandwidth can be larger than that of an Internet connection of most corporate systems.[6]

An attack of this nature can be difficult to resolve as many machines belonging to several organisations may be involved. The German Honeynet project analysed traffic and results showed that machines using Windows operating systems carried the highest number of targets, totalling 80%. The most common attacks were:

- Port 445/TCP – used for resource sharing in Windows 2000+.
- Port 139/TCP – NetBIOS session service; as with Port 445, this port is used for resource sharing.
- Port 137/UDP – provides information on network devices such as system name and name of file shares
- Port 135/TCP – implement RPC. A remote procedure call (RPC) allows a computer program running on one machine to execute code on another host.

Honeynets are an emerging technology and the law surrounding them is also evolving. One of the main issues is that of honeynet operation liability. Some argue that it is negligence on the part of the operator to fully secure their system that results in attacks; in the case of honeypots we deliberately facilitate the misuse of the machine in question.[7] The approach taken by the majority of honeypot operators is to lure potential attackers to their system, inviting them in. The bait is given in the hope of learning the behaviour of hackers so that the Internet community can better protect itself. A further ethical quandary is that we are acting as a big brother to the hacker, inviting them in and watching their tactics under laboratory conditions. Dornseif *et al.* make a comparison with other real-life situations where it is generally unacceptable to carry out experiments on non-consenting adults.[7] Ethics remainn for the particular organisation involved. Ethics are often fostered from the legal implications that might ensue once an action is taken, so legal obligations or consequences can colour ethical behaviour. In Germany, to be liable for the actions of an attacker using your honeypot to attack others the legal system most prove that there was the intent on the part of the organisation to attack the third party. The law also comes down on the side of the honeypot operator as regards liability for damages. The operator cannot be made liable as long as they have put some measure in place, such as limiting outward connections to prevent attacker misuse. Although these measures may not be totally secure, the fact that they have been attempted to restrain an attacker's activities means is not liable for damages to the party attacked.[8]

Honeypot tools

Many different honeypot software products have been developed, some to work on UNIX, others for Windows and a number that have been successful on one platform have been exported to others. We now examine a number of different products, looking at their features and also their limitations.

Honeynet Project – Roo

Honeynets are a valuable source of information about malicious attacks, but the configuration and installation of such systems has considerable demands and risks involved. It is not trivial to install and set up a honeynet and care must be taken with configuration that no weaknesses are left for an attacker to exploit. To tackle this problem the Honeynet project developed a piece of software called Honeywall. The first version was called Eeyore and the latest version is called Roo. The Honeynet project put standards in place that defined how data capture and control should be employed. Data capture defines the methods of logging all the activity once the hacker enters the honeynet system. Data control defines the procedures for limiting the abilities of an attacker to sue the honeynet to further their own malicious agenda.

The core component of this honeynet is the honeywall, which is equipped with three interfaces (Figure 20.1). Two of the interfaces are not assigned IP addresses; of these two interfaces one is connected to the production system and the other is connected to the honeypots. Information flows directly between these two interfaces without any

Figure 20.1 Generation II honeynet layout

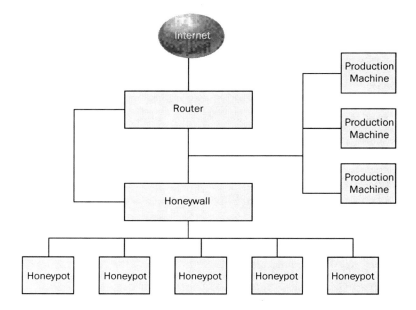

delay or latency, acting as a transparent bridge. The third interface is connected to the main router on the network and has no interaction with the honeynet. The honeywall implements both the data capture and control policies. Set up, installation and configuration of a honeynet takes a considerable amount of effort. The Honeynet project has taken steps to ease this deployment by creating a bootable CD which allows a honeywall to be set up straightforwardly. The latest version is a generation III honeynet called Roo. The honeywall is based on Fedora Core 3. The honeywall only creates the honeywall gateway; you are still required to set up the honeypots.[6] This method provides many advantages. Previously, it was necessary to download, install and configure all individual items. The CD alleviates this entire configuration allowing for faster deployment.

Honey-DVD

The Honeynet project Roo CD does alleviate or lessen the burden of setting up a honeynet but it does not automatically set up the honeypots themselves. The honey-DVD solution was developed in the University of Mannheim in Germany. It allows for a complete honeynet setup from a bootable DVD. The creators used multiple techniques to devise this technology. Dornseif sets out the technologies used and explains the feature of the DVD.[6] The first technology in use is Live Linux distributions capable of booting from a DVD and running completely within the bounds of memory without interactions with the machine's hard disk. The second technique is visualisation, which helps with better performance and instability of different operating systems. The final technique used it that of remote configuration. The honey-DVD is controlled by a central tool which allows the user to configure every component of the honeynet much like the honeypot operating system. The mixture of these three techniques allows the creation of an automatic honeynet with the following features:

- The honeynet can be booted from any PC with a bootable DVD drive
- Fully functioning generation III honeynet with honeywall and honeypots
- Simple set up allows for flexibility in configuring important values
- Allows for all maintenance and traffic analysis to be done from the DVD
- The honey-DVD is independent of the machine's underlying hard disk
- Honey-DVD is an open source tool and is freely available to download.

Honeyd

Honeyd is a low-interaction honeypot that works with Linux, Solaris and Windows platforms. The main function of Honeyd is to detect unauthorised access within a computer system. It can reply to all TCP and UDP ports and IP addresses and can be configured to emulate a fully functioning network. It monitors all unused IP addresses concurrently. When a connection attempt is made to an unused IP address, Honeyd assumes it is an attacker and tries to interact with whoever is making the connection. As a result of this methodology, if Honeyd detects any attackers it can be assumed that the attack is real and not a false alarm. The user is thus notified only of real attacks rather than all connections, which dramatically reduces the amount of information that needs to be analysed. Its strength lies in its modular design and the administrator's ability to choose what functionality they wish to implement.[9] Honeyd is one of the more useable honeynet implementations in a non-graphical user interface (GUI) environment although it is a difficult piece of software to install and configure properly. The user needs good technical and network knowledge and it also takes a significant amount of time to set up. Honeyd not only detects possible attacks but also allows for services to be emulated. This allows you to see what services are of interest to the attacker and what they are attempting to do. The emulation is created by using scripts to mimic a particular service using a particular port. These scripts can be written in a language of choice, commonly Perl, Shell script or Python. Example scripts that can be used are those to mimic FTP and Telnet services.[10] Honeyd can also be used to emulate operating systems, further adding to the pretence that the attacker is actually compromising an actual live system.

KFSensor

KFSensor[11] is a Windows-based honeypot system developed by Keyfocus Ltd. It is a commercial product offering standard, professional and enterprise editions. KFSensor simulates system services at the application layer of an open system interconnection (OSI) network model. The machine running KFSensor does not have to be dedicated to this task solely but conflict can arise if services are being carried out on certain ports that KFSensor wants to simulate. KFSensor emulated ports will not be active if services are being carried out on those ports by other applications on the machine (see Figure 20.2).

Figure 20.2 KFSensor architecture

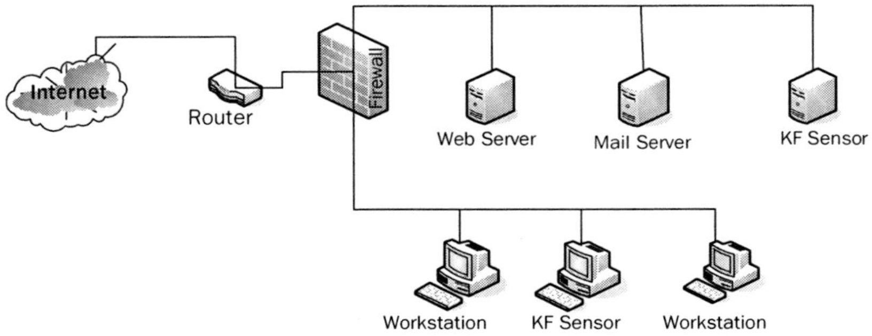

At the core of the KFSensor application is an Internet daemon that has been built to handle multiple ports and IP addresses. Using the features built into the daemon this allows KFSensor to respond to connections in a variety of ways from port listening to complex emulation of system services. For example, KFSensor simulates responses to both valid and invalid requests to an IIS Server. This makes it that bit more difficult to be identified as a honeypot, thus preventing hackers from detecting its presense. A disadvantage is that KFSensor works at application layer level and has no IP stack. If a hacker pings a machine running KFSensor, they would identify the KFSensor host machine and not KFSensor itself. Pinging of course is not only a useful tool for network engineers but also for hackers in figuring out what is at the other end. This can alert a hacker that something is quite not what it seems. For example, if the KFSensor host machine is running an underlying operating system of Windows XP and the hacker sees Exchange Server supposedly running on the same machine then they could be alerted to its presence. KFSensor supports approximately 256 listeners; in comparison Honeyd has an IP stack and is thus able to support thousands of ports. The GUI interface to KFSensor is very user friendly, using colour and icons to donate attack types and their severity. There are two main components of KFSensor, the server and the monitor. The monitor provides the interface to the system and is configurable to allow a user to display the granularity of data which they require. The server provides the core functionality: it listens to both TCP and UDP ports and interacts with the visitors and generates responses. KFSensor provides both signature attack identification and detection of known threats; it responds in real time, which allows for identification of known attack patterns. But KFSensor does not rely solely on the signature engine, therefore allowing it to detect zero day attacks or internal threats. Once an attack has been identified it is reported and allows for immediate analysis. KFSensor also allows for remote administration in its enterprise edition and complements the security already in place in an organization such as firewalls, antivirus software and can simulate real servers such as FTP, SMB, POP3, HTTP, Telnet, SMTP and SOCKS.

PatriotBox

PatriotBox[12] is another GUI-based Windows honeypot and is much more affordable than KFSensor. It does not have the same power as KFSensor in that it has no database capabilities or scripting. It allows for some customisation, although depending on which emulation is chosen a number of default listeners on certain ports are put in place. The emulations used are not as good as with KFSensor as the emulations of certain services do not have the accuracy of responses and banners compared with KFSensor. PatriotBox offers a good entry-level honeypot and is much more affordable, although some functionality is missing and the overall look and feel is not as polished as with other products. PatriotBox offers all the basic functionality required for a start-up project but is light on the required functionality for its implementation in a security conscious production environment or to get long-term returns in terms of a good information.

Jackpot

Jackpot[13] is a honeynet dedicated to fighting spam and was developed using a combination of Java and HTML. It operates an SMTP sever decoy system. Jackpot is easy to install and is free of charge. Jackpot allows you to differentiate between spam relay test messages and regular spam. Jackpot can be configured to set the number of relay messages you will accept before refusing to relay more to other sites. Jackpot fools spammers into thinking it is relaying their messages when in fact it is sending them to a drop box. If a spammer sends a test spam message to clarify that their spam is being relayed the tester message will be let through but all other messages stopped. The tarpit delay can be set very low so as to irritate the spammer waiting for a response to return from their commands. Jackpot will save all the information collected on the spam for further analysis and will also trawl the spamming site to see if it can pick up clues as to the origin of the spam or spammer.

Conclusion

Honeypot technology can provide the knowledge that helps us defend our systems. The honeypot provides us with insights into the hacker's motivations and movements, thus allowing us the potential to sandbag and harden our production systems against attacks. Honeypots are being deployed globally in an attempt to be the 'recipients' of thousands of exploits from hackers on a daily basis. These honeypots provide invaluable data about hackers worldwide, which is then used to alert security personnel to the hackers' activities. This process acts as an early warning system, as a means of collecting evidence or, at the very least, as a tool that can be added to the security arsenal of any organisation.

Notes

1. Lodin, S. (1998) Intrusion detection product evaluation criteria, *http://www.cis.udel.edu/~zhi/www.docshow.net/ids.htm*
2. *http://www.honeynet.org*
3. Spitzner, L. (2004) Open source honeypots: learning with Honeyd, *http://www.securityfocus.com/infocus/1659*
4. Hall, M. (2004) 'Sticky security', *Computerworld*, 38:3, 48.
5. Curran, K., Morrissey, C., Fagan, C., Murphy, C., O'Donnell, B., Fitzpatrick, G. and Condit, S. (2004) A year in the life of the Irish Honeynet: attacked, probed and bruised but still fighting. *Information Knowledge Systems Management*, 4:2, 1–13.
6. Alliance Research, The Honeynet Project (2005) Know your enemy: tracking botnets, *http://www.honeynet.org/papers/bots/*
7. Dornseif, M., Freiling, F.C., Gedicke, N. and Holz, T. (2006) Design and Implementation of the Honey-DVD. *Proceedings of the 2006 IEEE Workshop on Information Assurance, http://pi1.informatik.uni-mannheim.de/publications/pdf/design-and-implementation-of-the-honey-dvd*
8. Dornseif, M., Gärtner, F.C. and Holz, T. (2004) Vulnerability assessment using honeypots. *Praxis der Infromationsverarbeitung und Lommunikation (PIK)*, 4:27, 195–201, *http://pi1.informatik.uni-mannheim.de/publications/pdf/vulnerability-assessment-using-honepots*
9. Honeynet Project (2005) Know your enemy: honeynets, *http://www.honeynet.org/papers/honeynet/*
10. Spitzner, L. (2004) Problems and challenges with honeypots, SecurityFocus, *http://www.securityfocus.com/print/infocus/1757*
11. *http://www.keyfocus.net*
12. *http://www.alkasis.com*
13. *http://www.jackpot.uk.net*

21

Wireless 802.11 security

Kevin Curran and Elaine Smyth

Wireless networks have a number of security issues. Signal leakage means that network communications can be picked up outside the physical boundaries of the building in which they are being operated, meaning a hacker can operate from the street outside or discretely from further afield. In addition, the wired equivalent privacy protocol is inherently weak. There are also various other attacks that can be initiated against WLANs, all with detrimental effects. This chapter outlines some of the issues surrounding security on WiFi 802.11 networks.

Introduction

On the surface, WLANs act much as their wired counterparts, transporting data between network devices. However, there is one fundamental, significant, difference; WLANs are based upon radio communications technology, as an alternat ive to structured wiring and cables. Data are transmitted between devices through the air by utilizing radiowaves. Devices that participate in a WLAN must have a network interface card (NIC) with wireless capabilities. This essentially means that the card contains a small radio device that allows it to communicate with other wireless devices, within the defined range for that card, for example the 2.4–2.4853 GHz range. For a device to participate in a wireless network it must, first, be permitted to communicate with the devices in that network and, second, it must be within the transmission range of the devices in that network. To communicate, radio-based devices take advantage of electromagnetic waves and their ability to be altered in such a manner that they can carry information, known as modulation. Information is transferred by mixing the electromagnetic wave with the information to be transmitted. At the receiving end, the signal is compared with an un-modulated signal to reverse the process (called demodulation). There are three main types of modulation techniques: amplitude modulation (AM), frequency modulation (FM) and phase modulation (PM). Because FM is more robust against interference, it was chosen as the modulation standard for high-frequency radio transmissions.[1] Radio devices utilised within WLANs operate in the 2.4–2.4845 GHz range of the unlicensed industrial scientific and medical (ISM) frequency band, using either frequency hopping spread spectrum (FHSS) or direct sequence spread spectrum (DSSS), which are special modulation techniques used for spreading data over a wide band of frequencies sacrificing bandwidth to gain signal-to-noise (S/N) performance.[1]

Wireless devices have the option of participating in two type of networks, namely ad hoc and infrastructure. An ad hoc (also known as peer-to-peer) network is the simplest form of WLAN. It consists of two or more nodes communicating without any bridging or forwarding capability; all nodes are of equal importance and may join and leave the network at any time, and each device also has equal right to the medium. Access points (APs) are not necessary. For this to work, the devices wishing to participate in an ad hoc network must be within transmission range of each other; when a nodes goes out of range it will lose connection with the other devices. The range of this type of network is referred to as a 'single cell' and is called an independent basic service set (IBSS).[2]

In an infrastructure network communications take place through an AP, in a many-to-one configuration, with the AP at the single end. In its simplest form it consists of one AP and a group of wireless clients/devices, which must be within transmission range of the AP, and be properly configured to communicate with the AP. This type of network is called a basic service set (BSS).[3] If two or more BSSs are operated in the same network, by linking the APs via a background network, this is then called an extended service set (ESS). Such a configuration can cover larger, multi-floor, buildings. However, support is required for 'roaming' between different APs on the network, i.e. the hand-off between a device leaving the range of one AP and going into the range of another.[4]

APs can be overlapped if they are each given a different channel, within the 2.4–2.4835 GHz range, to communicate on. There are 11 overlapping frequencies specified in IEEE 802.11, which means that with careful planning multiple networks can coexist in the same physical space without interfering with each other.[2] APs must also be configured with a service set identifier (SSID), also known as the network name. It is a simple alphanumeric string given to each ESS that identifies the wireless network and allows stations to connect to one desired network when multiple independent networks operate in the same physical area. It also provides a very basic way of preventing unauthorised users from joining your network, as all devices in an ESS must have the same ESSID to participate.

Most APs can provide additional, basic, security features, such as WEP and MAC address filtering. WEP, an abbreviation for wired equivalent protocol, is a protocol designed specifically for use on wireless networks and is supposed to provide the security equivalent of the cable in a wired network through the use of encryption. Communicating devices must use the same WEP key in order to communicate. MAC address filtering provides a basis for screening users wanting to connect to a network; for a client device to be able to communicate with the AP successfully, its name must appear on an access control list of MAC addresses held by that AP. However, both these methods have been shown to be weak in their ability to secure wireless networks; both can be easily broken.

Wired networks have always presented their own security issues, but wireless networks introduce a whole new set of rules with their own unique security vulnerabilities. Most wired security measures are just not appropriate for application within a WLAN environment; this is mostly due to the complete change in transmission medium. However, some of the security implementations developed specifically for WLANs are also not terribly strong. Indeed, this aspect could be viewed as a 'work-in-progress'; new vulnerabilities are being discovered just as quickly as security measures are being released. Perhaps the issue that has received the most publicity is the major weaknesses in WEP, and more particularly the use of the RC4 algorithm and relatively short initialisation vectors (IVs).

Signal leakage

WLANs suffer from all the security risks associated with their wired counterparts; however, they also have some unique risks of their own. The main issue with radio-based wireless networks is signal leakage. Due to the properties of radio transmissions it is impossible to contain signals within one clearly defined area. In addition, because data are not enclosed within a cable it makes it very easy to intercept without being physically connected to the network. This puts it outside the limits of what a user can physically control; signals can be received outside the building and even from streets away. Signal leakage may not be a huge priority when organisations are implementing their WLAN, but it can present a significant security issue, as demonstrated below. The same signals that are transmitting data around an organisation's office are the same signals that can also be picked up from streets away by an unknown third party. This is what makes WLANs so vulnerable. Before WLANs became common, someone wishing to gain unauthorised access to a wired network had to physically attach themselves to a cable within the building. This is why wiring closets should be kept locked and secured. Any potential hacker had to take great risks to penetrate a wired network. Today potential hackers do not have to use extreme measures, as there is no need to smuggle equipment on site when it can be done from two streets away. It is not difficult for someone to obtain the necessary equipment; access can be gained in a very discrete manner from a distance.

Wired equivalent protocol

To go some way towards providing the same level of security that cable provides in wired networks, WEP was developed. IEEE 802.11 defined three basic security services for the WLAN environment:[5]

- authentication (a primary goal of WEP)
- confidentiality (privacy – a second goal of WEP)
- integrity (another goal of WEP).

WEP was designed to provide the security of a wired LAN by encryption through use of the RC4 (Rivest Code 4) algorithm. Its primary function was to safeguard against eavesdropping ('sniffing'), by making the data that are transmitted unreadable by a third party who does not have the correct WEP key to decrypt the data. RC4 is not specific to WEP; it is a random generator, also known as a keystream generator or a stream cipher, and was developed in RSA Laboratories by Ron Rivest in 1987 (hence the name Rivest Code). It requires a relatively short input and produces a somewhat longer output, called a pseudo-random key stream. This key stream is simply added to the data to be transmitted, to generate what is known as a ciphertext.

WEP is applied to all data above the 802.11b WLAN layers (physical and data link layers, the first two layers of the OSI reference model) to protect traffic such as transmission control protocol/internet protocol (TCP/IP), Internet packet exchange (IPX) and hyper text transfer protocol (HTTP). It should be noted that only the frame body of data frames are encrypted and the entire frame of other frame types are transmitted in the clear, unencrypted.[5] To add an additional integrity check, an IV is used in conjunction with the secret encryption key. The IV is used to avoid encrypting multiple consecutive ciphertexts with the same key, and is usually 24 bits long. The shared key and the IV are fed into the RC4 algorithm to produce the key stream. This is XORed with the data to produce the ciphertext, and the IV is then appended to the message. The IV of the incoming message is used to generate the key sequence necessary to decrypt the incoming message. The ciphertext, combined with the proper key sequence, yields the original plaintext and integrity check value (ICV).[6] The decryption is verified by applying the integrity check algorithm on the recovered plaintext and comparing the output ICV with the ICV transmitted with the message. If it is in error, an indication is sent back to the sending station. The IV increases the key size; for example, a 104-bit WEP key with a 24-bit IV becomes a 128-bit RC4 key. In general, increasing the key size increases the security of a cryptographic technique. Research has shown that key sizes of greater than 80 bits make brute force[7] code breaking extremely difficult. For an 80-bit key, the number of possible keys is 10^{24}, which puts computing power to the test; but this type of computing power is not beyond the reach of most hackers. The standard key in use today is 64-bit. However, research has shown that the WEP approach to privacy is vulnerable to certain attacks regardless of key size.[5] Although the application of WEP may stop casual 'sniffers', determined hackers can crack WEP keys in a busy network within a relatively short period of time.

WEP's major weaknesses relate to issues such as the use of static keys, the length of the IV and the RC4 algorithm. Here we outline the weaknesses associated with static keys and IV length.

Static keys

When WEP is enabled in accordance with the 802.11b standard, the network administrator must personally visit each wireless device in use and manually enter the appropriate WEP key. This may be acceptable at the installation stage of a WLAN or when a new client joins the network, but if the key becomes compromised and there is a loss of security, the key must be changed. This may not be a huge issue in a small organisation with only a few users, but it can be impractical in large corporations, who typically have hundreds of users. As a consequence, potentially hundreds of users and devices could be using the same, identical, key for long periods of time. All wireless network traffic from all users will be encrypted using the same key; this makes it a lot easier for someone listening to traffic to crack the key as there are so many packets being transmitted using the same key. Unfortunately, there were no key management provisions in the original WEP.

IV length

This is a 24-bit initialisation vector that WEP appends to the shared key. WEP uses this combined key and IV to generate the RC4 key schedule; it selects a new IV for each packet, so each packet can have a different key. This forms a family of 2^{24} keys. As described, each packet transmission selects one of these 2^{24} keys and encrypts the data under that key. On the surface, this may appear to strengthen protection by lengthening the 40-bit WEP key, but this scheme suffers from a basic problem; if IVs are chosen randomly there is a 50% chance of reuse after fewer than 5,000 packets.[8] The problem is a numerical restriction; because the IV is only 24 bits long, there are a finite number of variations of the IV for RC4 to pick from. Mathematically there are only 16,777,216 possible values for the IV. This may seem like a huge number, but given that it takes so many packets to transmit useful data, 16 million packets can easily go by in hours on a heavily used network. Eventually the RC4 algorithm starts using the same IVs repeatedly. Thus, someone passively 'listening' to encrypted traffic and picking out the repeating IVs can begin to deduce what the WEP key is. Made easier by the fact that there is a static variable (the shared key), an attacker can eventually crack the WEP key.[9] For example, a busy AP, which constantly sends 1500-byte packets at 11 Mbps, will exhaust the space of IVs after $1500 \times 8/(11 \times 10^6) \times 2^{24} = 18,000$ seconds, or 5 hours. (The amount of time may actually be smaller as many packets are smaller than 1500 bytes). This allows an attacker to collect two ciphertexts that are encrypted with the same key stream. This reveals information about the two messages. XORing two ciphertexts that use the same key stream would cause the key stream to be cancelled out and the result would be the XOR of the two plaintexts.[10]

There is an additional problem that involves the use of IVs, and more specifically weak IVs. Some numbers in the range 0–16,777,215 do not work to well with the RC4 algorithm. When these weak IVs are used, the resulting packet can be run through a series of mathematical functions to decipher part of the WEP key. By capturing a large number of packets an attacker can pick out enough weak IVs to reveal the WEP key.[11] Tools such as AirSnort[12] specifically exploit this vulnerability to allow hackers to obtain the above information relatively easily. The cracking process within AirSnort works by collecting packets thought to have been encrypted using a weak IV and then sorting them according to which key byte they help expose. A weak IV can assist in exposing only one key byte. The Flurer attack states that a weak IV has about a 5% chance of exposing the corresponding key byte.[13] So, when a sufficient number of weak IVs have been collected for a particular key byte, statistical analysis will show a tendency towards a particular value for that key byte. The cracking process makes a key guess based on the highest ranking values in the statistical analysis. Tests conducted by Stubblefield *et al.* show that between 60 and 256 weak IVs were needed to recover a key.[14]

War-driving

'War-driving' is a term used to describe a hacker, who, armed with a laptop, a wireless NIC, an antenna and sometimes a global positioning system (GPS) device travels, usually by car, scanning or 'sniffing' for WLAN devices, or more specifically unprotected or 'open' and easily accessed networks. There is a website where war-drivers can upload any information they obtain. This site is called Wigle and can be found at *http://www.wigle.net*.[10] As early as November 2001, the BBC took to the streets of London to observe how lax wireless security was. In one short trip around London they found that two-thirds of the networks discovered were wide open.[15] It was noted that some of the networks were using DHCP,[16] making it even easier for an unauthorised individual to join the network, because users are automatically issued with a valid IP address and other network information.

Due to the increased use of WLANs in recent years, it is quite possible that the number of unsecured devices has also risen in tandem, thus providing potential hackers with more choice. Even given all that has been written about the insecurities of WLANs, some users/organisations still insist on implementing them with their default settings and no encryption.[17] A worldwide war-drive, held in August–September 2002, discovered that 70% of APs were running without using any encryption, and worse that 27% were doing so while using the default SSID that came with the hardware, leaving them wide open for use by anyone in range with a wireless NIC and a note of all vendors' default SSIDs. These are rather disturbing figures; leaving an AP at its default settings is the equivalent of putting an Ethernet socket on the outside of the building so anyone passing by can plug into the network.[18] There are a plethora of hacking tools widely available to download from the Internet for any potential war-driver to use. Table 21.1 lists some of the more popular tools and a brief description of their function.

There has been much press globally, and many articles and papers written about wireless networks and their security vulnerabilities. However, despite all the literature, some enterprises still make the mistake of believing that they do not have to worry about wireless

Table 21.1 Wireless network hacking tools

Tool name	Description
NetStumbler (*http://www.netstumbler.com*)	Wireless AP identifier; listens for SSIDs and sends beacons as probes searching for APs.
Kismet (*http://kistmetwireless.net*)	Wireless sniffer and monitor; passively monitors wireless traffic and sorts data to identify SSIDs, MAC addresses, channels and connection speeds. Also identifies data with weak ICs that can be used by AirSnort to crack WEP.
Wellenreiter (*http://www.wellenreiter.net*)	LAN discovery tool; uses brute force to identify low traffic APs, hides real MAC address and integrates with GPS.
THC-RUT (*http://packetstormsecurity.nl/ filedesc/thcrut-1.2.5.tar.html*)	WLAN discovery tool; uses brute force to identify low traffic APs.
Ethereal (*http://www.ethereal.com*)	Network analyser; interactively browses the captured data, viewing summary and detail information for all observed network traffic.
WEPCrack (*http://wepcrack.sourceforge.net*)	Encryption breaker; cracks 802.11 WEP encryption keys using the discovered weaknesses of the RC4 key scheduling.
AirSnort (*http://airsnort.shmoo.com*)	Encryption breaker; passively monitors transmissions, computing the encryption key when enough packets have been gathered with real initialisation vectors.
HostAP (*http://hostap.epitest.fi*)	Converts a WLAN station to function as an AP (available only for WLAN cards that are based on Intersil's Prism 2/2.5/3 chipset).

security if they are running non-critical systems with non-sensitive information across their WLANs. All information is sensitive, and what an enterprise may class as being non-sensitive to them may be very useful to a hacker. In addition, most WLANs will connect with the wired enterprise backbone at some point, thus providing hackers with a launch pad to the entire network. The havoc an unwelcome third party could cause from here would be unlimited and very difficult to trace. Aside from the various attacks they could instigate [denial of service (DoS) and viruses], the loss of confidentiality, privacy and integrity that would occur if someone where able to steal, alter or delete information on your customer database is damaging enough. Access to sensitive information would be made relatively easy, perhaps even to customer credit card details. This could have an un-quantifiable effect on business, perhaps resulting in the loss of customers/clients and future revenue.[19]

Types of attack

This section deals with the various attacks that can be performed against WLANs (aside from the WEP crack), how they are carried out and what effect they have in relation to authentication, confidentiality and integrity, the three basic security requirements within networks. All of the attacks can be categorised into two general types, namely passive and active.

Passive attacks

A passive attack is an attack on a system that does not result in a change to the system in any way; the attack is purely to monitor or record data. Passive attacks affect confidentiality, but not necessarily authentication or integrity. Eavesdropping and traffic analysis fall within this category. When an attacker eavesdrops, they simply monitor transmissions for message content. This usually takes the form of someone listening in to the transmissions on a LAN between stations/devices.

Eavesdropping

Eavesdropping is also known as 'sniffing' or wireless 'footprinting'. As already mentioned, there are various tools available for download that allow the monitoring of networks and their traffic; these tools were developed by hackers, for hackers. NetStumbler, Kismet, AirSnort,

WEPCrack and Ethereal are well-known names in wireless hacking circles, and all are designed specifically for use on wireless networks, with the exception of Ethereal, which is a packet analyser and can also be used on a wired LAN. NetStumbler and Kismet can be used purely for passive eavesdropping; they have no additional active functions, except perhaps their ability to work in conjunction with GPSs to map the exact locations of identified wireless LANs. NetStumbler is a Windows-based sniffer, whereas Kismet is primarily a Linux-based tool. NetStumbler uses an 802.11 probe request sent to the broadcast destination address, which causes all APs in the area to issue an 802.11 probe response containing network configuration information, such as their SSID, WEP status, MAC address of the device, name (if applicable), the channel the device is transmitting on, the vendor and the type, either peer or AP, along with a few other items of information. Using the network information and GPS data collected, it is then possible to create maps with tools such as StumbVerter and MS Mappoint. Kismet, although not as graphical or user friendly as NetStumbler, is similar to its Windows counterpart, but it provides superior functionality. While scanning for APs, packets can also be logged for later analysis. Logging features allow for captured packets to be stored in separate categories, depending upon the type of traffic captured. Kismet can even store encrypted packets that use weak keys separately to run them through a WEP key cracker after capture, such as AirSnort or WEPCrack.[20] Wireless network GPS information can be uploaded to the Wigle site. Therefore, if Wigle data exist for a particular area, there is no need to drive around that area probing for wireless devices; this information can be obtained in advance from the Wigle website. All that remains is to drive to a location where known networks exist to observe traffic. Wigle currently has a few hundred thousand networks on its database.

Traffic analysis

Traffic analysis gains intelligence in a more subtle way by monitoring transmissions for patterns of communication. A considerable amount of information is contained in the flow of messages between communicating parties. Airopeek NX, a commercial 802.11 monitoring and analysis tool for Windows, analyses transmissions and provides a useful node view, which groups detected stations and devices by their MAC address and will also show IP addresses and protocols observed for each. The Peer Map view, within Airopeek NX, presents a matrix of all hosts discovered on the network by their connections to each other. This can make it very easy to visualise AP and client relationships, which could be useful to hackers in deciding where to try and gain access or target an attack.[21] Some attacks may begin as passive but cross over to active attacks as they progress. For example, tools such as AirSnort or WEPCrack may passively monitor transmissions, but their intent is to crack the WEP key used to encrypt data being transmitted. Ultimately the reasons for wanting to crack the key are so that an unauthorised individual can access a protected network and then launch an active attack of some form. These types of attack are classed as passive decryption attacks.

AirSnort exploits the key weaknesses and uses this to crack WEP keys, as does WEPCrack. These are tools that put hackers on the first step towards an active attack. However, WEPCrack, unlike AirSnort, must be used in conjunction with a separate packet sniffer as it does not have the ability to capture network traffic. These tools utilise what is known as a brute force technique to break codes. Brute force is a method of breaking a cipher by trying every possible key until the correct one is found. The feasibility of this attack depends on the key length of the cipher, and/or the amount of computational power available to the attacker, and of course time. Another type of passive decryption attack is what is known as a dictionary attack, which is also a form of brute-force technique. A dictionary attack refers to breaking a cipher, or obtaining a password by running through a list of likely keys, or a list of words. The term dictionary attack initially referred to finding passwords in a specific list, such as an English dictionary. Today, a brute-force approach can compute likely passwords, such as all five-letter combinations, 'on-the-fly' instead of using a pre-built list. The most recent brute-force, passive decryption, attack is called a table. It is a method which involves using a relatively small number of Initialisation Vectors (IVs) (24-bit) to build decryption tables. Once the contents of a single encrypted packet are known, the hacker can work backwards and build a table of all the keys possible with a particular IV.[22]

Active attacks

An active attack, also referred to as a malicious attack, occurs when an unauthorised third party gains access to a network and proceeds to perform a DoS attack, to disrupt the proper operation of a network, to intercept network traffic and either modify or delete it, or inject extra traffic onto the network. There are many active attacks that can be launched against wireless networks; the following few paragraphs outline almost all of these attacks, how they work and what effect they have.[5] DoS attacks are easily the most prevalent type of attack against

802.11 networks, and can be waged against a single client or an entire WLAN. In this type of attack the hacker usually does not steal information, but rather simply prevents users from accessing network services, or causes services to be interrupted or delayed. Consequences can range from a measurable reduction in performance to the complete failure of the system. Some common DoS attacks are outlined below.

Man-in-the-middle (MITM) attack

This attack is carried out by inserting a malicious station between the victim station and the AP, the attacker becoming the 'man in the middle'; the station is tricked into believing that the attacker is the AP and the AP into believing that the attacker is the legitimate station. The perpetrator passively monitors the frames sent back and forth between the station and the AP during the initial association process with an 802.11 analyser. As a result, information is obtained about both the station and the AP, such as the MAC and IP address of both devices, association ID for the station and SSID of the network. With this information a rogue station/AP can be set up between the two unsuspecting devices. Because the original 802.11 does not provide mutual authentication, a station will happily re-associate with the rogue AP. The rogue AP will then capture traffic from unsuspecting users; this can expose information such as user names and passwords. After gleaning enough information about a particular WLAN, a hacker can then use a rogue station to mimic a valid one. This enables the hacker to deceive an AP by disassociating the valid station and reassociating again as a rogue station with the same parameters as the valid station. Two wireless cards are typically required for this type of attack.[23] Once the attacker has successfully inserted themselves between the AP and client station, they are free to modify traffic, selectively forward or even delete it completely, while logging every packet that comes through it. In addition, the attacker is also free to explore and use other areas of the network as a legitimate user.

Session hijacking

In this attack the intruder appears to be a legitimate user who has just connected with the AP that they have been disconnected from. Much like the second half of the MITM attack, the intruder then connects with the still active WLAN connection, thereby hijacking the session. The attacker must wait until the client has successfully authenticated to the network, then send a disassociate message to the client on behalf of the legitimate AP, using the MAC address of the AP. The disassociate message causes the legitimate client to become 'unattached' to the network. Therefore, once this disassociate occurs, the attacker can then send frames to the valid AP using the 'assumed' MAC address of the legitimate client. However, this attack assumes that no encryption is present, otherwise the radio perpetrating the attack would not be able to gain access to the network after the hijack because the AP would reject all packets that do not match an encryption key corresponding to a known user, unless the attacker has taken the time beforehand to crack the key. When no encryption is present, this attack will easily succeed, allowing the attacker to use the session until the next re-authentication takes place. At the next re-authentication, the attacker would not be re-authenticated and effectively kicked-off, and they would then have to hijack another valid session.[24]

MAC spoofing, or identity theft

To carry off this attack the intruder impersonates a legitimate device on the network by stealing their credentials. To do this the attacker must change the manufacturer-assigned MAC identity of their NIC to the same value as a legitimate user on the network; they assume the identity of this user by spoofing their MAC address. By analysing traffic, a hacker can easily pick off MAC addresses of authorised users. The hacker then connects to the wireless LAN as an authorised user. This is similar in principle to the initial stage of the MITM attack, in which a device impersonates or masquerades as someone they are not. This attack enables the hacker to transmit and receive data within the network as an authorised member; because they are using the identity of an authorised user it will hide their presence on the network and bypass any MAC address-based ACLs.[25]

Other MAC vulnerabilities

A utility known as Interframe spacing can also be utilised to launch malicious attacks. As every transmitting node must wait at least the shortest interframe space (SIFS) interval before transmitting, if not longer, an attacker could completely monopolise the channel by sending a short signal just before the end of every SIFS period. Although this attack could be highly effective, it also requires the attacker to expel considerable energy; an SIFS period is only 20 microseconds on 802.11b networks, leading to a cycle of 50,000 packets per second in order to disable all access to a network.[26] However, a more serious vulnerability arises from the virtual carrier-sense mechanism used to mitigate collisions from hidden terminals.[27] Each 802.11 frame carries a duration field that indicates the number of microseconds that the channel is reserved. This value, in turn, is used to program the network allocation vector (NAV) on each node. The NAV keeps stations quiet until the first acknowledgement of a transmission is received. Only when a node's NAV reaches zero is it allowed to transmit. This feature is principally used in the ready-to-send/clear-to-send (RTS/CTS) handshake that can be used to synchronise access to the channel when a hidden terminal may be interfering with transmissions. During this handshake the sending node first sends a small RTS frame that includes a duration large enough to complete the RTS/CTS sequence, including the CTS frame, the data frame and the subsequent acknowledgement (ACK) frame. The destination node replies to the RTS with a CTS, containing a new NAV value, updated to account for the time already elapsed in the sequence. After the CTS is sent every station in radio range of either the sending or the receiving station will have updated their NAV and will hold all transmissions for the defined duration. Although the RTS/CTS feature is rarely used in practice, respecting the virtual carrier sense function indicated by the NAV field is mandatory in all 802.11 implementations. An attacker may exploit this feature by stating a large duration field, thereby preventing stations from gaining access to the channel. Although it is possible to use almost any frame type to control the NAV, using the RTS with CTS, legitimate stations will propagate the attack further than it could on its own by passing the large NAV value to all stations within range. To cause a noticeable degradation in network performance, this attack can be carried out repeatedly, to disrupt network functioning, resulting in a DoS.[26]

Malicious association

Using a freeware tool called HostAP to create what is known as a 'soft AP', hackers can force unsuspecting stations to connect to an undesired 802.11 network or alter the configuration of the station to operate in ad-hoc mode. The HostAP software enables a station to operate as a functioning AP. As the victim station broadcasts a probe to associate with an AP, the attacker's malicious AP responds and starts a connection between the two. At this point, the attacker can exploit the vulnerable victim station. It could be used as a launch pad to the rest of the network, viruses could be unleashed and a so-called backdoor could be left for later use. This type of attack highlights how vulnerable client stations are; they are not always aware that the AP they connect to is legitimate, which can be attributed to the lack of mutual authentication.[28]

De-authentication

Part of the communications framework between an 802.11 AP and client is a message which allows them to explicitly issue a request for de-authentication from one another at any stage. Even if some form of key authentication does exist, this message is not authenticated, which makes it relatively simple for a third party to spoof this message on behalf of either device and direct it to the other party. In response, the AP or client will exit the authenticated state and will refuse all further packets until authentication is re-established. By repeating the attack persistently a client may be kept from transmitting or receiving data indefinitely.[26]

Association flood

This is a resource starvation attack. When a station associates with an AP, the AP issues an associate identification number (AID) to the station in the range 1–2007. This value is used for communicating power management information to a station that has been in a power-save state. This attack works by sending multiple authentication and association requests to the AP, each with a unique source MAC address. The AP is unable to differentiate between the authentication requests generated by an attacker and those created by legitimate clients, so it is forced to process each request. Eventually, the AP will run out of AIDs to allocate and will be forced to de-associate stations to reuse previously allocated AIDs. In practice, many APs will restart after a few minutes of authentication flooding, but this attack is effective in bringing down entire networks or network segments; if repeatedly carried out, they can cause a noticeable decrease in network up time.[25]

Power save vulnerability

Much as a PC or laptop enters stand-by mode after a period of inactivity, a client station within a WLAN is also permitted to enter a stand-by state, known as power save mode. In this state clients are unable to transmit or receive. Before entering power save mode the client is required to announce its intention so that the AP can start buffering any inbound traffic for the node. Occasionally, the client will awaken to poll the AP for any traffic destined for it. If there are any buffered data, the AP delivers the data and subsequently discards the contents of its buffer. By spoofing the polling message on behalf of the client, an attacker can cause the AP to discard the client's packets while it is in power save mode. Along the same lines, it is potentially possible to trick the client station into thinking there are no buffered packets at the AP when in fact there are. The presence of buffered packets is indicated in a periodically broadcast packet called the traffic indication map, or TIM. If the TIM message itself is spoofed, an attacker may convince a client that there are no buffered data for it and the client will immediately revert back to stand-by state.[26]

Jamming

Jamming is a ridiculously simple, yet highly effective method of causing a DoS on a wireless LAN. Jamming, as the name suggests, involves the use of a device to intentionally create interfering radio signals that effectively 'jam' the airwaves, resulting in the AP and any client devices being unable to transmit. Unfortunately, 802.11b WLANs are easily jammed – intentionally or otherwise – owing to the crowded frequency band that they operate in. This provides a would-be attacker with plenty of opportunity, and tools, to jam wireless network signals.[29]

Conclusion

Wireless networks have a number of security issues. Signal leakage means that network communications can be picked up outside the physical boundaries of the building in which they are being operated, such that a hacker can operate from the street outside or discretely further afield. In addition, wireless networks have various other weaknesses. WEP, the protocol used within WLANs to provide the equivalent security of wired networks, is inherently weak. The use of the RC4 algorithm and weak IVs makes WEP a vulnerable security measure.

Notes

1. Harte, L., Kellog, S., Dreher, R. and Schaffinit, T. (2000) *The Comprehensive Guide to Wireless Technologies: Cellular, PCS, Paging, SMR and Satellite.* North Carolina: APDG Publishing.

2. Tourrilhes, J. (2000) *Wireless Overview – The MAC Level. http://www. hpl.hp.com/personal/Jean_Tourrilhes/Linux/Linux.Wireless.mac.html.* Accessed 10 October 2003.

3. Sikora, A. (2003) *Wireless Personal and Local Area Networks.* Chichester: John Wiley & Sons Ltd.

4. Geier, J. (1999) *Wireless LANs, Implementing Interoperable Networks.* USA: MacMillan Technical Publishing.

5. Karygiannis, T. and Owens, L. (2003) *National Institute of Standards and Technology, Special Publication 800-48*, Draft, *http://csrc.nist.gov/ publications/drafts/draft-sp800-48.pdf.* Accessed 18 August 2003.

6. Tyrrell, K. (2003) *An Overview of Wireless Security Issues. http://www.giac. org/practical/GSCE/Kevin_Tyrrell_GSEC.pdf.* Accessed 19 October 2003.

7. A method that relies on sheer computing power to try all possibilities until the solution to a problem is found; usually refers to cracking passwords by trying every possible combination of a particular key space.

8. Walker, J. (2000) *Unsafe at any Key Size; An analysis of the WEP encapsulation. http://www.dis.org/wl/pdf/unsafe.pdf.* Accessed 23 October 2003.

9. iLabs, Wireless Security Team. (2002) *What's Wrong with WEP? http:// www.nwfusion.com/research/2002/0909wepprimer.html.* Accessed 23 October 2003.

10. Vines, R.D. (2002) *Wireless Security Essentials, Defending Mobile Systems from Data Piracy.* Indiana: Wiley Publishing Inc.

11. PCQuest. (2003) *WEP Security Cracked. http://www.pcquest.com/content/ topstories/wireless/103081102.asp.* Accessed 7 November 2003.

12. Airsnort (2009) *http://airsnort.shmoo.com/*

13. Airsnort FAQ (2009) *http://airsnort.shmoo.com/faq.html*

14. AirSnort FAQ. (2003) *How the crack process works. http://airsnort.shmoo. com/faq.html.* Accessed 25 October 2003.

15. BBC News. (2001) *Welcome to the era of drive-by hacking. http://news.bbc. co.uk/1/hi/sci/tech/1639661.stm.* Accessed 29 October 2003.

16. Dynamic host control protocol; governs the dynamic allocation of IP addresses to network devices/clients.

17. Ulanoff, L. (2003) Get free Wi-Fi, while its hot. *PC Magazine*, July.

18. Griffth, E. (2002) *Mapping the Lack of Security. http://www.wi- fiplanet.com/news/article.php/1488541.* Accessed 19 September 2003.

19. AirDefense. (2003) *Wireless LAN Security – What Hackers Know That You Don't. http://ssl.salesforce.com/servlet.Email/AttachmentDownload?q=00m 0000000003Pr00D00000000hiyd00500000005k8d5.* Accessed 18 August 2003.

20. Sutton, M. (2003) *Hacking the Invisible Network.* iDefense, iAlert White Paper, *http://www.rootshell.be/~doxical/download/docs/misc/Idefense_ Hacking_the_invisible_network_(wireless).pdf.* Accessed 18 August 2003.

21. McClure, S., Scambray, J. and Jurtz, G. (2003) *Hacking Exposed: Network Security Secrets and Solutions*, 4th edn. McGraw-Hill.

22. Franklin, C. (2001). *A Cracked Spec. http://www.internetweek.com/reviews01/ rev031201-2.htm.* Accessed 7 November 2003.

23. Wi-FiPlanet (2002) *Minimising WLAN Security Threats. http://wi-fiplanet. com/tutorials/article.php/1457211.* Accessed 5 November 2003.

24. Proxim, Wireless Networks. (2003) *Wireless Network Security.* http://www.proxim.com/learn/library/whitepapers/wireless_security.pdf. Accessed 7 November 2003.
25. Wright, J. (2003) *Detecting Wireless LAN MAC Address Spoofing.* http://home.jwu.edu/jwright/papers/wlan-mac-spoof.pdf. Accessed 5 November 2003.
26. Bellardo, J. and Savage, S. (2003) *802.11 Denial of Service Attacks: Real Vulnerabilities and Practical Solution.* http://www.cs.ucsd.edu/users/savage/papers/UsenixSec03.pdf. Accessed 5 November 2003.
27. A problem that occurs when one or more stations cannot 'hear' all other stations. These stations cause collisions by transmitting at the same time as another station.
28. SyDisTyKMoFo (2003) *Wireless Attacks Explained.* http://www.astalavista.com/library/wlan/wlansecurity.htm. Accessed 7 November 2003.
29. Computer Associates. (2003) *Who's Watching Your Wireless Network?* http://wp.bitpipe.com/resource/org_943197149_209/wireless_network_wp_bpx.pdf. Accessed 27 September 2003.

22

The problem of spam email

John Honan and Kevin Curran

As a communications medium, email has become very useful and practically universal. However, the usefulness of email and its potential for future growth are jeopardised by the rising tide of unwanted email, both spam and viruses. This threatens to wipe out the advantages and benefits of email. An important flaw in current email standards (most notably SMTP) is the lack of any technical requirement that ensures the reliable identification of the sender of messages. A message's domain of origin can easily be faked, or 'spoofed'. This chapter investigates the problem of email spam and provides an overview of the methods used to minimise it.

Introduction

Spam can be defined as unsolicited email, often of a commercial nature, sent indiscriminately to multiple mailing lists, individuals or newsgroups. Spam can be categorised as follows:

- Junk mail – mass mailings from legitimate businesses that are unwanted.

- Non-commercial spam – mass mailings of unsolicited messages without an apparent commercial motive, including chain letters, urban legends and joke collections.

- Offensive and pornographic spam – mass mailings of 'adult' advertisements or pornographic pictures.

- Spam scams – mass mailings of fraudulent messages or those designed to con people out of personal information for the purpose of identity theft and other criminal acts.

- Virus spam – mass mailings that contain viruses, Trojans, malicious scripts, etc.

Spoofing[1] is a technique often used by spammers to make them harder to trace. Trojan viruses embedded in email messages also employ spoofing techniques to ensure the source of the message is more difficult to locate.[2] Spam filters and virus scanners can eliminate only a certain amount of spam and also risk blocking legitimate emails. As the SoBig virus has demonstrated, virus scanners themselves actually add to the email traffic through notification and bounceback messages.[3] SMTP is flawed in that it allows these email headers to be faked, and does not allow for the sender to be authenticated as the 'real' sender of the message. If this problem can be solved, it will result in a reduction in spam email messages, more security for existing emails, and allow email viruses to be tracked down and stopped more effectively.[4] This approach is known as 'trusted email'. The simple mail transport protocol (SMTP) is the basic protocol used by servers to send email messages to each other.[4] It defines how the conversation should take place, and the format of the data that are exchanged during the conversation. The email is composed in the sender's mail user agent (MUA), usually a piece of software on the sender's PC such as Outlook or Eudora, but can also consist of a web-based email systems such as Yahoo or Hotmail. The message might look as follows:

Date: Thursday, 1 Apr 2004 12:40:30 -0000
From: you@yourhost.com
To: John & Kevin <jhonan@silveronion.com>
Subject: Party on Sat night
There's a party on Saturday night, would you like to go?

There are two parts to the above message, the header and the body. The header contains information about the message, such as who it is to be sent to. The body contains the actual text of the message itself. When the sender clicks the 'Send' button in their MUA, some additional headers are automatically added to the message by the MUA. For example (the new headers added by the MUA are in bold):

Date: Thursday, 1 Apr 2004 12:40:30 -0000

From: you@yourhost.com

To: John & Kevin < jhonan@silveronion.com>

Subject: Party on Sat night

Message-Id: <002d01c444ca$bdaa3e70$5b92cbc1@

yourhost.com>

X-Mailer: Microsoft Outlook Express 6.00.2800.1409

There's a party on Saturday night, would you like to go?

The message-Id is a unique identifier added by the MUA, and the X-Mailer is the name and version of the MUA software used to compose the email. To deliver the email, the MUA needs to contact a mail transport agent (MTA). The MTA is responsible for routing and delivering email. In the example above, the MTA at yourhost.com (the sender's domain) needs to establish an SMTP conversation with the MTA at silveronion.com (the recipient's domain). The SMTP conversation takes place as follows. When silveronion.com receives the email, it adds a header of its own, the *Received* header. This is like a postmark. Every MTA that handles a message adds this received header.[5,6] This is how the message might look after silveronion.com has received it:

Received: from yourhost.com (HELO yourhost.com) (193.203.

146.91) by silveronion.com with SMTP; 1 Apr 2004 12:40:40

Date: Thursday, 1 Apr 2004 12:40:30 -0000

From: you@yourhost.com

To: John & Kevin < jhonan@silveronion.com>

Subject: Party on Sat night

Message-Id: <002d01c444ca$bdaa3e70$5b92cbc1@

             yourhost.com>

X-Mailer: Microsoft Outlook Express 6.00.2800.1409

There's a party on Saturday night, would you like to go?

The Received header shows from which server the message was received; it often includes the IP address, in case the server supplied an incorrect or faked hostname (yourhost.com). Other information stored in the

Received header includes the name of the receiving MTA server, and may include other information such as the version of the MTA software the server is running. Each server involved in forwarding the message will add its server information to the received portion of the message, and thus a message may have many received headers. They are read in reverse order. The header at the top indicates the last server which added its received header. Finally, if the email message has reached its eventual destination, an SMTP *From* header is added:

From: you@yourhost.com Thurs Apr 1 2004 12:40:30

Received: from yourhost.com (HELO yourhost.com) (193.203. 146.91) by silveronion.com with SMTP; 1 Apr 2004 12:40:40

Date: Thursday, 1 Apr 2004 12:40:30 -0000

From: you@yourhost.com

To: John & Kevin <jhonan@silveronion.com>

Subject: Party on Sat night

Message-Id: <002d01c444ca$bdaa3e70$5b92cbc1@ yourhost.com>

X-Mailer: Microsoft Outlook Express 6.00.2800.1409

There's a party on Saturday night, would you like to go?

The From header lists the address as supplied by the sender in the MAIL part of the SMTP conversation. Some MTA agents store this in a 'Return-Path:' header instead. This final message is how it looks when it reaches the inbox of jhonan@silveronion.com. The recipients email client software parses the header and presents the mail to the user in a more readable format (the final recipient often does not see all the headers in their email software, being mainly interested in the 'From', 'Subject' lines, and the body.) The headers as described above are standard SMTP headers. Any header beginning with 'X-' (such as X-Mailer) is a freeform header, and can be used for any purpose.[6] Spammers exploit SMTP through a number of flaws in the SMTP protocol, for example:

1. No verification of identify – the server accepts who you say you are without question

2. No consequences for dishonest addressing ('From' line can be anything you want)

3. Content filtering requires delivery (the email has to be received by the server before it can be filtered)

4. Nothing on which to base delivery routing options (no generic flags in the header or elsewhere to allow an email to be flagged as an advertisement, adult content, newsletter, or otherwise)

5. No consequences for dishonest content (the actual message contents do not match the subject line).

The main flaw in SMTP is that it allows 'untrusted' communications to take place.[5] There is no requirement to prove you are who you say you are when an SMTP communication is instigated. SMTP is also very effective at sending email as quickly as possible to its destination, meaning the spammer is only slowed down by the speed of their connection to the Internet. These problems offer the spammer two main advantages which allow them to continue spamming unhindered, namely anonymity and volume of spam.[7]

Apart from the obvious methods of supplying incorrect information in the email header, many spammers go to great lengths to remain anonymous. Anonymity is important to a spammer, because if spammers can be tracked down to an ISP they risk having their email server shut down or their web-hosting account terminated. In light of new 'Can-Spam' anti-spam legislation, spammers are even more determined to remain unaccountable. An additional technique used by spammers is exploitation of open email relays. These are SMTP servers that are mis-configured and allow email to be forwarded to addresses outside of the server's domain. On inspecting the email headers, it appears as if the relay server is the source of the email.[8] In order to trace the spammer, the owner of the open relay needs to be made aware of the activity. However, some sites are either reluctant to act or willingly abet spammers. Furthermore, even when spammers are identified and an ISP removes their account, spammers will often open a new one immediately and carry on their activities. Many system administrators are aware of tricks that spammers use and have configured email servers correctly and securely. However, spammers have discovered the capability of using common Web mail form handling software as open relays. Many websites provide form applications such as mailto and the FormMail Perl scripts to allow users to construct forms, input to which can be forwarded to a specified email address for collecting information. Spammers write software that exploits security holes in FormMail scripts to enable them to forward email to a specified address. This results in the spam appearing to originate from the website of the FormMail software, an undesirable outcome.[7]

Spammers email in bulk using automatic sending programs. Spammers must first obtain email addresses; sources include joining mailing lists to gather addresses from the mailing list software, purchasing mail lists from other spammers on CD-ROM (which can contain millions of addresses) and spambots (or harvesters), which scan Internet newsgroups and webpages for email addresses. Spammers ensure their spam is not blocked by spam-filtering software by making the spam look like legitimate email, by avoiding excessive use of HTML or exclamation marks, or by misspelling commonly used spam phrases and words.[9]

Existing anti-spam methods

This section discusses a number of technical anti-spam methods currently in use along with the advantages and disadvantages of each. There are also industry proposals which attempt to address the shortcomings of the current anti-spam approaches. The industry proposals suggest a more robust, future-proof, all-encompassing solution to stopping spam. These proposals often comprise hybrid approaches, i.e. combinations of a number of methods, and are generally more complex to implement as they require changes to email infrastructure.

Requirements of anti-spam systems

Ideally, the system should block all spam. This may not be achievable in practice, as there may always be a small quantity of spam that bypasses whatever system is in place. The number of spam messages getting through should be perhaps 1 in 1000. If a person is sent 200 spam emails a day, then if 1 spam gets through to their in-box per 5-day working week, this equates to 0.1%, an acceptable level to most email users.

The system should not block legitimate email. Not receiving email you are expecting, or important email being blocked by a spam filter is considered worse by many people than receiving large quantities of spam. It is therefore important that any anti-spam system ensures that 100% of legitimate email gets through.

The system should block spam with little or no user interaction. The spam blocking ideally should occur before the email even reaches the client computer (any filtering that happens on the client computer means the spam has to be downloaded, which results in additional network traffic for the user, and possibly a noticeable delay while the spam is filtered). The system should ideally exist on the email server itself, not on the client computer.

Finally, the user should not be aware of any delays in either sending or receiving and filtering email. Users may be tolerant of certain performance issues if they know it is preventing spam reaching their inbox, but they will not be as accepting if this starts affecting the normal day-to-day operation of their PC to send and receive emails.[10]

Existing methods used to minimize spam

Below are the main methods being used to prevent spam, together with their pros and cons.[11]

Complain to the spammer's ISP

When spam volumes were quite low, it was often effective to send a complaint email to the ISP of the spammer. The ISP could then investigate and close down the relevant account. The advantages of this approach are that it can achieve direct action from the ISP to get the spammer shut down fairly quickly. The disadvantages are that the volumes of spam are now too high to allow a complaint to be sent and followed up on for every spam that is sent. In addition, it is often difficult to determine from the header information who the ISP of the spammer is. Spammers shut down in one ISP or hosting company will just open accounts with someone else. This method has a medium level of spam blocking efficiency. It may block one spammer, but others will get through. False positives, however, do not occur.[9]

Mail server IP blacklists

An IP blacklist is a list of the IP addresses of spammers' mail servers, or relay servers (unsecure servers that allow spammers to forward email). These lists are maintained by volunteer groups and anti-spam organisations. ISPs can then subscribe to these lists and refuse to accept email from any listed IP addresses. This is a very precise method of blocking potential spam, although such blacklists can never hope to list every single IP address that spammers use. Spammers often end up listing legitimate IP addresses, or blacklisting an entire domain (1000 ordinary users could be blacklisted as a result of the actions of one spammer). The source IP is spoofable by the spammer, which means the spammer can bypass the blacklist. Spam blocking efficiency with this method is high. It blocks all spam from given IP addresses but false positives are likely. If a legitimate sender uses a blacklisted IP block, their email will be stopped.

Signature-based filtering

This method compares incoming emails against a signature database of known spam emails. The system calculates a checksum signature of an incoming spam message, and adds it to the database. Any incoming emails are then compared against this database to see if the email is spam. The advantages of this are that it is an accurate way of matching spam. It can achieve very low 'false positives' as only definite spasm emails are matched based on the hash signature of their contents. The disadvantages are that in order to be detected as spam, the message will have to exist in the database of pre-sent spam messages. If the spam is new, it may not exist in the database at this stage, and therefore will not be blocked. The database must be kept up to date.[11] The main problem, however, is that signature filtering is easily bypassed by making minor modifications to each message to avoid signature matches, and therefore this technique is no longer that useful anymore. Spam blocking efficiency with this method is low.

Bayesian filtering

This method uses a statistical analysis technique to analyse the words contained in each email received. It uses predefined lookup tables to determine the probability that an email is spam. For example, the word 'Viagra' would have a high weighting, as it commonly appears in spam emails. Bayesian filtering is a new approach to spam prevention. This approach seems to trigger fewer false positives than other types of filtering, as it is self-training based on spam it receives. In some cases the user can update the filter if it misclassifies an email, thus improving the detection accuracy. Spammers, however, often bypass these types of filters by making the spam look less spammy, using fewer spam-related words (often making the email read like a personal email from a friend), or putting random non-spam words at the end of the message to cause the Bayesian calculation to misclassify them as non-spam. Another technique spammers use is to misspell spam-related words. Spam blocking efficiency with this method is high. Bayesian filters are quite accurate but false positives are quite likely.[11]

Rule-based filtering

Rule-based filters look for patterns that indicate spam: specific words and phrases, lots of uppercase letters and exclamation points, malformed headers, dates in the future or the past, etc. This is how nearly all spam filters worked until 2002. Until Bayesian filtering was introduced, this was probably the most flexible method to help identify spam but this method is very easy for the spammer to bypass. More adept spammers even run their spam through rule-based filters before sending it to ensure it does not trigger the spam alert. Many spammers have now learnt to make their email not 'look' like spam to the filters, and use techniques to ensure it is at least opened by the recipient when it reaches their in-box. (e.g. making the 'From' look like a normal name, and making the 'Subject' something like 'Hi' or 'Long time no see'). Rule-based filtering is often used in conjunction with Bayesian filtering. Spam blocking efficiency is high. False positives are quite likely as an email which contains certain words or formatting can be mistakenly flagged as spam. Performance can suffer as each email needs to be scanned.[11]

Challenge-response filtering

When you receive an email from a new sender, a challenge-response filter sends an email back to them, telling them they must go to a webpage and fill out a form before the email is delivered. Once the sender has verified themself, they will be added to a senders' 'whitelist' to ensure any future emails get through without requiring verification. This method ensures you only receive email from people who really want to correspond with you. The chances are that a spammer is not going to spend the time filling out the web form. However, this can be quite inconvenient for the sender, as they have to remember to fill in the form before the recipient receives the email. In some cases the sender might not bother, and this method will always result in email being delayed. This approach has not been widely adopted, and the level of spam blocking efficiency is medium. Spammers can fill out the forms too, and may use automated scripts. There may be false positives. If the sender does not accept the challenge then their email stays in the 'spam' box.

Legal approach (Can Spam Act)

In 2003 the US Senate passed into law the 'Can Spam' act as an attempt to cut down spam.[12] This should have been an effective deterrent against spammers but weaknesses exist in the Can Spam legislation. A loophole in spam laws, however, is usually in the exact definition of spam. Most spam laws allow the sending of unsolicited email to recipients who have a prior relationship with the sender. This is reasonable, but what a prior relationship consists of needs to be defined carefully. There is a type of spammer ('permission-based email marketers') who obtains email addresses by buying them from websites with unethical privacy policies. By calling the site a spammer bought your email address from a 'partner' or 'affiliate', the spammers can claim that they too have a 'prior relationship' with you, and are therefore exempt from spam laws.

In November 2004,[13] the USA held its first criminal trial concerning spam in Leesburg, Virginia, which resulted in the conviction of Jeremy Jaynes. The case was brought under Virginia's state anti-spam law, not the weaker Federal Can Spam act. Virginia's law makes it a crime to send unsolicited bulk mail using forgery, so the Commonwealth had to show first that Jaynes sent lots of unsolicited mail and second that it was sent using forgery. The mail in question was sent on three days in October to AOL, which is why the case was heard in Leesburg, the seat of Loudon County in which AOL's mail servers are located. Although most of society welcomes rulings such as that in Virginia, it must be noted that spammers are often based in different countries, which have different Internet laws. Applying a law on an international basis or prosecuting spammers in other countries is problematic. Spam blocking efficiency with this method is high as it stops spam being sent at source.

Slow down spammers (proof of work)

Spam has low response rates (on the order of 15 per million) but spammers make up for it with high volumes, sending millions of emails per day.[4] If you could slow down the rate at which spammers send email, you could put them out of business. One way to do this would be to make any computer used to send email perform an easily verifiable time-consuming computation before you would accept that email. Whatever these computations are, they should be within acceptable, controllable levels of complexity, because legitimate corporate email servers have to be able to send high volumes of email. And corporate email servers would be running on standard hardware. Many computations can be made hundreds or thousands of times faster by custom hardware.

This is the first approach that directly attacks the spammers' profitability model; instead of trying to block or filter spam that has already been sent, it makes it more costly for the spammer to send each message. It also helps reduce false positives caused by other types of spam filtering. It is likely that if an email has a 'proof of work' stamp, then it has been sent by a genuine sender, and can bypass standard Bayesian filters. For this idea to work, it is necessary to determine the type of computation that could not easily be speeded up by custom hardware. Even with a suitable computation, this idea would require new email protocols. And any new protocol has one fundamental problem: no one is inclined to adopt it until everyone else does. As a result, it is practically impossible to get a new protocol adopted. How are we to get system administrators who will not install patches for years-old security holes to switch to a new email protocol? Spammers already have highly tuned systems and would not be deterred by the need for custom hardware. Spam blocking level of efficiency of this method is medium. If spammers actually performed the proof-of-work test, then the email would get through. False positives may still occur. If a legitimate sender does not perform a proof-of-work test to stamp their email, then it could be flagged as 'possible spam'. Performance would be poor at the sender end, as it requires CPU cycles for proof of work, but good at the recipient end.

Proposed industry solutions

Most of the above approaches take a 'technology-only' approach to the problem of spam emails. What is required is an approach that encompasses technology with a policy-based solution. Any approach also needs support from the major ISPs (such as Yahoo, Hotmail and AOL), and should be aligned with existing anti-spam laws. There are a number of industry proposals, most of which encompass hybrid multi-layer spam blocking/filtering technologies with trust-based systems and often cover the areas of policy as well.

Trusted email open standard

On 30 April 2003, ePrivacy Group announced the trusted email open standard (TEOS) to fight spam, spoofing and email fraud.[14] TEOS is a staged approach towards a trusted email system built upon and extending the SMTP protocol. TEOS takes a two-track approach comprising an identify verification system, content assertions (flags in the subject line which identify the type of content) in conjunction with a policy-based trust and accountability process. TEOS creates a framework of trusted identity for email senders based on secure, fast, lightweight signatures in email headers, optimised with domain name system (DNS)-based systems for flexibility and ease of implementation. TEOS also provides a common-language framework for making trusted assertions about the content of each individual message. ISPs and email recipients can rely on these assertions to manage their email.[15]

Microsoft coordinated spam reduction initiative

Microsoft's proposal covers a number of areas, but the main focus is on a system called Caller ID.[16] Microsoft and the Internet Engineering Task Force have proposed changes to the way SMTP verifies the sender of an email by looking up the source via DNS. This involves modifications of DNS standards (a central part of the Internet itself). Caller ID allows Internet domain owners to publish the IP address of their outgoing email servers in an XML format email 'policy' in the DNS record for their domain. Email servers can query the DNS record and match the source IP address of incoming email messages to the address of the approved sending servers. This results in email being verifiable as coming from who it says it is from.

Domain Keys and Sender Policy Framework (SPF)

These proposals (supported by Yahoo and AOL) are essentially the same as the Caller ID proposals. They use a DNS challenge/response mechanism to allow look-up and verification of the sender of the email to ensure they are who they claim to be. However, weaknesses are already becoming apparent in this system. This approach was implemented by Yahoo in the first quarter of 2004, but it has resulted in no reduction in spam volumes to Yahoo email addresses. The spammers are validating themselves as legitimate email senders to ensure their emails get through, and legitimate emailers are sending from servers that have not actually implemented the Domain Keys technology. Although spammers no longer have anonymity on their side, there is no solid legal framework in place, or even a way to prevent spammers from continuing to send spam if they are using Domain Keys. Systems such as Domain Keys and Caller ID only offer a part of the anti-spam solution. They ensure the email sender can be identified but they do not offer a way to stop a spammer sending spam.[17]

Spammer profitability

At present, a spammer is limited only by the speed of their uplink and their available hardware as to how many spam messages they can send a day. Spammers are usually specialists in their field. They are employed on a cost per email or sometimes a response commission basis.[18] In order to make it unprofitable for the spammers to stay in business, it is necessary to reduce the amount of spam they send, or make it costly to send each message. It should be possible based on existing knowledge about spammers' business models to calculate how much the rate of spamming needs to be slowed down. There are two approaches to calculating spammer profitability and breakeven points: based on economic calculations, and a simpler model based on a 'slowdown rate'.[9]

Computation time per message

The key fact here is that resolving spamming involves both monetary expenditure (in the form of the amortised yearly cost of a CPU) as well as the expenditure of a certain amount of time. These two ideas are connected. Consider the following four variables:

- *secondsPerMessage*, the amount of CPU time spent per message in solving the puzzle (actually this is per message per recipient, but for brevity hereafter we simply say 'per message').

- *messagesPerResponse*, the number of messages that must be sent to get one actual successful response. For example, if only one in 10 thousand spam messages generates a successful response, then the value of this variable is 10,000.

- *revenuePerResponse*, the amount of revenue generated by each successful response. In our analysis here, this should be thought of as the revenue net of both the actual cost of goods and any amortised overhead.

- *cpuCostPerYear*, the burdened cost of a CPU: the amount of money necessary to acquire, house, power, air-condition, maintain and administer a CPU for a year.

With these definitions in hand, we can derive a formula to indicate spammer breakeven points:

$$SecondsPerMessage =$$
$$31557600 * revenuePerResponse/cpuCostPerYear * messagesPerResponse.$$

What this says is that given reasonable values for the three variables *messagesPerResponse*, *revenuePerResponse* and *cpuCostPerYear*, the expenditure of an amount of CPU time per message beyond the threshold indicated is *guaranteed* to deter a profit-driven spammer. (Note that this equation is independent of any particular currency: it simply requires that *revenuePerResponse* and *cpuCostPerYear* be denominated in the same units.) This equation can be understood in one of two ways, depending on when one considers a response to have occurred. Specifically, *messagesPerResponse* is an indication of either:

1. the *click-through* rate, i.e. the rate at which the content of spam messages is actively acted upon by their recipients, or

2. the *conversion* rate, i.e. the rate at which spam messages actually result in a sale or other transaction involving a transfer of money.

Actual figures for response rates to spam emails are rare, although there is a lot of 'what if' speculation. In 2002 the *Wall Street Journal* gave real-world examples of spam response rates of 0.013% and 0.0023%.[19] If the rate per email did indeed return to 0.1 cents then at a 0.0023% response rate advertisers would need to be selling goods with a profit margin of at least $4.35. This is not implausible: mortgage leads are worth $50, cell phone sales about $85 and there are examples of companies selling fake medicines worth $2.50 for $59.95. Hence, a price of 0.1 cents per email could be viable, especially if the senders of spam were to improve response rates by applying presentation from legitimate marketers. Thus we must look to restrict spammers to just 1,750 emails per day per machine. Of course this would also limit legitimate emailers to the same level of sending. Depending on the viewpoint one chooses, the *revenuePerResponse* must be adjusted accordingly. Rreal-world estimates for each of the two interpretations of the *messagesPerResponse* rate together with their corresponding profit levels can be gleaned from various and sundry sources, especially the many press interviews of spammers that have appeared. These sources indicate with high probability that the following are not unreasonable estimates for these parameters for the majority of spammers (Table 22.1).

In order to get a sense of the implications of what this means in concrete terms, if we assume for that *cpuCostPerYear* for the average spammer is approximately USD $200, then using the equation above we can conclude that:

- at a 1-in-2000 click-through rate, 78 seconds of computation deters $1 per click;

- at a 1-in-10,000 click-through rate, 31 seconds of computation deters $2 per click;

Table 22.1 Parameter approximate value range

	Low	High
Click-through rate	1-in-2000	1-in-10,000
Revenue per click	USD $1	USD $2
Conversion rate	1-in-50,000	1-in-100,000
Revenue per conversion	USD $1	USD $80

- at a 1-in-50,000 conversion rate, 78 seconds of computation deters $25 per transaction;
- at a 1-in-100,000 conversion rate, 63 seconds of computation deters $40 per transaction.

Given the uncertainty in our parameter estimates and the fact that our model here actually omits several factors of cost to the spammer, it seems reasonable to believe that around 1 minute of computation is a highly significant spam deterrent, and probably a level that will guarantee that a majority of spammers are not profitable. Moreover, for these values the numbers illustrated are an absolute *upper bound*: it is very possible that significantly smaller thresholds are also quite effective deterrents. It is worthwhile recalling that in deployed systems puzzles need not be solved if the sender of a message is on their recipient's known-sender list. The average machine will only need to send about 75 emails, which gives some headroom for legitimate activity, but when one starts to consider variations in sending activity and differences in puzzle-solving speeds, this method of estimating computation times does not give much insight into the value of how much spam will continue to arrive. The difficulty is that the effect will be to suppress the least profitable forms of spam and we have no idea what proportion this might be. However, if spam is more convincingly presented, or the spammer can make a profit from not only emailing but owning other parts of the marketing chain, then it will certainly not be possible to raise the computation time sufficiently to have an impact without starting to affect legitimate email.[9]

Conclusion

It is becoming increasingly clear that a single technology is not going to solve the problem of spamming.[2,20] An intelligent combination of technologies might be much more effective. There are a quartet of complementary technologies to consider, namely proof of work, signatures with whitelist, domain certificates and content filters. This cocktail of anti-spam measures is known as the 'hybrid' system. They are inadequate when used individually, but when used together can compensate for the inadequacies inherent in each part of the system. An all-encompassing anti-spam system needs to address a number of additional areas, however, and ideally consists of a multi-layered approach:

- Policies – mass-mailers agree to conform to certain standards

- Accountability – if spammers do not conform, then some sort of Internet 'sanctions' should be applied

- Traceability – email should be verifiable as coming from who it says it is from, to ensure senders can be traced

- Legal – for repeat spammers or those who refuse to comply with any of the policies, then legal discourse can be used as the fall-back position

- Technical – proof-of-work stamps to minimise spam volumes. Traditional Bayesian filters to trap anything that gets through (this is the point where false positives could occur – so whether Bayesian filters are still required in this model is debatable)

- Whitelists and signatures to ensure ease of communication and establish trust between verified correspondents.

Domain certificates provide a good first line of defence to reduce forgery. This is a highly recommended goal regardless. They can be implemented at the SMTP level, separately from the remainder of the filters, which must operate at the message level. The two reasons for going to a key (whitelist signature) system instead of proof of work system is to provide a mechanism that will allow stamp size to be set to a level to hurt spammers without hurting ordinary users, as well as giving a mechanism for mailing lists to be able to deliver traffic to all users quickly and efficiently. Currently the main stumbling block with any of these proposed industry solutions is achieving agreement between partners on the best way forward. Spammers have learned to adapt to overcome many of the anti-spam measures used against them, thus the greater urgency for industry partners to work together to implement a global hybrid solution.

Notes

1. Templeton, S. and Levitt, K. (2003) Detecting spoofed packets. *IEEE DARPA Information Survivability Conference and Exposition* Volume I, April 22–24, 2003, Washington, DC, pp. 164–77.

2. Ishibashi, H., Yamai, N., Abe, K. and Matsuura, T. (2001) *Protection Method against Unauthorised Access and Address Spoofing for Open Network Access Systems*, pp. 10–13.
3. Wikpedia (2009) Sobig computer worm. *http://en.wikipedia.org/wiki/Sobig_* (computer_worm)
4. Schwartz, A. and Garfinkel, S. (1998) *Stopping Spam*. O'Reilly.
5. Tserefos, P., Smythe, C., Stergiou, I. and Cvetkovic, S. (1997) A comparative study of simple mail transfer protocol (SMTP), POP and X.400 email protocols. *22nd Annual IEEE Conference on Local Area Networks, Minneapolis, USA*, pp. 545–55.
6. Clyman, J. (2004) The problem with protocols. *PC Magazine*, February.
7. Simpson, P. (2002) Putting spam back in the can. *ITsecurity.com*, 13 May,
8. Hastings, N. and McLean, P. (1996) TCP/IP spoofing fundamentals. *IEEE IPCCC'96, IEEE International Phoenix Conference on Computers and Communications*, Phoenix, Arizona, pp. 218–24.
9. Goodman, J. and Rounthwaite, R. (2004) Stopping outgoing spam. *ACM Conference on Electronic Commerce, EC'04*, New York, pp. 20–39.
10. Bass, T, and Watt, G. (1997) Simple framework for filtering queued SMTP mail (Cyberwar Countermeasures). *Proceedings of IEEE MILCOM '97*.
11. Graham, P. (2003) Different methods of stopping spam. *http://www.secinf. net/anti_spam/Stopping_Spam.html*
12. Baker, W. and Kamp, J. (2003). Summary of Can Spam Act. *http://www.wrf. com/publications/publication.asp?id=1623481222003*
13. Levine, J. (2004) Putting a spammer in jail. *CircleID*, 16 November, *http://www. circleid.com/article/804_0_1_0_C/*
14. Schiavone, V., Brussin, D., Koenig, J., Cobb, S. and Everett, R. (2003) Trusted email open standard – a comprehensive policy and technology proposal for email reform. Federal Trade Commision, Workshop on SPAM, Washington, 2003 Available at: *http://www.ftc.gov/bcp/workshops/spam/ Supplements/eprivacygp.pdf*
15. ePrivacy Group (2003) TEOS proposal document, *http://www.eprivacygroup. net/teos/*
16. Microsoft (2004) The Coordinated Spam Reduction Initiative – A technology and policy proposal. Microsoft Corporation. 13 February 2004. *http://www.microsoft.com/downloads*
17. Geer, D. (2004). Will new standards help curb spam? *IEEE Computer Magazine*, February, *http://www.computer.org/computer/homepage/0204/ TechNews/index.htm*
18. Boutin, P. (2004) Interview with a Spammer. *InfoWorld*, 16 April, *http://www. infoworld.com/article/04/04/16/16FEfuturerichter_1.html?s=feature*
19. Schryen, G. (2004) Approaches addressing spam. *Proceedings of IPSI*, Hawaii.
20. Roberts, P. (2004) Experts question Microsoft's Caller ID patents. *InfoWorld*, March, *http://www.infoworld.com/article/04/03/05/HNcalleridpatents_1.html*

23

Computer hacking

Kevin Curran, Peter Breslin, Kevin McLaughlin and Gary Tracey

Many self-proclaimed hackers would actually consider themselves to be performing a service to businesses as they claim they are simply showing businesses the flaws within their systems so that they can implement methods of prevention. They state that if it was not for hacking, security software would not be where it is today. An ethical hacker will tell you that someone who hacks into a system for purposes of self-benefit is a cracker rather than a hacker, as it is the former that give cause for security software in the first place. This chapter reviews the role of tools, methods and rationale of hackers.

Introduction

'Access' is defined in Section 2(1)(a) of the Information Technology Act[1] as 'gaining entry into, instructing or communicating with the logical, arithmetical, or memory function resources of a computer, computer system or computer network'. Unauthorised access would therefore mean any kind of access without the permission of either the rightful owner or the person in charge of a computer, computer system or computer network. Thus, not only would accessing a server by cracking its password authentication system be unauthorised access, but so too would switching on a computer system without the permission of the person in charge. Eric Raymond, compiler of *The New Hacker's Dictionary*[2] defines a hacker as a clever programmer. Although hacking, according to many hackers themselves, is beneficial to the development of systems security, it is still known as a crime under the computer misuse act. Categories of misuse under this act include: Computer fraud – Unauthorised access to information, Computer hacking, Eavesdropping, Unauthorised use for personal benefit, Unauthorised alteration or destruction of data, Denying access to authorised user and Unauthorised removal of data. The law does not distinguish between a hacker and a cracker. In regard to this, reformed hacker John Draper states:

> 'Hackers are very important for the Internet community as a whole because they are the ones who will be buttoning up the holes in the system. Governments should be a little more tolerant of what is going on and hackers should be willing to contact a company and say "I found bugs in your system".'

He believes that without hackers, security would not be where it is today, that hackers are playing a valuable part in the development of highly effective security systems, and that the government and the law should recognise this and try to distinguish more carefully between a hacker whose intent is to identify security flaws for a company, and a cracker whose intent is malicious.

Crackers use various methods to maliciously attack a computer's security, one such method being a 'virus'. A computer virus is defined as a piece of programming code usually disguised as something else that causes some unexpected and usually undesirable event. A computer virus attaches itself to a program or file so it can spread from one computer to another, leaving infections as it travels. The severity and effects of a computer virus can range much the same as a human virus. Some have only mild affects that simply annoy the host, whereas more severe viruses can cause serious damage to both hardware and software. Almost all viruses are attached to an executable file, which means the virus may exist on your computer but it cannot infect it unless you run or open the malicious program.[3] It is important to note that a virus cannot be spread without action. Users continue the spread of a computer virus, generally unwittingly, by sharing infected files or sending emails with viruses as attachments.

Another method is to use a 'worm'. A worm is similar to a virus in both design and the damage it can cause. Like a virus, worms spread from system to system, but unlike a virus, it has the ability to travel without any help from the user. It does this by taking advantage of the files and information already present on the computer. The biggest danger with a worm is its ability to replicate itself on your system, so rather than your computer sending out a single worm, it could send out hundreds or thousands of copies of itself, creating a devastating effect. For example, it is common for a worm to be sent via email; it is then possible for the worm to use the information in your email address book to send duplicates of itself to your contacts, and their contacts, etc. Due to the copying nature of a worm and its ability to travel across networks the end result in most cases is that the worm consumes too much system memory (or network bandwidth), causing Web servers, network servers and individual computers to stop responding. In more recent worm attacks, such as the much talked about Ms.Blaster worm, the worm has been designed to tunnel into your system and allow malicious users to control your computer remotely.

Eavesdropping

Eavesdropping can be thought of as another form of hacking. In many cases it involves unlawfully accessing a computer system in order to listen to (gather) information. This is invasion of privacy. Eavesdropping can be used by a hacker to gain information such as passwords and bank account details, although not all forms of eavesdropping are used for malicious purposes; governments use computer eavesdropping as a means of surveillance. They use this technique to identify paedophiles and other people who could be holding illegal information. Increasing numbers of employers are investing in surveillance software (eavesdropping software) that allows them monitor or eavesdrop on everything their employees type on their computers, be it email, Web surfing or even word processing. Not all forms of eavesdropping are illegal. And more and more eavesdropping software is being developed.

This kind of surveillance (eavesdropping) software is very similar to so-called Trojan software already used illegally by some hackers and corporate spies. Trojan software is a very common hacking and eavesdropping tool used by many hackers. Trojan horse software allows the hacker to enter your system and even take control of it. It gives the hacker remote access. At first glance, the Trojan horse will appear to be useful software but will actually do damage once installed or run on your computer. Those who are at the receiving end of the Trojan will have to activate it (by opening it) for the hacker to gain access; they are normally tricked into doing so because they appear to be receiving legitimate software or files from a legitimate source. Once the Trojan is activated on your computer, the hacker can then gain access. The effects of the Trojan can vary much like a virus; sometimes the affects can be more annoying than malicious (changing your desktop, adding unwanted active desktop icons) and sometimes the effects can be severe, causing serious damage by deleting files and destroying information on your system. The Trojan opens a 'back door' to your system, which allows the user to view personal and confidential files; this kind of information can then be used for purposes such as blackmail.

Electronic eavesdropping is perhaps the most sinister type of data piracy. Even with modest equipment, an eavesdropper can make a complete transcript of a victim's actions – every keystroke, and every piece of information viewed on a screen or sent to a printer. The victim, meanwhile, usually knows nothing of the attacker's presence, and blithely goes about his or her work, revealing not only sensitive information, but the passwords and procedures necessary for the hacker to obtain even more. In many cases, you cannot possibly know if you are being monitored. Sometimes you will learn of an eavesdropper's presence when the attacker attempts to make use of the information obtained: this is often too late to prevent significant damage. There are different methods of eavesdropping, a few of which are detailed below.

Electrical wires are prime candidates for eavesdropping (hence the name wiretapping). An attacker can follow an entire conversation over a pair of wires with a simple splice – sometimes the hacker does not even have to touch the wires physically: a simple induction loop coiled around a terminal wire is enough to pick up most voice and RS-232 communications. Ethernet and other local area networks are also susceptible to eavesdropping; unused offices should not have live Ethernet or twisted-pair ports inside them. You may wish to scan periodically all of the Internet numbers that have been allocated to your subnet to make sure that no unauthorised Internet hosts are operating on your network. You can also run LAN monitoring software and have alarms sound each time a packet is detected with a previously unknown Ethernet address. Some 10Base-T hubs can be set to monitor the IP numbers of incoming packets. If a packet comes in from a computer connected to the hub that does not match what the hub has been told is correct, it can raise an alarm or shut down the link. This capability helps prevent various forms of Ethernet spoofing.

Key loggers

Another method of computer systems eavesdropping is to use what is know as a key logger. A key logger is a program that runs in the background, recording all keystrokes used. Once keystrokes are logged, they are hidden in the machine for later retrieval, or sent automatically back to the attacker. The attacker can use the information gained by the key logger to find passwords and information such as bank account details. It is important to remember that a key logger is not just used as a hacking tool. Many home users and parents use key loggers such as Invisible Key to record computer and Internet activities. These key loggers are helpful in collecting information that will be useful when determining if your child is talking to the wrong person online or if your child is surfing inappropriate website content and it again can be used by businesses to monitor employees' work ethics. Normally there may be many files to key loggers and this means that it can be difficult to remove them manually; it is best to use anti-virus software or try to use methods such as firewalls to prevent them from getting onto the system in the first place.

On 17 March 2005 it was revealed that one of the largest bank robberies in Britain had been foiled by police in London. The target was the London branch of the Japanese bank 'Sumitomo Mitsui'. The bank robbers planned to steal an estimated £220 million. The stolen money was to be wired electronically from the bank into 10 different offshore bank accounts. This planned robbery was unlike any traditional bank robbery in Britain's history. It did not involve running into the bank with handguns, taking hostages and leaving in a getaway car. This was far more high-tech.[4] The bank robbers uploaded a program onto the bank's network that recorded every keystroke made on a keyboard. The program recorded the websites that were visited on the network, the passwords, bank account numbers and PIN numbers that were entered on these websites, and it then saved them to a file. This file was accessed by the robbers and they were later able to visit sites that the bank's employees had been surfing and reuse their login information so as to 'break' into their accounts. The site had no reason to think that the person logging on was not authorised to do so.

Key-logging software can record all sorts of computer operations, not just keystrokes. It can also record emails received and sent, chats and instant messages, websites, programs accessed, and peer-to-peer file sharing and it can also take screenshots. Key logging can occur in two ways. A specially coded program can be uploaded onto a network from anywhere in the world. The other involves a piece of hardware that is about the size of a battery. This is plugged into the computer from the keyboard and records the keystrokes made. This has to be physically installed onto the machine by a person and in order to retrieve the information gathered by the mini-hard drive the person also has to remove the hardware physically.[5] The key-logging software at Sumitomo Mitsui was uploaded to the network more than 6 months prior to the planned robbery. It was first noticed on the network in October 2004. The National Hi-Tech Crime Unit (NHTCU) then monitored the situation closely. The foiled robbery was the biggest and most high-profile coup in the Unit's short history.

Password grabbers, however, are useful to the owners of systems as well as to crackers as they provide them with the ability to monitor transactions carried out by the users for security auditing purposes. There are several types of password grabbers available such as Keycopy, which copies all the keystrokes to a file using timestamp, Keytrap, which copies all the keyboard scan codes for later conversion to ASCII, and Phantom, which logs keys and writes them to file every 32 keystrokes.

Spyware

The most common form of computer systems eavesdropping is provided by adware and spyware software. Spyware software covertly gathers user information through the user's Internet connection without his or her knowledge, usually for advertising purposes. Spyware applications are typically bundled as a hidden component of freeware or shareware programs that can be downloaded from the Internet; however, it should be noted that the majority of shareware and freeware applications do not come with spyware. Once installed, the spyware monitors user activity on the Internet and transmits that information in the background to someone else. Spyware can also gather information about email addresses and even passwords and credit card numbers.[6]

Spyware software is quite similar to a Trojan horse in that the user will unknowingly install the software themselves. The software can also cause a decrease in bandwidth as it runs in the background sending information to and receiving information from the software's home base. The most common way in which spyware software is installed onto a machine is when the user has downloaded certain freeware peer-to-peer file swapping software such as 'WarezP2p' or 'Kazaa'. Spyware software can be used by companies for advertising purposes as well as being used by hackers to gain user information. Adware is very similar to spyware. It affects your computer in much the same way, the main difference being that adware is used more for advertising purposes. Adware can result in numerous pop ups appearing once you have connected to the Internet, and it can allow icons to be added to your desktop and add websites to your Internet favourites. Both adware and spyware can be difficult to remove, as they will attach themselves to various parts of the system registry. Adware and spyware can be removed by downloading software tools from the Internet, although prevention via a firewall is recommended.

Unauthorised computer access and computer eavesdropping are potentially illegal, although in many cases eavesdropping is used simply by parents to monitor a child's Web history and the content of the sites they have visited, or by an employer to check that an employee is working and is doing his or her job.

Packet sniffing

Packet sniffing is a technology used by crackers and forensics experts alike. Data travel in the form of packets on networks. These packets, also referred to as data-grams, are of various sizes depending on the network bandwidth as well as the amount of data being carried (bytes). Each packet has an identification label called a 'header'. The header carries information of the source, destination, protocol, size of packet, total number of packets in sequence and the unique number of the packet. The data carried by the packet are in an encrypted format, not as much for the sake of security as for the sake of convenience in their transmission. This cipher text (encrypted form) is also known as the hex of the data. When a person 'A' sends a file to 'B' the data in the file are converted into hex and then broken into many packets. Finally, headers are attached to all packets and the data are ready for transmission.

When being transmitted, the packets travel through a number of layers [open systems interconnection (OSI) model]. Amongst these layers, the network layer is responsible for preparing the packet for transmission. This is the level where most hackers like to attack as the packets are usually not secured and are prone to spoofing and sniffing attacks. When an adversary (a person trying to hack into a system) 'C' wishes to intercept the transmission between 'A' and 'B', he or she would have intercept the data packets and then go on to translate them back from hex to the actual data. The hacker would normally use a technology called 'packet sniffing'. When the adversary uses this technology he or she is able to intercept all or some of the packets leaving the victim (sender) computer. The same deception can also be practised at the point of the intended recipient of the message before it can actually receive the packets. To use the sniffing technology the adversary only needs to know the IP address (e.g. 202.13.174.171) of either of the parties involved in the communication. The adversary would then instruct the sniffer to apply itself to the network layer of the victim's IP address. All packets leaving that IP address would then be 'sniffed' and the data being carried will be reported to the adversary in the form of logs. The sniffed data would still be in hex format, although most sniffers now provide conversion of hex into readable data, with varying levels of success.

Web server hacking

Web server hacking is when a hacker detects and takes advantage of the vulnerabilities of web server software or of add-on components, for example when worms 'Nimba' and 'Code Red' exploited the vulnerabilities of Microsoft's ISS Web server software. Source code disclosure allows the cracker to view the source code of application files on a vulnerable Web server and together with other techniques gives the attacker the ability to access protected files containing information such as passwords.[7] Computer and network resources can often be addressed in two ways. Canonicalization resolves resources name to standard form. Applications that make their security decisions based on the resource name can be extremely vulnerable to being duped into executing unexpected actions known as canonicalization attacks. Web distributed authoring and versioning is an extension to the HTTP protocol that enables distributed Web authoring through a set of HTTP headers and methods that allow such capabilities as creating, copying, deleting and searching for resources; this would be a major threat to a company if it was available to an attacker. Web field over flow involves an attacker bringing down a Web server through use of a Web browser. This vulnerability exists because Web developers often prefer to concentrate on functionality rather than security. One solution would be for developers to employ an input sanitisation routine in every program. The developer could move the administration page to a separate directory. Web server scanners are available that can scan and detect a wide range of well-known vulnerabilities.[7]

Password cracking

Cracking a password involves its decryption, or bypassing a protection scheme. When the UNIX operating system was first developed, passwords were stored in the file '/etc/passwd'. This file was readable by everyone, but the passwords were encrypted so that a user could not determine another person's password. The passwords were encrypted such that a person could test a password to see if it was valid, but could not decrypt the entry. However, a program called 'crack' was developed that would simply test all the words in the dictionary against the passwords in '/etc/passwd'. This would find all user accounts whose passwords where chosen from the dictionary. Typical dictionaries also included people's names as a common practice is to choose a spouse or child's name. Password crackers are utilities that try to 'guess' passwords. One method, also known as a dictionary attack, involves trying out all the words contained in a predefined dictionary. Ready-made dictionaries of millions of commonly used passwords can be freely downloaded from the Internet. Another form of password cracking attack is 'brute force'. In this form of attack, all possible combinations of letters, numbers and symbols are tried out one by one until the password is found out. Brute-force attacks take much longer than dictionary attacks.

Conclusion

Computer eavesdropping and hacking can both be considered forms of the general term unauthorised computer access. Unauthorised access can be described as an action in which a person accesses a computer system without the consent of the owner; this may include using sophisticated hacking/cracking software tools to gain illegal access to a system or simply be a case of a person guessing a password and gaining access. There are many methods that can be employed to prevent unauthorised computer access, such as regularly changing passwords, ensuring anti-virus software is up to date and ensuring that an up-to-date firewall exists on each system.

Notes

1. *http://www.stpi.soft.net/itbill2000_1.html*
2. Raymond, E. (1996) *The New Hacker's Dictionary*, 3rd edn. Cambridge, MA: MIT Press.
3. Dr-K (2000) *Complete Hacker's Handbook*. London: Carlton Book Ltd.
4. *http://news.bbc.co.uk/2/hi/technology/4357307.stm*
5. *http://searchsecurity.techtarget.com/sDefinition/0,,sid14_gci962518,00.html*
6. Wikipedia. *http://en.wikipedia.org/wiki/Spyware*
7. McClure, S., Scrambray, J. and Kurtz, G. (2003) *Hacking Exposed: Network Security Secrets & Solutions*, 4th edn. New York: McGraw-Hill/Osborne.

24

The invisible Web

Edwina Sweeney and Kevin Curran

A Web crawler or spider crawls through the Web looking for pages to index and when it locates a new page it passes the page on to an indexer. The indexer identifies links, keywords and other content and stores these within its database. This database is searched by entering keywords through a interface and suitable Web pages are returned in a results page in the form of hyperlinks accompanied by short descriptions. The Web, however, is increasingly moving away from being a collection of documents to a multidimensional repository for sounds, images, audio and other formats. This is leading to a situation where certain parts of the Web are invisible or hidden. The term known as the 'Deep Web' has emerged to refer to the mass of information that can be accessed via the Web but cannot be indexed by conventional search engines. The concept of the Deep Web makes searches quite complex for search engines. Google states that the claim that conventional search engines cannot find such documents as PDFs, Word, PowerPoint or Excel files or any non-HTML page is not fully accurate and they have taken steps to address this problem by implementing procedures to search items such as academic publications, news, blogs, video, books and real-time information. This chapter provides an overview of the 'hidden Web'.

Introduction

Eighty-five per cent of Web users use search engines to find information about a specific topic. However, nearly an equal amount state that the inability to find desired information is one of their biggest frustrations.[1] Because so much information is available on the Internet and the inadequacies of search engines mean that much of this is not accessible explain why search engines are an obvious focus of much investigation. Conventionally, indexing a document so that it can be found by a search engine means that the crawler must follow a link from some other document. Therefore, the more links to your document the more chance a document has of been indexed. This leaves a major loophole for documents that are generated dynamically. Because no links exist to these documents, they will never be located to be indexed. In addition, for websites that host databases, subscriber information or registration information are sometimes required before access is given to their resources. Typically, this type of information is never accessed because the crawler does not have the ability to submit registration or subscriber information. Millions of these documents exist on the Internet and thus a substantial amount of valuable information is never read by Internet users. Steve Lawerence of the NEC Research Institute states:

> 'Articles freely available online are more highly cited. For greater impact and faster scientific progress, authors and publishers should aim to make their research easy to access. Evidence shows that usage increases when access is more convenient and maximizing the usage of the scientific record benefits all of society.'[2]

The Surface Web[3] contains an estimated 2.5 billion documents, growing at a rate of 7.5 million documents per day.[1] The Deep Web is estimated to comprise in excess of 307,000 sites, with 450,000 online databases. Furthermore, the content provided by many Deep Web sites is often of very high quality and can be extremely valuable to many users.[4] However, general search engines are the first place a typical user will go to for information. There are common approaches implemented by many indexed search engines. They all include three programs, namely a crawler, an indexer and a searcher. This architecture can be seen in systems including Google and FAST. Some search engines also offer directory categories which involve human intervention in selecting appropriate websites for certain categories. Directories naturally complement search engines. There is now a trend towards the use of directories because, in addition to their classification, their content is pre-screened, evaluated and annotated by humans.[5] Search engines do not search the Web directly. In fact, when searching for a Web page through a search engine, the engine is always searching a somewhat stale copy of the real page. It is only when that page's URL is returned via a results page that a fresh copy of the page is made available. A Web crawler or spider crawls through the Web looking for pages to index. Its journey is directed by links within Web pages. Through the process of following links from different Web pages, the spider's journey can become infinite. When a spider locates a new page it passes the page to another program called an indexer. This program identifies links, keywords and other content and stores these within its database. This database is then searched by entering keywords through a search interface and a number of suitable Web pages will be returned in a results page in the form of hyperlinks accompanied by short descriptions (see Figure 24.1).

Chang and Cho claim that although

> 'The surface Web has linked billions of static HTML pages, an equally or even more significant amount of information is "hidden" on the deep Web, behind the query forms of searchable databases'.[6]

Conventional search engines create their indices by crawling static Web pages. In order to be discovered, the page must be static and linked to other pages.[7] It is thought that Web crawlers cannot browse or enter certain types of files, for example dynamic Web pages, and therefore cannot index the information within these files. However, claims have now been made that conventional search engines have the ability to locate dynamic Web pages, i.e. those that are generated in an ad-hoc manner.[8] Index Web crawlers cannot index pages that are in non-HTML format. Examples of non-HTML pages include PDFs, spreadsheets, presentations and some word processing files, script-based pages which include Perl, JavaScript and computer-generated imaging, and pages generated dynamically by active server pages, for example database files and images, video and music files.

Figure 24.1 Conventional search engine configuration

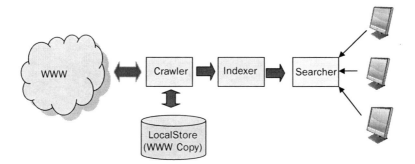

The biggest problems faced by search engines to date are their inability to login, to subscribe or enter relevant keywords to specialised databases or catalogues. When you use a search form to query a back-end database, the information generated is just in response to your particular query. It is much more cost effective to use these Web resources in this manner as opposed to entering all possible queries and then storing all the generated content in some repository. There are also pages that the search engine companies exclude for specific non-technical reasons. Some pages would not provide a financial benefit to store while other pages would not be of great interest to many people. There are thousands of public, official and special purpose databases containing government financial, and other types of information that is needed to answer specific inquiries. This information may include a stable link, although many search engines do not consider them to be sufficiently important to store.[8] The Web is increasingly moving away from being a collection of documents and becoming multidimensional repository for sounds, images, audio and other formats. This has led to a situation where certain parts are invisible or hidden. The term known as the 'Deep Web' has been used repeatedly by many writers to refer to the mass of information that can be accessed via the Web but cannot be indexed by conventional search engines. Most people accessing the Web through a search engine assume that all documents available on the Internet will be found through an efficient search engine such as Google. In August 2005, Google claimed to have indexed 8.2 billion Web pages.[1] This figure sounds impressive. However, when it is compared with the estimated size of the deep or hidden Web, it becomes apparent that a whole wealth of information is effectively hidden to Internet users. Extensive research was carried out by the BrightPlanet Corporation in 2001.[7] Its comprehensive findings were that:

1. Public information on the Deep Web is currently 400–550 times larger than the commonly defined World Wide Web

2. The Deep Web contains nearly 550 billion individual documents compared with the 1 billion of the surface Web

3. More than 200,000 Deep Web sites exist

4. Sixty of the largest Deep Web sites collectively contain about 750 terabytes of information, sufficient by themselves to exceed the size of the surface Web 40-fold

5. On average, Deep Web sites receive 50% greater monthly traffic that surface sites

6. The Deep Web is the largest growing category of new information on the Web

7. Total quality content of the Deep Web is 1,000–2,000 times greater than that of the surface Web

8. More than half of the Deep Web resides in topic-specific databases

9. A full 95% of the Deep Web is publicly accessible information and is not subject to fees or subscription.

Table 24.1 represents the subject coverage across all 17,000 Deep Web sites used in their study. The table shows uniform distribution of content across all areas, with no category lacking significant representation, illustrating that that Deep Web content has relevance to every information need and market.[7]

The Deep Web also holds a greater 'quality' of documents. The BrightPlanet Corporation conducted a series of tests to measure the quality of documents returned from the Deep Web. Using computational linguistic scores, they posed five queries across various subject domains to the surface Web and the Deep Web. Table 24.2 indicates the five queries that were issued to three search engines, namely AltaVista, Fast and Northern Lights, and three well-known Deep Web sites. The results show that a Deep Web site is three times more likely to provide 'quality'[9] information than a surface Web site. Professional content suppliers typically have the kinds of database sites that make up the Deep Web; static HTML pages that typically make up the surface Web are less likely to be from professional content suppliers.[7]

Table 24.1 Distribution of Deep Web sites by subject area[7]

General	Coverage (%)	Specific	Coverage (%)
Humanities	13	Agriculture	2.7
Lifestyles	4	Arts	6.6
News, media	12.2	Business	5.9
People, companies	4.9	Computing	6.9
Recreation, sport	3.5	Education	4.3
Travel	3.4	Government	3.9
Shopping	3.2	Engineering	3.1
Employment	4.1	Health	5.5
Science, maths	4	Law	3.9

Table 24.2	'Quality' documents retrieved from the Deep and Surface Web[7]

	Surface Web			Deep Web		
Query	Total	Quality	Yield (%)	Total	Quality	Yield (%)
Agriculture	400	20	5.0	300	42	14.0
Medicine	500	23	4.6	400	50	12.5
Finance	350	18	5.1	600	75	12.5
Science	700	30	4.3	700	80	11.4
Law	260	12	4.6	320	38	11.9
Total	2210	103	4.7	2320	285	12.3

The concept of the Deep Web makes searches quite complex for search engines. Even Google has attempted to integrate the Deep Web into its centralised search function. Google provides specific searches to, for example, academic publications, news, blogs, video, books and real-time information. However, even a search engine such as Google provides access to only a fraction of the Deep Web.[10] When the Internet evolved, Web pages were structured HTML documents. Managing such static documents was relatively simple. Since then, the growth rate of the Web has been 200% annually.[7] Since 1996, three developments within the Web have taken place. First, database technology was introduced; second, the Web became commercialised; and third, Web servers became capable of delivering dynamic information through Web pages. It is now quite common for most organisations, public and private, to transfer, seek and provide information through a database-driven application. Governments at all levels around the world have made commitments to making their official documents and records available on the Web through single-access portals.[1] An increasing amount of the Deep Web has now become available on the Web. As publishers and libraries make agreements with commercial search engines, undoubtedly more content will be searchable through a centralised location. Also, as the amount of online information grows, the amount of dynamically generated Web pages will grow. Search engines cannot ignore and exclude these pages.

State of the art in searching the Deep Web

Currently many tools exist that allow Internet users to find information. However, a large number of Web pages require Internet users to submit a query form. The information generated from these query forms is not indexable by most search engines as they are dynamically generated by querying backend databases.[11] The majority of these resources are within the Deep Web and therefore are rarely indexed.[5,12] When examining the contents of the Deep Web, it became very obvious that much of the information stored was accurate and relevant, for example scientific, historic and medical data that would dramatically improve communication, research and progress in these areas.[2] This section provides an overview of research addressing the problem of the Deep Web. Each project proposes a different method; however, there are some similarities between them.

Although autonomous heterogeneous sources are seemingly independent, the information that they provide is revealed through the query user interfaces. A search form within a book sales website such as Barnes & Noble contains attributes such as author, title, ISBN and edition. This would indicate that this site is about books. Within an airline site, attributes such as from, to, departure date and return date would reveal that the site is about flights. Kabra *et al.* have built a *source selection system* which examines user queries with regard to 'deep' Web sources.[12] Given the huge number of heterogeneous Deep Web sources, Internet users may not be aware of all the sources that can satisfy their information needs. Therefore, the selection system developed by Kabra *et al.* attempts to find the most relevant Deep Web resources from a given simple imprecise query. It designs a co-occurrence-based attribute graph for capturing the relevance of attributes. It employs this graph to rank sources in order of relevance to a user's requirement. The system counteracts the impreciseness and incompleteness in user queries. It assumes that the user may not be aware of the best attributes to enter as a query and so therefore limit themselves in the results that will be returned to them. The main contributions of the work by Kabra *et al.* are an attribute co-occurrence graph for modelling the relevance of attributes and an iterative algorithm that computes attribute relevance given an imprecise query. A methodology was created in which the relevance of an attribute was determined using the relevance of other attributes. There may be some attributes that are not included in a user's query but which do appear in many of the data source query interfaces. These co-occurring attributes will also be relevant to the search. In addition, there are similar attributes that co-occur with the other attributes that are likely to have some relevance to the query in question. Therefore, any relevant attribute will increase the relevance of its co-occurring attributes. In order to quantify this approach, a relevance score was associated with each attribute which represented how likely a query interface containing the attribute will provide appropriate information to the Internet user. The results indicated that the system frees users from worrying about finding the right set of query attributes. Even with a set of attributes that might not necessarily best describe the type of information required, the algorithm will direct the Internet user to the most appropriate set of Web sources.

The actual Deep Web is at a nascent stage.[13] Many systems would assume that the Internet user is aware of the appropriate Web resource and would ignore the need to help users to find the desired website that they want to extract information from. Finding the most relevant website to a given user query is the main objective of most search engines. Manually administered measures seem to have the highest percentage of success. Google has always favoured the algorithmic approach to searching because of the obvious scaling advantages over the human editorial approach. Computer algorithms can evaluate many times more Web pages than humans can in a given time period. 'Of course the flip side of this argument is that machines lack the ability to truly understand the meaning of a page.'[14]. The fact that Internet users are now aware of the 'Deep Web' should have a profound effect on the development of search tools. Search engines such as Yahoo integrate categories into their user interface which aids in the selection of appropriate Web resources. The Google search engine, which indexes approximately 8 billion pages, has created a development forum which allows access to Google APIs. In essence this allows developers to interact with the Google database and search engine to retrieve Web pages which can be filtered using a number of different techniques. It also enables developers to create custom search engines which direct their search to specific sites. Coverage of the 'Deep' Web is not easily accessed through conventional search engines and therefore an invaluable amount of information is never accessed by many Internet users. By directing specific or well-defined queries to a Deep Web resource, users can make their own determination of 'quality' documents. The implementation of a system to achieve this could be done through use of Google APIs and the Google Custom Search Engine tool.

Google Custom Search Engine

Google recognises that there are inherent limitations in the use of link-based ranking schemes to provide optimal search results.[14] In 2006, Google launched a new development tool which enables Web users to create their own search engine. The Custom Search Engine (CSE) provides a form-based interface for building a specific search engine on top of the Google search platform. This means that the Web user can focus on selecting valuable trusted content, while Google does the crawling, indexing, ranking and displaying of results. The main function of building a CSE is to determine which sites are searched, and to define a set of rules that guide the ranking of results. Specifically, the CSE program allows four major methods for altering the search results: (1) which sites will be included in the displayed results; (2) sites whose ranking should be raised; (3) sites whose ranking should be lowered; and (4) sites which should be excluded from the results. Theoretically, the CSE program enables knowledgeable experts to provide editorial oversight of the results. Google recognises that there are limitations in the use of link-based ranking schemes to provide best possible search results. Knowledgeable experts can now define search engines whose results are manually tweaked. Web designers can also use more than one knowledgeable expert to build a CSE. The program includes a collaboration feature, from which other experts can be recruited to contribute their expertise. When a user performs a search, they are brought to a Web page that looks like the traditional Google results page. However, there are significant differences in that the site owner can choose to have the search results appear on their own Web page or, alternatively, they can be hosted by Google on Google.com. The CSE owner can customise the look and feel of the page to make it look more like their existing site. The implication of introducing such a tool is that Google has effectively recruited a number of 'knowledgeable experts' to help improve their search results. The potential exists for a substantial amount of search volume to take place through highly trusted resource sites across the Web, where trusted and recognised experts put together vertically orientated CSEs that provide superior results in their area of expertise.[14] Google offers the designers of these CSEs revenue based on the number of visitors to the site. Google shares in this advertising revenue; therefore, there is an incentive for them to promote third-party custom search engines. This practice is significant to the whole notion of Google creating a distributed search platform; while distributing the work of CSEs, it still retains its ability to monetize searches. To design a CSE, a developer has to decide on the name, a description, whether to limit the CSE solely to the sites they specify or to include results from the entire Web, and whether you want third-party contributions, to be by invitation only or to be open to anyone who is interested.

Conclusion

Conventional search engines index a document such that it can be found by searchers. This is done through a 'crawler' following a link from some other starting point. This means that the more links to your document the more chance a document has of been indexed. This, however, can be a problem for documents that are generated dynamically as no links exist to these documents, and therefore they will never be located to be indexed. In addition, for Web sites that host databases, subscriber information or registration information is sometimes required before access is given to their resources. Typically, this type of information is never accessed because the crawler does not have the ability to submit registration or subscriber information. Google is a widely used and reputable search engine. It has released an exciting feature through its Google custom search engine. Allowing Internet users the ability to filter their own search engine is a positive approach to gaining access to the Deep Web. Typically, Internet users will more freely use this technology to search before attempting to subscribe to individual Deep Web sources. Providing a Google technology that can comparably return results as if from a Deep Web site will be very useful.

Notes

1. Kay R. (2005) QuickStudy: Deep Web. *ComputerWorld*, 4 June, *http://www.computerworld.com/action/article.do?command=viewArticleBasic&articleId=293195&source=rss_dept2*
2. Lawrence, S. (2001) Online or invisible. *Nature*, 411, no. 6837, p. 521.
3. A term which is used to describe information that is indexed and accessible through conventional search engines.
4. Ntoulas, A., Zerfos, P. and Cho, J. (2005) What's new on the Web?: the evolution of the Web from a search engine perspective. *International World Wide Web Conference, Proceedings of the 13th international conference on World Wide Web*, pp. 1–12. ACM Press.
5. Lackie, R. (2006) *Those Dark Hiding Places: The Invisible Web Revealed*. NJ: Rider University.
6. Chang, K. and Cho, J. (2006) Accessing the Web: from search to integration. *25th ACM SIGMOD International Conference on Management of Data / Principles of Database Systems*, pp. 804–5. ACM Press.
7. Bergman, M. (2001) The Deep Web: surfacing hidden value. *Journal of Electronic Publishing*, *http://www.press.umich.edu/jep/07-01/bergman.html*
8. Berkeley (2007) *What is the Invisible Web, a.k.a. the Deep Web*, Berkeley Teaching Guides, *http://www.lib.berkeley.edu/TeachingLib/Guides/Internet/InvisibleWeb.html*

9. Quality is a metric value that can be difficult to determine or assign.
10. Cohen, L. (2006) Internet tutorials, the Deep Web, FNO.com, From Now on. *The Educational Technology Journal*, 15: 3.
11. Broder, A., Glassman, S., Manasse, M. and Zweig, G. (1997) Syntatic clustering of the Web. *6th International World Wide Web Conference.* *http://proceedings.www6conf.org/HyperNews/get/PAPER205.html.*
12. Kabra, G., Li, C. and Chen-Chuan Chang, K. (2005) *Query Routing: Finding Ways in the Maze of the Deep Web.* Department of Computer Science, University of Illinois at Urbana-Champaign.
13. Wang, J. and Lochovsky, F. (2003) Data extraction and label assignment for web databases. *International World Wide Web Conference, Proceedings of the 12th international conference,* Budapest, Hungary, pp. 187–96. ACM Press.
14. Seth, S. (2006) *Google muscle to power custom search engines,* CRIEnglish. com. *http://english.cri.cn/2906/2006/10/24/272@154396.htm*

25

Digital watermarking and steganography

Kevin Curran, Xuelong Xi and Roisin Clarke

Digital imaging companies lose revenue each year to people who are illegally copying and using their images. One prevention mechanism is to encode images digitally, making it difficult for others to copy. This can be achieved using digital fingerprinting or simply by adding a visible watermark. The information is encoded within a host image, so that the actual appearance of the image does not change, but within the image there is a watermark or secret message, which prohibits the attacker from making an exact copy. The objective of steganography is not to change the actual message, or to make it difficult to read, as cryptography does, but rather to hide the existence of the message without distorting the carrier or the actual information. This chapter describes the results of implementing a least significant bit (LSB) digital watermarking system.

Introduction

The objective of steganography is to send a message through media known as a carrier, to a receiver, while preventing anyone else from knowing that the message exists. The carrier can be one of many different digital media, but the most common is the image. The image should not attract any attention as a carrier of a message and should compare as closely as possible to the original image by the human eye. When images are used as the carrier in steganography, they are generally manipulated by altering one or more bits of the byte that make up the pixels of the image. The LSB may be used to encode the bits of the message. These LSBs can then be read by the recipient of the steganography image and put together as bytes to reproduce the hidden message, providing they have the appropriate key – the password for the steganography image.[1]

Steganography is derived from the Greek word *steganos*, which means covered or secret, and *graphy*, meaning written or drawn. The art of steganography originated from a Greek man named Histiaeus, who was a prisoner of a rival king. He needed a way of transmitting a secret message to his people. He had the idea of shaving a willing slave's head and tattooing the message onto his scalp. When the slave's hair grew back, he was sent to deliver the message to Histiaeus' army.[2] Steganalysis is the art of discovering such a message. Breaking a steganographic system involves detecting that steganography has been used, reading the embedded message and proving that the message has been embedded to third parties. Steganalysis methods are also used by the steganographer to determine whether the message is secure and whether the process has been successful.[3] Detection involves observing relationships between combinations of cover, steganography media and steganography tools. This can be achieved by passive observation of patterns or unusual exaggerated noise and visual corruption. The patterns visible to the human eye could broadcast the existence of the message and point to signatures of certain methods or tools used. If numerous comparisons are made between the cover images and the steganography images, patterns can begin to emerge. Some of the methods of carrying out steganography produce characteristics that act as signatures for that particular method. Detection might involve looking at areas in the image where colour does not flow well from one area to the next. The attacker should obviously not be familiar with the cover image, as this would make comparisons easier.

Today steganography is used for transmitting data, as well as hiding trademarks in images and music. This is known as digital watermarking. Cryptography and steganography are different in their methods of hiding information. Cryptography scrambles a message and hides it in a carrier, so that if intercepted it is generally impossible to decode. Steganography hides the very existence of the message in the carrier. When the message is hidden in the carrier a stego-carrier is formed, for example a stego-image. If successful, it would be perceived to be as close to the original carrier or cover image by the human eye. Images are the most widespread carrier medium.[1,4] They are used for steganography in the following way.

- The message may first be encrypted. The sender (or embedder) embeds the secret message to be sent into a graphic file.[5] This results in the production of what is called the stego-image. Additional secret data may be needed in the hiding process, e.g. a stego-key.[6] The stegoimage is then transmitted to the recipient.

- The recipient or the extractor extracts the message from the carrier image. The message can only be extracted if there is a shared secret between the sender and the recipient. This could be the algorithm for extraction or a special parameter such as a key (the stego-key).

To make the stegonographic process even more secure the message may be compressed and encrypted before it is hidden in the carrier. Figure 25.1 illustrates the principles behind steganography, in which a carrier message has a message added and put through a stegosystem encoder. The stego-image is then sent through the appropriate channels to a stegosystem decoder.[7]

For greyscale images each pixel has a value between 0 and 255. The image is broken down into coordinates and pixels. The carrier image must be either the same size or larger than the message. The LSB of each pixel of the carrier is changed to the LSB of each pixel of the message to be hidden. This has the effect of hiding the message but making it appear to be the carrier. The human eye cannot detect the message or any difference to the carrier. It then has to be passed through a stego-image decoder for the hidden message to be extracted. A username and password is required at this stage. This is where cryptography and steganography can be used together. When the message is compressed it takes up less space in the carrier and will minimise the amount of information to be sent. It also limits the chances of being seen or detected in the carrier. The random message resulting from encryption and compression would be easier to hide than a message with a high degree of regularity.[8] Encryption and compression are recommended in conjunction with steganography, as this

Figure 25.1 Steganographic system[7]

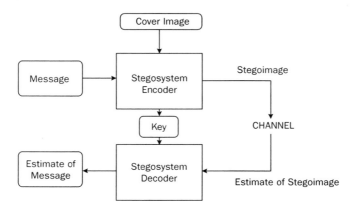

offers a higher degree of security and reliability. There are a variety of digital carriers or places where data can be hidden. Data may be embedded in files at imperceptible levels of noise and properties of images can be changed and used in a way particular to the user's aim. Features such as luminescence, contrast and colours can be changed according to which one is most useful to the particular application. This chapter focuses on bit values of pixels in the greyscale range which can be altered to embed hidden images inside other images, without changing the actual appearance of the carrier image.

Image steganography

In LSB substitution, the LSB is changed because this has little effect on the appearance of the carrier message, as shown in Figure 25.2.

This shows that the greyscale image would change significantly if there were any other bit changed than the LSB. It changes increasingly the closer you get to the maximum significant bit (MSB). When the LSB is changed, the pixel bit value changes from 128 to 129, which is actually undetectable to the human eye. With the MSB is changed, the pixel bit value changes from 128 to 0, which makes a significant change to the greyscale view. The theory is that if you take two greyscale images, and change the LSB of image 1 to the LSB of image 2 for each coordinate or pixel, image 1 will be hidden in image 1, as illustrated in Figure 25.3.

When the second image is embedded in the first, there should be no detectable change or alteration to the appearance of the first image. A digital image is the most common type of carrier used for steganography.

Figure 25.2 **LSB and MSB substitution**

Image 1:

1	0	0	0	0	0	0	0

The grayscale pixel bit size is: 128

Image 2:

1	0	0	0	0	0	0	1

The grayscale pixel bit size here is: 129 with the LSB changed.

Image 3:

0	0	0	0	0	0	0	0

By changing the MSB here the bit size has changed from 128 to 0.

Figure 25.3 Image processing results

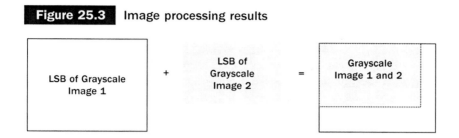

A digital image is produced using a scanner, camera or other digital device. The digital representation is an approximation of the original source.[9] The system used for producing the images focuses two-dimensional patterns of varying light intensity and colour onto a sensor. The pattern, in this case a greyscale pattern, has a coordinate system with the origin in the upper left corner of the image. The pattern can be described by a function $f(x,y)$. The pattern can be described as an array of numbers that represent light intensities at various points. These are known as pixels. Sampling is the process of measuring the value of the image function, $f(x,y)$, at discrete intervals. Each sample is the small square area of the image known as the pixel. The raster data of an image are the part of the image that can be seen on screen. Pixels are indexed by x and y coordinates (x and y are integer values). Dense sampling produces high-resolution images in which there are many pixels, each contributing to a small part of the image. Coarse sampling results in a low-resolution image in which there are fewer pixels.

Application of steganography to images

When an image is used as a carrier in steganography, it is generally manipulated by changing one or more bits of the byte, in our case the LSB. If it corresponds to the bit to be hidden or embedded it is left unchanged. Otherwise it is changed to correspond to the hidden bit. These LSBs can then be read by the recipient of the stego-image and put together as bytes to reproduce the hidden message. In a greyscale image, each pixel is either black or white and has a level of between 0 and 255, as each pixel has 8 bits. Steganography is carried out by changing the low-order bit of a pixel, and using it to encode 1 bit of a character. There are two stages in the steganalysis system:

- detecting that steganography has been used
- reading the embedded message.

Steganalysis is used by a steganographer in order to determine whether a message is secure and consequently whether the steganographic method has been successful. The aim of a stegoanalyst is to detect stego-images, find and read the embedded message, and prove that the message has been embedded to third parties. Detection involves observing relationships between combinations of cover, message, stego-media and steganographic tools.[10] Active interference by the stegoanalyst involves removing the message without altering the stego-image too much, or removing the image or message without consideration of the appearance or structure of the stego-image.[6] There are two necessary conditions to be fulfilled for a secure steganographic process. The key must remain unknown or undetectable to the attacker, and the attacker should not be familiar with the cover image.[11] If the cover image is known and it is impossible to keep it unknown from the attacker, the message could be embedded in a random way so that it is secure, as long as the key remains unknown. However, it is preferable that the cover image remains unknown to maintain maximum security.

Digital watermarking

Digital watermarking is the process of hiding information in a carrier in order to protect the ownership of text, music, films and art.[9] Watermarking can be used to hide or embed visible or hidden copyright information.[12] Steganographic techniques can be used for the purposes of digital watermarking. Often information about the carrier itself is hidden, providing further information that is not explicitly displayed.[10] Watermarks in images are hidden generally so that they do not disturb or distort the image rather than to avoid detection. They are generally hidden in more significant areas of the image and are not lost by compression. The main aim of watermarking is to prevent unlawful reproduction of a product. The ID of the author can be hidden so that if the image is circulated, this still remains embedded in the image. In some cases watermarks are clearly visible – they are not a type of steganography, but are part of the actual image.

Watermarking does not impair the image. This is the main concern with visible watermarking. Although the watermark can be seen, it must be inserted in such a way that it does not interfere with the original image. The underlying image must still be legible. If the watermark blocks large portions of the original image or the entire image, it is not an effective watermark. There is also no point to a watermark that can be removed easily. The typical litmus test with the watermark is that if the watermark is removed then the image should be impaired or destroyed. Even though only a small amount of data are to be embedded, it should be inserted in more than one place so that it is more difficult to remove. Someone who is trying to remove the watermark would be unlikely to detect all of the watermarks from the original image.

There are two types of digital watermarking, visible and invisible (Figure 25.4).[13] Unlike steganography, it is irrelevant if a digital watermark is detected. Some companies prefer their watermarks to be visible to deter possible thieves. It is essential, however, that the watermark cannot be removed or tampered with.

Figure 25.5 illustrates how an image undergoes the watermarking process and appears at the end apparently unaltered to the user. In an

Figure 25.4 (a) Visible watermarking; (b) invisible watermarking

(a)   (b)

Figure 25.5 Coloured watermarking process

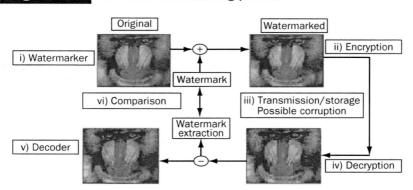

image such as this, the least significant 4 bits could be changed without any perceptual change in the resultant image, allowing enough space to hide a secret message.[3]

Invisible watermarks

In visible watermarking, a pattern is applied to a file or image so that it is undetectable by the human eye. Certain pixels in an image are changed so the human eye cannot tell the difference from the original image. A computer program can, however, detect such discrepancies. Another factor to consider when applying an invisible watermark is the actual size of the pixels. The smaller the pixel, the less chance there is of detecting a change in colour. The strength of invisible watermarks is that the image quality is not degraded or changed according to the user or consumer. When looking at the image, there is no way of telling that there is a watermark, yet the digital image is still protected. But invisible watermarks are effective only while the image is in digital form. If a digital image that has an invisible watermark is printed, and then rescanned, the watermark is effectively removed.

Visible watermarking

A visible watermark makes slight modifications to an image. The transformation is such that the image can still be seen, but the watermark is effectively laid over the top of it. One of the advantages of visible watermarks is that even if an image is printed and scanned the watermark is still visible. A visible watermark image will usually make use of a light greyscale tone or simply make the pixels that contain the watermark slightly lighter or darker than the surrounding area. When applying a visible watermark, it is essential that the watermark is applied to enough of the image that it cannot be removed, and the original image can still be seen and is still legible. If you apply too much of the watermark, all you will see is the watermark and little of the actual image. Complex mathematical formula can be used to make watermarks more robust, but at a general level a watermarking program finds a group of pixels and adjusts the pixels in a way that the watermark can be seen but the image is not destroyed. The usual way of performing this operation is to make the colour of specific pixels darker.

Table 25.1 Steganography vs. watermarking

Characteristic	Steganography	Digital watermarking
Amount of data	As much as possible	Small amount
Ease of detection	Very difficult to detect	Not critical with visible watermarks
Ease of removal	Very important it cannot be removed	Important it cannot be removed
Goal of attacker	To detect the data	To remove the data
Goal of user	To hide information so it cannot be removed	To embed a signature to prove ownership
Current uses	Covert communications	Protecting rights of owners

Attacks on watermarks

Attacks on watermarks involve trying to remove or distort them. The hidden information should be made such an integral part of the image that it is impossible to remove it without destroying the image. If the watermark is hidden in the LSB, all the individual has to do is flip one LSB and the information cannot be recovered. Various image processing techniques may be used to attack a watermark. Attacks can be particularly successful when using the same algorithm as was used to produce the existing watermark. A common problem with watermarks is that their existence is often advertised so that potential users know that the image has copyright information embedded.

Table 25.1 shows the differences between steganography and digital watermarking. Which should be used depends on use; each has its advantages and disadvantages. The user will know best which one to choose depending on the application and situation.

Requirements of a steganographic system

There are a number of ways of hiding information in image pixels. In some methods the objective is to store the message in a random way so as to make it more difficult to detect. These methods typically involve the use of a key – the stego-key. The best types of images to use are black and white, greyscale or natural photographs. Redundancy within the data helps to hide the existence of a secret message. A cover image should contain some randomness. It should contain some natural uncertainty or noise, as hiding information may introduce enough noise to raise suspicion. Therefore, the carrier or cover image must be carefully selected. Once it has been used, the image should not be used again and should be destroyed. A familiar image should not be used – it is better for steganographers to create their own images. Below is a list of desirable properties of a watermarking system:

- *Perceptual transparency*. The watermark should not affect the quality of the original image. Where possible, the watermark should be undetectable, as this increases security. Attackers find detectible watermarks much easier to remove or manipulate.

- *Robustness*. This is a measure of how well the watermark withstands various methods of image processing. The image may be subjected to filtering, rotation, translation, cropping, scaling, etc., as part of the image processing. The more robust the watermark the better it will perform when these methods are applied. If the watermark algorithm is embedded using the spatial or frequency domain, it will withstand the image processing much better. There is also a watermark type called 'Fragile', which is intentionally non-robust as such watermarks are used for authentication of original material rather than tracing it back to the source after processing.

- *Security*. To improve security, it is important that third parties cannot alter the watermark even if they know the algorithm for embedding and recovering.

- *Payload of watermark*. The amount of data that can be stored in a watermark depends on the application. For example, in copyright a payload of 1 bit is sufficient, but for intellectual copyrights such as ISBN a payload of 60–70 bits is required. Watermarking granularity is a term used to represent the number of bits that are actually needed to represent a watermark within an image.

- *Oblivious vs. non-oblivious*. In copyright and data protection applications, the extraction algorithm can use the original unwatermarked data or image to find the watermark. This is non-oblivious watermarking. In other applications such as indexing or copy protection the watermark extraction algorithm cannot access the original image, making detection and extraction very difficult for possible attackers. This type of watermarking is known as oblivious.

Implementation of steganography

An effective way to implement steganography is to use images as the carrier and hidden message and use the pixel values as the method by changing the LSB. A simple method could be to use greyscale images to transfer the data through embedding images in carriers. Image processing can be done through a program such as Matlab. As mentioned earlier, LSB substitution involves embedding a watermark by replacing the LSB of the image data with a bit of the watermark data. Detection can be done visually or by correlation methods. One of the drawbacks of this method is that if the algorithm is discovered, it is relatively easy for someone to alter it and overcome the watermark. This is why the watermark is often placed in more than one place in the original image.

Figure 25.6(a) shows an actual image and Figure 26.6(b) shows a watermark that can be used. Figure 26.6(c) shows the watermark recovered when the code is implemented with the LSB method. This shows the repetitive nature of this method, making it more difficult for attackers to manipulate. There are, however, a number of drawbacks with LSB substitution. LSB substitution can survive simple operations such as cropping, as it is placed in numerous locations, but any addition of noise or compression of the image will overcome the effects quickly. Also, if the watermark is detected, an attacker would only have to replace all LSB bits with a '1', fully defeating the effects. One solution to improve the robustness of the watermark is to use a pseudo random number generator to determine the pixels to be used for embedding. Security is increased, but this does require effectively a password or key

Figure 25.6 (a) The image; (b) the watermark; (c) the recovered watermark

(a)   (b)   (c)

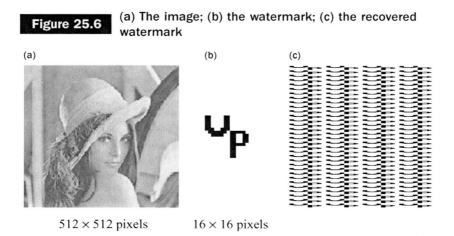

512 × 512 pixels   16 × 16 pixels

to be sent with the image, or shared among users. Provided the attacker does not receive the password it would be very difficult to manipulate the watermark.

Conclusion

Digital watermarking is used by those who wish to prevent others from stealing their material. LSB substitution is not a particularly good candidate for digital watermarking, but it is very useful in steganography owing to its lack of robustness. LSB-embedded watermarks can be removed easily using techniques that do not affect the image visually to the point of being noticeable. Furthermore, if one of the other embedding algorithms is used, the encoded message can be recovered easily and even altered by an attacker. It would appear that LSB will remain in the domain of steganography.

Notes

1. Martin, A., Sapiro, G. and Seroussi, G. (2005) Is IMAGE STEGANography natural? *IEEE Trans on Image Processing*, 14:12, pp. 2040–50.
2. Cole, E. (2003) *Hiding in Plain Sight*. New York: John W. Wiley.
3. Cheddad, A., Condell, J., Curran, K. and Mc Kevitt, P. (2007) A comparative analysis of steganographic tools. *Proceedings of the Seventh IT&T Conference*, pp. 29–37. IET Publishers.
4. Westfield A. and Pfitzmann, A. (1999) Attacks on steganographic systems. *Proceedings of Third International Workshop, IH'99. Computer Science*, 1768, pp. 61–76.
5. Zollner J., Federrath, H., Klimant, H., Pfitzmann, A., Piotraschke, R., Westfeld, A., Wicke, G. and Wolf, G. (1998) Modelling the security of steganographic systems, information hiding. *2nd International Workshop, IH'98. Computer Science*, 1525, 344–54.
6. Pfitzmann, B. (1996) Information hiding terminology collected by Birgit Pfitzmann. *Information Hiding First International Workshop*. LNCS 1174, pp. 347–50. Berlin: Springer-Verlag,
7. Marvel, L., Boncelet, C. and Retter, C. (1999) Spread-spectrum image steganography. *IEEE Transact. Image Process* 8:8, 1075–83.
8. Fridrich, J., Goljan, M. and Hogeg, D. (2002) Steganalysis of JPEG images: breaking the F5 algorithm. *Proceedings of Information Hiding: 5th International Workshop, IH 2002*, pp. 310–23, Revised Papers. Lecture Notes in Computer Science 2578. Berlin: Springer.
9. Hashad, A.I., Madani, A.S. and Wahdan, A.E.M.A. (2005) A robust steganography technique using discrete cosine transform insertion.

Proceedings of IEEE/ITI 3rd International Conference on Information and Communications Technology, Enabling Technologies for the New Knowledge Society, pp. 255–64. IEEE Press.

10. Johnson, N.F. and Sushil, J. (1998) Steganalysis of images created using current steganography software, Centre for secure Information Systems, George Mason University, Fairfax, Virginia. *Information Hiding Second Workshop, IH'98. Computer Science*, 1525, 273–89.

11. Cheddad, A., Condell, J., Curran, K. and Mc Kevitt, P. (2008) Securing information content using a new encryption method and steganography. *Third International Conference on Digital Information Management.* ICDIM publishers

12. Wayner P. (2002) *Disappearing Cryptography, Information Hiding: Steganography and Watermarking*, 2nd edn. Morgan Kaufmann.

26

Vertical search engines

Kevin Curran and Jude McGlinchey

This chapter outlines the growth in popularity of vertical search engines, their origins, the differences between them and well-known broad-based search engines such as Google and Yahoo. We also discuss their use in business to business, their marketing and advertising costs, their revenue streams and who uses them.

Introduction

A search engine is a program that will search for keywords in documents and then return a list of the documents that contained those keywords. Typically, it works by sending out a 'spider' or 'web crawler' that returns all the documents it can find. Each returned document is read and indexed based on its word content by a program known as an 'indexer'. The indices are created using an algorithm so that in most cases only results that are relevant for the query are returned. The Interactive Television Dictionary & Business Index[1] defines vertical search engines as:

> 'Web sites which focus on particular topics and which especially allow you to search for information relating to those topics. The "vertical" term comes out of the idea that these are places where instead of searching horizontally, or broadly across a range of topics, you search vertically within only a narrow band of interest.'

A vertical search engine can be defined as one that contains only content gathered from a particular narrowly defined Web niche, and therefore the search results will only be relevant to certain users. Vertical search engines are also referred to as vertical portals – vortals – specialty search engines and topical search engines. When we think of a search engine we automatically think of a 'broad-based' search engines such as Yahoo, Google, MSN, Altavista, Ask and Dogpile. Currently, these engines dominate the online search market; however, specialized search engines for niche markets are increasing in popularity. One of the biggest specialisd engines at present is LookSmart (see Figure 26.1).

Although vertical search engines are not new, what has changed is their increased popularity. Like consumers, businesses use the Internet for a variety of needs. Sometimes they are looking for all the information they can get, for which search engines such as Google and Yahoo will suffice. More often, however, they are looking for something very specific related to their business needs. That is where vertical search sites come in. Vertical search engines deliver to businesses what the larger sites cannot without the use of complex keyword combinations. This results in relevant and essential content rather than an exhaustive return of information. Some examples of vertical search engines include

- *Jobs* – SimplyHired.com, Indeed.com, Eluta.ca, Recruit.net
- *Travel* – Sidestep.com, Kayak.com, Mobissimo.com, Pinpointtravel.com, Farechase.com

Figure 26.1 LookSmart

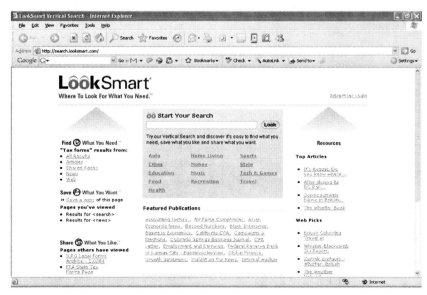

- *Health* – Amniota.com, GenieKnows.com, Healia.com, Healthline.com, MammaHealth.com
- *Classifieds* – Edgeio.com, Oodle.com
- *Blogs* – Technorati, Bloglines, Blogger Search, Sphere, Feedster
- *Source Code* – Koders.com, Krugle, Google Code
- *Academic/teen* – Answers.com, Teenja.com, Gradewinner.com, Scholar.google.com.
- *People* – Zoominfo.com, Ziggs.com
- *Shopping* – Become.com, Oodle.com, PinpointShopping.com.

Vertical and broad-based search engines

Broad-based search engines such as Google are not the ultimate in Web searching as they are cluttered with all the information matching the words in the original query however relevant or irrelevant. There is a typical search failure rate of 31.9% on broad-based search engines among business users.[2] It has also been demonstrated that professionals using broad-based search engines were unable to find important work-related information because they were not trained in their use and the search engines were not designed as business tools. This resulted in a low business user satisfaction rating of 40% for broad-based search engines. Additionally, for businesses the broad-based search engine has resulted in lower productivity from the failure of users to find critical information. This has created a gap that is being filled by vertical search engines that have the advantage that they can produce more relevant results.[3] Second-generation broad-based search engines have tried to overcome this productivity loss by ranking using various human element factors. Yahoo Mindset[4] allows the user to set the commercial vs. non-commercial bias on the results returned via the use of a slide rule (see Figure 26.2).

As broad-based search engines are becoming ever broader, so too are their search results, with the result that business users in particular are starting to make the switch to vertical search engines. Consider the example of a dentist who is looking for information on ceramics, a common material used in dental work. If the dentist performs a Google search on the keyword 'ceramics', Google will serve up millions of results, but most of the entries on the first few pages will concern hobbies such as pottery. By contrast, if the dentist performs the same search on DentalProducts.net, it will return far more relevant results. It would

Figure 26.2 Yahoo Mindset

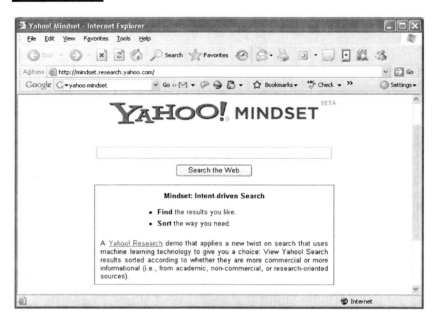

appear that Web users are starting to access/use the Internet much as they do with multi-channel television, namely opting for specialised channels that give them the particular information that they want; for example, a child wanting to see cartoons will go directly to the cartoon channel.

Vertical search engine advertising

Vertical search engines are attracting professionals and business users looking for niche topics and are providing them with a satisfactory user experience. The high cost of advertising on mainstream search engines is causing those in marketing to switch to vertical search engines because the space inventory is less crowded and they can negotiate better rates, possibly receive more custom through increased site visits and receive a better return on investment for their campaigns. Trends to consider include:

- $7.4 billion was spent on search engine marketing in 2005 (16% of which was B2B).
- More than 40% of the average marketer's budget is devoted to searches.

- Nearly 38% of Yahoo's and 50% of Google's advertisers are defined as B2B.

- Nearly 64% of search engine users search for business information first.[5]

Local online advertising is on the upswing. eMarketer's current estimate shows US local online advertising spending at $1.3 billion in 2006, representing 7.9% of a total US online adverstising spending of $16.7 billion.[3] A cost-effective way for smaller businesses to compete in pay-per-click (PPC) advertising is through vertical search engines. Broad-based search engines such as Google and Yahoo! have mainstream advertisers like Amazon who spend millions each week on search advertising, buying every possible term related to their strategic keywords. This prevents smaller businesses from competing for these key terms.

For instance, a search on Google for the term 'wholesale toys' will feature results such as AOL and the Discovery Channel. AOL and Discovery are not wholesalers but they will buy every term that people use to purchase toys because it attracts traffic and because, quite simply, they can afford to. This creates a problem for smaller advertisers. When companies such as AOL and Amazon start bidding on search terms without regulation, bid prices and the ability of real businesses to compete become distorted, making it difficult for small businesses to buy these terms. Although many small businesses might actually be the most relevant source for a term such as 'wholesale toys', they can never compete with $50 million a year search budgets. That is the primary reason why vertical search engines are gaining a toehold and are becoming known as category killers. Many vertical search engines have forums, blogs, fresh content and huge networks set up around a niche topic, providing many attractive promotional opportunities for advertisers. The cost to compete on a vertical search engine is much lower than on general search engines, and marketers can expect much higher clickthroughs and conversions on their search ads, as well as a higher return on investment on their marketing campaigns. There are many benefits of advertising on vertical search engines versus Google AdWords if you pick the right engine for your product or service. Examples of how vertical search engines can be used to good advantage are:[2]

- *Clickthrough rates*. You can get higher clickthrough rates because the audience is segmented and highly qualified

- *Banner ads*. You can request custom positioning for your banners on vertical search engines. Most verticals offer users highly relevant content with targeted banners.

- *Direct links.* Link directly to the client's site or requested URL which gives the advertisers a Search Engine Optimisation (SEO) benefit because engines can now associate the advertiser with a highly ranked vertical search engine.

- *Special ad placement.* Vertical search engines can accommodate a client's request quickly and on the fly. They are lean and versatile; they can react quickly to changing market conditions and industry trends.

- *User-generated media.* Vertical search engines cover issues related to specific topics or industries. Therefore, they can enable customers to blog on their sites, encouraging industry participation. Blog and story links provide great SEO benefits if a customer is linked to them.

- *Email marketing.* Many vertical search engines have email lists, and these databases consist of recipients interested in the niche. These opt-in email lists can be more relevant than any mass-market offerings. Users look forward to receiving weekly newsletters with stories on the industry.

- *B2B ad advantage.* The main difference is that vertical search engines provide an ad advantage for B2B marketers because their ads are exposed to a highly motivated, targeted audience. Clickthroughs can be fewer, saving you money, and conversions can be higher.[2]

Research analysts at Forrester Research, Jupiter Research and Marketing Sherpa have identified a new tier in search dubbed 'specialised search', which includes 'local', 'topical' and 'vertical' search.[5]

- *Local.* This is of geographical or place-based relevance, for example *www.chicago.com*

- *Topical.* This relates to consumer niches such as travel, sport and hobbies, for example *www.kayak.com*

- *Vertical or B2B.* This concerns search engines designed to serve the needs of businesses in specific industries. In terms of design and implementation, several models are emerging in vertical search, including:

   The vertical search engine as a destination or 'portal'. An example of this is *http://www.VetMedSearch.com.* Often media companies that own these destination sites optimise them and buy keywords on Google to drive their audience to visit.

   Vertical search as a complementary Web site application. This model entails embedding a search engine on an existing, already trafficked site, such as *www.CertMag.com.*

Parametric search. This tool, more prevalent in engineering and other product-specific, information-intensive, procurement-driven industries, allows for face-to-face product and manufacturer comparison.

In terms of revenue that these vertical search engines generate, a variety of advertising programs are gaining favour, including: *cost per click*, in which the advertiser pays only for each time that a user clicks on its ad; *cost per action*, an emerging model in which the advertiser pays, not on click, or for impressions, but only if the consumer performs a specific action, such as purchasing a good; and finally, *flat fee/fixed fee*, which is the most popular early ad model for most vertical search engines.

With vertical search engine advertising revenue expected to reach $1 billion by 2009[6] and their continued growth rate it would not be unexpected for such engines to become more important owing to their specialised nature, unless broad-based search engines such as Google fight back with a more advanced form of content control. As it is virtually impossible to have a vertical search engine for every speciality, and it is highly likely that vertical search engines specialising in shopping, financial services, media and entertainment, and travel have the best chance of survival, it is no surprise to find that advertisers are already spending large amounts of money within these sectors.[7]

Conclusion

A vertical search engine contains content gathered from a particular narrowly defined Web niche so that the search results will only be relevant to specific users. Vertical search engines are also referred to as vertical portals or topical search engines. Broad-based search engines include Yahoo, Google, MSN and Altavista. Currently, these engines dominate the online search market, although specialised search engines for niche markets are increasing in popularity. Broad-based search engines such as Google are not the ultimate in Web searching as they are cluttered with all the returned information that matches the words in the initial query however relevant or irrelevant. One of the largest specialised engines at present is LookSmart. The cost to compete on a vertical search engine is much lower than on general search engines, and marketers can expect much higher clickthroughs and conversions on their search ads, as well as a higher return on investment on their marketing campaigns. There are many benefits of advertising on vertical search engines versus Google AdWords if you pick the right one for your product or service.

Notes

1. ITV Dictionary – Definition (2007) *http://www.itvdictionary.com/definitions/ vertical_portals_vortals_specialty_search_engines_topical_search_engines_ definition.html*
2. Prescott, J. (2007a) Why Google will lose dominance. *iMedia Connection*, 12 February, *http://www.imediaconnection.com/content/13634.asp*
3. Prescott, J. (2007b) Find your niche with specialized search. *iMedia Connection*, 26 March, *http://www.imediaconnection.com/content/14149.asp*
4. *http://mindset.research.yahoo.com/*
5. Zillmer, N. and Furlong, B. (2006) *The Emerging Opportunity in Vertical Search*. A White Paper From SearchChannel & Slack Barshinger, *www.slack barshinger.com/verticalsearch/pdf/0505_vertical_search.pdf*
6. Richard, C. (2006) *Vertical Search Delivers What Big Search Engines Miss*. Outsell White Paper, August, *http://www.outsellinc.com/store/products/289*
7. Kopytoff, V. (2005) New search engines narrowing their focus. *San Francisco Chronicle*, 4 April, *http://sfgate.com/cgi-bin/article.cgi?file=/c/a/2005/04/04/ BUGJ9C20VU1.DTL*

27

Web intelligence

Kevin Curran, Cliona Murphy and Stephen Annesley

Web intelligence combines the interaction of the human mind and artificial intelligence with networks and technology. This chapter attempts to define and summarise the concept of Web intelligence, highlight its key elements and explore the topic of Web information retrieval with particular focus on multimedia/information retrieval and intelligent agents.

Introduction

The Web has increased the availability and accessibility of information to such a large audience that an intelligent system is required to construct a meaningful reply to a query for information. The field of study that is Web intelligence (WI) involves a combination of artificial intelligence (AI) and information technology (IT) to produce an intelligent system. WI investigates the important roles that the latter two components have to play on the World Wide Web while being concerned with the practical impact they will have on the new and upcoming generation of Web-empowered products, systems, services and activities.[1] The study of WI draws from a range of diverse disciplines such as mathematics, linguistics, psychology and IT.[2] The Web intelligence Consortium (WIC) is an international non-profit organisation dedicated to the promotion of worldwide scientific research and industrial development in the era of Web and agent intelligence.[3] The WIC identifies nine key topics in the area of WI. One of those topics is Web information retrieval (Figure 27.1).

These nine key topics are further divided into 75 subsections. Multimedia retrieval is one of the subsections in the Web information retrieval category (Figure 27.2). The following paragraphs provide brief summaries of the predominant subjects discussed in this chapter.

Figure 27.1 Web intelligence

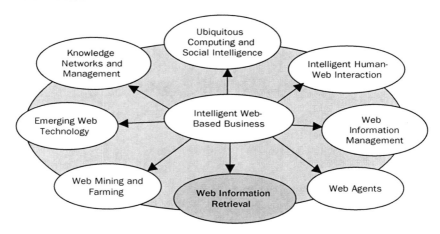

Figure 27.2 Web information retrieval

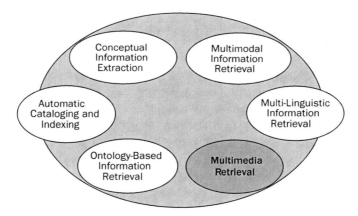

Web intelligence is a new direction for scientific research and development that explores the fundamental roles as well as practical impacts of AI and advanced IT on the next generation of Web-empowered products, systems, services and activities. Goetzel describes the Web of today as having 'an infantile mind' and believes that over the next couple of decades we will see 'its growth and maturity into a fully fledged, largely autonomous, globally distributed intelligent system'.[4]

Artificial intelligence is concerned with the design of intelligent computer programs, which simulate different aspects of intelligent human behaviour.

In particular, the focus has been on representing knowledge structures that are utilised in human problem solving. In other words, AI is the simulation of human intelligence processes by machines, especially computer systems. These processes include learning (the acquisition of information and rules for using the information) and reasoning (including the rules to reach approximate or definite conclusions, and self-correction). Particular applications of AI include expert systems, speech recognition and machine vision.

Web information retrieval comprises conceptual information extraction, automatic cataloguing and indexing, ontology-based information retrieval, multimodal information retrieval, multi-linguistic information retrieval and multimedia retrieval.

Intelligent multimedia information retrieval is a multidisciplinary area that lies at the intersection of AI, information retrieval, human computer interaction and multimedia computing.[5] It goes beyond traditional hypertext or hypermedia environments to provide content-based indexing of multiple media (e.g. text, audio, imagery, video) and management of the interaction with these materials.

Multimedia information retrieval

With the popularity of multimedia technology, contents of the World Wide Web have been far more versatile than a few years ago. However, although more information is available on the Web, the efficient and effective retrieval and management of these Web documents are still very challenging research issues.[6] Intelligent multimedia information retrieval involves much more than retrieving free text; it 'involves systems that enable users to create, process, (e.g., index, profile) summarise, present (e.g., visualise, customise), interact with (e.g., query, browse, navigate), and organise information within and across heterogeneous media such as text, speech, non-speech audio, graphics, imagery, animations, and video.'[5]

With the rapid development of Internet technology, the number of Internet users and the amount of multimedia information on the Internet is ever increasing. Recently, websites such as e-business sites and shopping centre sites deal with lots of image information. To find a specific image from these image sources, we usually use image database engines or Web search engines. However, the feature-based retrieval capabilities of these systems are quite limited, especially for the Web images.[7]

When navigating the Web, with such a vast collection of linked multimedia documents, users can easily get lost in its depths. Multimedia retrieval also poses users problems in finding appropriate resources and extracting information from within multimedia documents. Text and relational databases can be searched on content and indexing terms. However to find information in images, video and speech the user is dependent on the extent of the semantic description of the resource assigned by the database indexer. We need to identify users search methods to develop the technology they will use. And of course the Web needs to become much smarter if it is to optimise its own performance, as well as package knowledge to answer our ever-increasing number of questions. Some users know what they are looking for and try to satisfy their needs by following appropriate links. These users may or may not find something of interest, but may easily miss other, more relevant documents far from their current browsing paths.

There exists a great demand for retrieval and management tools for visual data, as visual information is a more capable medium of conveying ideas and is more closely related to human perception of the real world. However, image contents are more complicated to retrieve than say textual data stored in traditional databases. Image retrieval techniques should provide support for user queries in an effective and efficient way, just as conventional information retrieval does for text retrieval.

Intelligent agents

Another aspect of WI concerns the study and application of Web agents and intelligent agents. An agent on the Web can be described as a program that assembles information or performs some other service without your immediate presence and on some regular schedule. Usually an agent program, using parameters provided by the user, will search all or some part of the Internet, gather information the use is interested in, and present it to him or her on a predefined periodic basis.[8] In general, agents can be defined as programs used extensively on the Web that perform tasks such as retrieving and delivering information and automating repetitive tasks. Agents are designed to make computing easier and are currently used as Web browsers, news retrieval mechanisms and shopping assistants. By specifying certain parameters, agents will 'search' the Internet and return the results directly back to your PC. In fact, one of the more important roles of information retrieval agents is that of searching and filtering information from distributed Web sources. Thus, understanding and developing the correct information foraging behaviuor for information retrieval is a challenge. It is important to understand how people search for information.[9] Liu outlines a foraging agent model which takes into account Web topology, information distribution and agent interest profile.[9] Research into Web agents by the WIC has also suggested that agents could be broken down into a number of subcategories. Examples include semantic agents, information filtering agents and remembrance agents. Intelligent Web agents can use the problem solver mark-up language (PSML)[10] to specify their roles, settings and relationships with any other services. An intelligent Web will have the ability to process and understand natural language. It must understand and correctly judge the meaning of concepts expressed in words, such as 'good', 'best' and 'season'. Furthermore, the intelligent Web must grasp the granularities of these terms' corresponding subjects and the location of their ontology definitions.[9] In addition to the semantic knowledge that an intelligent search can extract and manipulate, intelligent Web agents will incorporate a dynamically created source of *metaknowledge* that deals with the relationships between concepts and the spatial or temporal constraint knowledge that planning and executing services use, allowing agents to self-resolve their conflicts. To solve specific problems, intelligent Web agents must be able to *plan*. The planning process uses goals and associated subgoals, as well as constraints.[9]

Semantic agents

Semantic agents operate on the Semantic Web. The Semantic Web operates on the object-orientated model of classes and objects each with their own properties. It is an extension of the current Web in which information is given well-defined meaning.[11] A semantic agent introduces the concept of ontology. Ontology is a means of describing information. It is a set of descriptors, including the vocabulary, the semantic interconnections and some simple rules of inference and logic, for a particular topic. Ontologies allow information on the Web to be precisely defined. This better enables computers, using agents, to return a more meaningful set of results to the user. Conversational agents, or 'chatterbots', such as Microsoft Agent[12] or Virtual Personalities Inc.[13] are basically speech-activated agents that can direct a computer-generated facial animation and that includes a learning element.[14] For such a system to operate a means of understanding natural language is required. This is undertaken in three stages of analysis: syntax, semantics and pragmatics. Syntax analysis is concerned with the structure of a sentence in terms of the relative positions of words and their parts of speech. Semantic analysis examines the meaning of words and begins to build an internal representation of the meaning of the sentence. This task cannot be completed without pragmatics, i.e. knowledge about the domain of discussion. An understanding of the pragmatics is needed to resolve uncertainty and fill in assumed knowledge about the domain. Conversational agents therefore can be used as front ends for database products, allowing the user to provide a query in a more natural context, although their use is limited.

Information filtering agents

A bot – an abbreviation for *robot* – is a relatively small and focused computer application that runs continuously, in the background as other programs are being run, and responds automatically to a user's activity. Current research into agents is also being undertaken in the field of email filtering and automatic handling agents/bots. These include such innovations as the approach being taken by A-Life BotMail,[15] which has developed a product that allows senders to deliver an interactive and intelligent bot that can converse with the recipient of the email and intelligently present the contents of the message instead of sending a plain document. Snoop[16] is another type of email agent that can automatically inspect and evaluate incoming mail messages and based on what it finds can take certain actions such as generate an automatic response. It can also forward emails, control your PC via email by launching certain applications in response to an email, and parse messages and log information to text files for storage. Other examples of Web agents include 'Copernic Agent'[17] for information retrieval on the Web, 'Emailrobot',[18] an email manager and automater, allowing you to process, route, track and manage messages, and 'NewsRover',[19] a tool for extracting information from Usenet newsgroups automatically. The large number of information sources on the Internet present users with the hard task of gathering relevant and useful information from a query. Such a task is too difficult to solve without some form of high-level filtering of information.[20] Intelligent agents can aid in this area, passing on to the user only those items that they are interested in.[21] One solution to this problem is to integrate different AI technologies such as scheduling, planning, text processing and interpretation problem-solving into a single information-gathering agent, called BIG (resource-bounded information gathering), that can take the role of the human information gatherer.[20] Agents have evolved to the point that complex Web agents now exist that can learn their user's preferences and actively seek out Web pages that could be of interest to them. To provide personal assistance, an agent needs information about the user's interests and needs.[22] Agents can suggest information sources and products to users based on learning from examples of their likes and dislikes. Such an agent is termed a 'reccomender agent'. Two modes of operation exist for recommender agents. Most existing recommender systems use social (collaborative) filtering methods that base recommendations on other users' preferences from websites. By contrast, content-based methods use information about an item itself to make suggestions. A content-based approach has the advantage of being able to recommended previously unrated items to users with unique interests and to provide explanations for its recommendations.

Remembrance agents

A remembrance agent is a program that aids human memory by displaying a list of documents that might be relevant to work the user is doing. Unlike most information retrieval systems, the agent runs continuously without any user intervention. Its unobtrusive interface allows a user to follow up or ignore the suggestions as desired. The front end of the agent program continuously watches what the user types and reads. It then sends this information to the back end. The back end finds old emails, notes files and online documents that it thinks relevant to the user's context. This information is then displayed by the front end, in such a way as not to distract the user from their current task.[23] Agents termed 'shop bots' can aid the user in their purchase of an item of interest over the Internet. They compare prices from a number of online stores but currently are not very comprehensive, except in the computing industry. PriceSCAN[24] offers a service allowing the user to compare the price of any tem from a number of different online stores before making a purchase. Shopping agents can compare prices on a number of different items or they can be specific to the field that they search in. Dealpilot[25] searches over 20 online bookstores for the lowest price and then returns the results to the user.

Profiling agents

Profiling agents are used to build dynamic sites with information and recommendations tailored to match the individual taste of each visitor. The main purpose of the agent software is to build customer loyalty and profitable one-to-one relationships. Learn Sesame[26] learns about users automatically from their browsing behaviour, adapting to changes in the users' interests over time. Agent programs can allow the user to have data sent automatically or 'pushed' to their computer at regular intervals, such as every hour, or when triggered by an event, such as when a Web page is updated. This is accomplished using what is known as 'push technology'. Desktop News[27] keeps the user informed by delivering a continuous stream of news and information from chosen websites direct to their desktop in a compact ticker toolbar. Push technology is an alternative to the way the World Wide Web currently operates in that information is presented to the user without their intervention, whereas ordinarily the user goes online to search for information.

Navigation agents

Navigation agents are used to navigate through external and internal networks, remember short cuts, pre-load caching information, and automatically bookmark interesting sites. IBM's Web Browser Intelligence[28], pronounced Webby, is an example. In addition, agents can help in the development and maintenance of a website. CheckWeb[29] scans user-generated HTML pages and explores all the links for errors. When finished the program generates a log file with all the errors it has found. IseekTraffic[30] submits a site to over 157,000 search engines, directories and links pages in its database. The software will submit all URLs to all of the top search engines and directories.

The categories of agents discussed up to now have been engineered to operate in one particular field or mode of information retrieval. Agents can also undertake a variety of features, not being restricted to just one function. Agents such as Ultra Hal[31] can cover a range of functions such as remind you of important dates, start programs on your behalf, browse the Internet and answer emails.

Many image retrieval systems have been developed, such as QBIC,[32] VisualSEEK[33] and Photobook.[34] For instance, MultiMediaMiner[35] is a prototype of a data mining system for mining high-level multimedia information and knowledge from large multimedia databases. Some systems rely on keyword-only retrievals and others support image content-based retrievals. In the latter approach, the systems support image retrievals based on image feature information, such as average colours, colour histograms, texture patterns and shape objects. However, most have been developed for image database applications. Multimedia applications such as video conferences or Web collaboration bundle several means of communication (language, text, image). Speech recognition, or speech-to-text, involves capturing and digitising sound waves, converting them to basic language units or phonemes, constructing words from phonemes, and contextually analysing the words to ensure correct spelling for words that sound alike (such as 'write' and 'right'). The multimedia revolution brings a challenge for us to create an intelligent Web capable of interacting and even understanding the user. This chapter has only skimmed the surface of the topic of Web intelligence; we all have a part to play in its definition.

Conclusion

The success of Web intelligence will not hinge on available technology alone, but rather on the widespread acceptance of the medium to meet the needs of the user at large. Web intelligence developers will essentially need to combine teams of people with varied perspectives to develop and design an intelligent Web that will effectively address the ultimate requirements of the user. In doing so we may witness a growth and adoption of Web intelligence, encompassing every area of commercial enterprise and every aspect of human endeavour, resulting in the proportional displacement of conventional methods of communication. All categories of intelligent agents discussed in this chapter, although diverse, have one thing in common. They are all constructed to allow the user to query the Internet and its vast array of back-end databases and bring back a meaningful set of results which are relevant to the user and allow them to carry out their tasks more efficiently and effectively. Intelligent information retrieval is a small part of Web intelligence that gives us the opportunity to improve the quality and effectiveness of interaction for everyone who communicates with a machine in the future.

Notes

1. The Web intelligence Consortium (2003) *http://wi-consortium.org/*
2. Yao, Y. (2001) Web intelligence (WI) *Research Challenges and Trends in the New Information Age.* Knowledge Information Systems Laboratory, Japan, Technical Report online at *http://kis.maebashi-it.ac.jp/wi01/pdf/wi_intro/wi-intro-new.pdf*
3. *http://wi-consortium.org/*

4. Goertzel, B. (2002) The emergence of global web intelligence and how it will transform the human race. *http://www.goertzel.org/papers/Webart.html, 2002*
5. Maybury, M. (1997) *Intelligent Multimedia Information Retrieval.* London: AAAI Press/MIT Press.
6. Pringle, G., Allison, L. and Dowe, D. (1998) *What is a tall poppy among Web pages? Proc. 7th IWWWC,* Brisbane, pp. 369–77. ICANN Publishers.
7. Hong, S., Lee, C. and Nah, Y. (2002) *An Intelligent Web Image Retrieval System.* Department of Computer Engineering,Dankook University, Seoul, Korea. Technical report available at *http://dblab.dankook.ac.kr/SPIE2.pdf, 2002*
8. Browne, C. (2002) *Web Agents.* Report online at *http://cbbrowne.com/info/agents.html, 2002*
9. Liu, J. (2003) Web Intelligence (WI): What makes wisdom web?. *18th International joint conference on Artificial Intelligence,* Acapulco, Mexico, pp. 1596–601.
10. Menasalvas, E., Segovia, J. and Szczepaniak, P.S. (2003) Advances in Web Intelligence. *First International Atlantic Web Intelligence Conference AWIC 2003.* Heidelberg: Springer-Verlag.
11. Hendler, J., Berners-Lee, T. and Miller, E. (2002) Integrating applications on the semantic web. *Journal of the Institute of Electrical Engineers of Japan,* 122:10, 676–80.
12. Microsoft Agents. (2002) *http://www.microsoft.com/msagent/*
13. Verbots. (2002) *http://www.verbots.com/.*
14. Sammut, C. (2002) *Conversational agents.* University of New South Wales, Australia. Report online at *http://www.cse.unsw.edu.au/~claude/projects/nlp.html*
15. *http://www.artificial-life.com/v5/Website.php*
16. *http://www.smalleranimals.com/snoop.htm*
17. *http://www.copernic.com/index.html*
18. *http://www.gfisoftware.com/*
19. *http://www.newsrover.com*
20. Lesser, V., Horling, B., Klassner, F., Raja, A., Wagner, T. and Zhang, S. (2000) BIG: a resource-bounded information gathering agent. *Journal of Artificial Intelligence,* Special Issue 118:1–2, 197–244.
21. Harper, N. (1996) Intelligent Agents and the Web. Online *http://osiris.sunderland.ac.uk/cbowww/AI/TEXTS/AGENTS3,*
22. Payne, T. and Edwards, P. (1995) Learning mechanisms for information filtering agents. *Proceedings of the UK Intelligent Agents Workshop,* pp. 163–83. Oxford: SGES Publications.
23. Rhodes, B. and Starner, T. (1995) Remembrance Agent. A continuously running automated information retrieval system. *Proceedings of The First International Conference on The Practical Application Of Intelligent Agents and Multi Agent Technology (PAAM '95),* pp. 487–95. Cambridge, MA: MIT Media Lab.
24. *http://www.pricescan.com/*
25. *http://www.dealpilot.com/*
26. *http://www.aminda.com/mazzu/ls.htm*
27. *http://www.desktopnews.com/*

28. IBM (2000) *Web Browser Intelligence – Agent Software, http:/lwww,raleigh. ibm.com/wbi/wbisoft.htm.*

29. *http://www.algonet.se/~hubbabub/how-to/check Weben.html*

30. *http://www.botspot.com/Intelligent_Agent/1986.html*

31. *http://www.agentland.com/*

32. *http://wwwqbic.almaden.ibm.com/*

33. *http://www.ctr.columbia.edu/VisualSEEk/*

34. *http://www-white.media.mit.edu/vismod/demos/facerec/*

35. Zaiane, O., Han, J. and Chee, S. (1998) MultiMediaMiner: A System Prototype for MultiMedia Data Mining. *Proc. of SIGMOD98, Seattle, Washington, USA, June 2–4th 1998.* ACM Publishers.

28

Summary

Kevin Curran

I am reminded of the Arabic saying which states 'Those who claim to forecast the future are lying, even if by chance they are later proved correct' as I make my predictions for the future of the Internet. I guess it is safe to say it will persist. Countries will also ban it and cyber law will continue to prove unwieldy to enforce and a source of great difficulty in many diplomatic incidents. I do expect a tiered Internet to evolve. The current flatline approach could prove to be unsustainable given the increases in fuel (servers need to be powered ...) and the costs to ISPs of leasing bandwidth and implementing tighter data security. The obvious trends are for the mobile phone to become the iniquitous surfing device but it will always be hampered by the small screen and even smaller keyboard, so serious surfing may always be done on a more traditional desktop client. As I write, 'cloud computing' is the flavour of the month but are large corporations willing to hand over their entire data stockpile to third-party organisations? Security issues will always be there. There is no silver bullet fix for security. Rather, it involves a constant cycle of vigilance and upgrade. The killer applications of the future will be location-aware: those that remind us about buying milk just when we are passing the shop door or remind us that we do need to repair our car when we are passing our mechanic. The integration of GPS, cellular GSM and indoor location technologies that allow us to more easily determine our location in the real world can truly open up a wonderful door to an ambient intelligent world where devices and electronics become 'fused' with our desires so that they work in tandem to provide us with intelligent inspired support, which can offset the otherwise complicated lives that we lead.

Section I provided an overview of protocols and how they provide the necessary functionality to move packets of information from source to destination. Protocols are the building blocks of the Internet, 'rules' that are implemented in many languages in order to allow the shipping of data from a client to source(s) and also enforce all the error correction, security and management features associated with such a task. Here we also looked at why delays happen in the Internet. Obviously it is a shared medium and this can mean that packets have to compete not just at quiet times but also at busy times when there may be too many packets arriving at a router, leading to some being discarded. Mesh networks are where nodes communicate with each other, via other nodes within the network or directly depending on the position of the source node to the destination node. The area covered by the mesh network of nodes is called a mesh cloud and is only effective if the nodes are listening and communicating with each other. This is closely related to ad-hoc networking. Finally, we looked at wireless sensor networks, which are used in many applications including traffic control, military operations and healthcare. Wireless sensor networks are made up of a number of small sensor nodes and a main routing node and when a signal is received by a sensor node, it sends it to the main gateway node and performs the necessary operation. Such networks provide the potential of gathering, processing and sharing data via low-cost, low-power wireless devices.

Section II included an overview of web operating systems. These are relatively new and have not yet become mainstream, although they may do with the influence of cloud computing. Really simple syndication (RSS) provides feeds from multiple sites simultaneously in an RSS viewer so that users do not need to visit multiple websites to follow site updates. RSS has become perhaps one of the most visible XML success stories to date. Asynchronous JavaScript and XML (AJAX) is a web development technique for creating interactive Web applications in order to make the Web experience interactive, faster and more user friendly. AJAX makes this possible by exchanging small amounts of data with the server behind the scenes, resulting in the Web page on the client side not needing to be reloaded when a user makes a change. VoiceXML is an exciting technology that can bring to life many automated voice-prompting systems and also has appeal as a technology for the visually impaired community. Finally, we looked at Web services, which are a standard means of interoperating between different applications, running on a variety of platforms. Web services represent the evolution of a human-orientated utilisation of the Web to a technology that is application driven, attempting to replace human centric searches for information with searches that are primarily application based.

Section III introduced Web 2.0, which is a social phenomenon referring to an approach to creating and distributing Web content itself, characterized by open communication, decentralisation of authority, freedom to share and re-use and 'the market as a conversation'. Web 2.0 is about making sure that users add value to a site as a side-effect of what they are actually using the site for. We covered mobile social software, which is software that supports user group interaction in online communities by overlaying a place and time element to the idea of digital networking. It enables users to find one another, in a particular vicinity and time, for social or business networking. Mobile social software has been largely targeted to cities, on the assumption that urban areas provide a sufficient density of people that users may serendipitously encounter as they go about their everyday lives. The long tail is the colloquial name for a long-known feature of statistical distributions. It is the theory that customer buying trends and the economy are moving away from the small number of hit products widely available in offline stores towards the huge number of one-off and niche products that are only available online. Finally, we looked at podcasting, blogging, videoblogging and screen casting. Podcasting allows users to listen to music files from podcasting websites or indeed from any website. Unlike Internet radio podcasting allows listeners to download the podcast so that they can listen to it later or store it on a mobile device. Screen casting has become popular with individual users who wish to document program bugs or oddities, as a visual demonstration showing how a program works can be much clearer than a verbal description. A blog is a website similar to an online diary where messages are posted describing items of interest to the blog author and a videoblog is a short video clip with sound posted on a website.

Section IV introduced WiMAX, which transmits data from a single location within a city to multiple locations throughout that city or cities. WiMAX is a high-speed Internet wireless technology planned purposely for outsized IP networks that provides superior coverage than its rival competitor Wi-Fi. Hybrid Web–desktop applications are simply those that can run seamlessly offline as if online. When in offline mode, users have exactly the same functionality as online users. We outlined the peculiarities of designing sites for visitors who will be browsing through mobile devices, as mobile communications is a continually growing sector in industry, and a wide variety of visual services such as video-on-demand have been created, although these are limited by low-bandwidth network infrastructures. Finally, we looked at the quest to provide mobile devices with the ability to detect and respond appropriately to changes in network connectivity, network connection quality and power consumption.

Section V provided an introduction to cryptography, encrypting data so that only a person with the right key can decrypt and make sense of the data. There are many forms of encryption, some more effective than others. This section provided a history of cryptography, some popular encryption methods, and also some of the issues regarding encryption, such as government restrictions. We also examined in depth how some of the security implementations developed specifically for WLANs are not terribly strong. Email has become very useful and practically universal. However, the usefulness of email and its potential for future growth are being jeopardised by the rising tide of unwanted email, both SPAM and viruses. An important flaw in current email standards is the lack of any technical requirement that ensures the reliable identification of the sender of messages.

Finally, section VI introduced the Invisible Web, which refers to the mass of information that can be accessed via the Web but cannot be indexed by conventional search engines. The concept of the Deep Web makes searches quite complex. We also examined digital fingerprinting/watermarking, which prevents unauthorised copying of media as the information is encoded within a host, so that the actual appearance of the host does not change, but within the host there is a watermark or secret message, which prohibits the attacker from making an exact copy. The objective of steganography is not to change the actual message, or make it difficult to read, as cryptography does, but rather to hide the existence of the message without distorting the carrier or the actual information. We looked at vertical search engines, which contain only content gathered from a particular narrowly defined Web niche, and therefore the search results will only be relevant to certain users. They are also referred to as vertical portals (vortals), specialty search engines and topical search engines. Finally, we provided an overview of Web intelligence, which involves a combination of artificial intelligence and information technology to produce an intelligent system. Web intelligence investigates the important roles that these two components have to play on the World Wide Web while being concerned with the practical impact they will have on the new and upcoming generation of Web-empowered products, systems, services and activities. The study of Web intelligence draws from a range of diverse disciplines such as mathematics, linguistics, psychology and information technology.

Index

9 781843 344995